PENGUIN BOOKS
SPEEDPOST

Shobha Dé (www.shobhade.net) is a Mumbai-based writer.

By the same author

Socialite Evenings
Starry Nights
Sultry Days
Sisters
Strange Obsession
Snapshots
Second Thoughts
Uncertain Liaisons: Sex, Strife and Togetherness in Urban India (co-edited with Khushwant Singh)
Shooting from the Hip
Small Betrayals
Surviving Men
Selective Memory: Stories from My Life

Shobha Dé

Speedpost

Letters to my children about living, loving, caring and coping with the world

PENGUIN BOOKS

PENGUIN BOOKS
Published by the Penguin Group
Penguin Books India Pvt. Ltd, 11 Community Centre, Panchsheel Park,
New Delhi 110 017, India
Penguin Group (USA) Inc., 375 Hudson Street, New York, New York 10014,
USA
Penguin Group (Canada), 90 Eglinton Avenue East, Suite 700, Toronto,
Ontario, M4P 2Y3, Canada (a division of Pearson Penguin Canada Inc.)
Penguin Books Ltd, 80 Strand, London WC2R 0RL, England
Penguin Ireland, 25 St Stephen's Green, Dublin 2, Ireland (a division of Penguin
Books Ltd)
Penguin Group (Australia), 250 Camberwell Road, Camberwell, Victoria
3124, Australia (a division of Pearson Australia Group Pty Ltd)
Penguin Group (NZ), 67 Apollo Drive, Rosedale, Auckland 0632,
New Zealand (a division of Pearson New Zealand Ltd)
Penguin Group (South Africa) (Pty) Ltd, 24 Sturdee Avenue, Rosebank,
Johannesburg 2196, South Africa

Penguin Books Ltd, Registered Offices: 80 Strand, London WC2R 0RL,
England

First published by Penguin Books India 1999

Copyright © Shobhaa Dé 1999

Cover photograph by Rajkumar
Inside photographs by Gautam Rajadhyaksha

All rights reserved

28 27 26 25 24 23 22 21

ISBN 9780140293173

For sale in the Indian Subcontinent only

Typeset in Sabon by Digital Technologies and Printing Solutions, New Delhi
Printed at Rashtriya Printers, New Delhi

Ranadip, Radhika, Aditya,
Avantika, Arundhati and
Anandita

. . . For a life-sentence of hard but joyful labour

God must be a mother . . .

Contents

Acknowledgements

I love children. My own and even other people's. I started this as a millenium gift for my kids. At some point, I decided to embrace kids everywhere . . . and a book happened. There are no 'off days' for parents. No vacations. No breaks. Even as I write these lines, I can hear one of my children summoning me urgently. I have to stop. But not before thanking David (must convince him to give parenting a shot), Karthika (bless her, she likes not just my kids but Tuts, our boxer, too) and of course, my husband Dilip, who keeps the 'wife' in me astonishingly alive.

Introduction

7 January 1999, the last day of the first week of a momentous year. I am squatting on the beige carpet of my bedroom in front of an old Chinese chest-of-drawers. This is where we store our albums—dozens of them. It is our unorganized memory bank, an instant reference system. I often find myself rummaging through the pictures. Sometimes, I'm in search of a specific image: Arundhati's first day at play school. Aditya's puzzled expression the morning his head was shaved for the mundan. Radhika with a live grasshopper parked proudly on her bare knee. Anandita with her birthday cake smeared all over her two-year-old face. Ranadip sticking a long, pink tongue out at the camera. Avantika making her photo face (head tilted, wide smile). Sometimes, I seek stray moments from a holiday, a celebration, an adventure, or even just a relaxed weekend in Alibag. Moments that may have been relegated to distant memory and need to be revived.

I get immense pleasure from our family albums. They are an easy reckoner of our lives. Often, I take in my breath at a forgotten photograph—good God, is that really me? And Dilip? How young we look. And there's Rana, so handsome and so awkward in his adolescent gangliness. Look at all of us caught at different times, in different moods, our old selves immortalized by a battered-up idiot-proof Minolta. Going just by the snapshots, we appear to have had a lot of fun together—which we most certainly have. But what is not reflected in these happy family pictures are the other, off-camera moments, when we've argued and fought and hurt and made up.

Some photographs are more revealing than others. Candid camera, as they say, doesn't lie. An unguarded expression, body language that gives the game away, a posture that's posed and far from relaxed. A grimace, a scowl, a frown. Tears. I look harder at these shots and try and remember what it was that might have triggered off that particular crisis.

These days, I spend quite a lot of time glancing through the albums. I haven't kept them terribly well, I must confess. They lie there in no particular order. Some are meticulously dated, others require guess-work. But each and every one of them captures and freezes for all time a special fragment of our lives. We laugh in most of them (as people generally do when a camera is aimed at them). But those which catch us unawares are the ones that interest me more. Of late, I've been systematically destroying my own 'bad' pictures. My kids tease me about this, but it took a shrewd actress to point out to me that it's bad pictures that everyone remembers once the person is dead and gone. 'Search and destroy,' she commanded. I shamefully admit I've done just that. Not too thoroughly, though. There are countless lousy prints still stuck in those albums—but I'm going to find them. And tear, tear, tear.

It was on one such mission that the idea of *Speedpost* came to me. I remember it being a late Saturday afternoon. My youngest children, Arundhati and Anandita, were sprawled on my bed watching *Small Wonder*. I was only half-listening, as I flipped through the latest batch of pictures—the ones taken on my fifty-first birthday. I looked at my own expression, and then at my children's, their eyes

brimming with mischief, their smiles wicked. I recalled the
few minutes early in the morning when I'd walked out of my
bedroom and into the dining room where they'd set up the
mini-celebration before leaving for school. On a large
yellow poster there was a caricature of me—their
mother—drawn by them. The lettering on my T-shirt read
'Born wild'. On the top half of the poster, perhaps as a
concession, were the words 'Fifty-one, and even more
fabulous'. I smiled at that. The previous night they'd
overheard me cribbing to a caller, 'These are my last few
hours of being able to claim I'm fifty and fabulous.
Somehow fifty-one and fabulous doesn't quite have the
same ring to it.' It was only a joke. Hell, who cares how it
feels after fifty anyway? One just stops counting. Not kids,
though.

I hugged them for trying to reassure me. It really was
sweet, and I guess I did need it. Now I was staring at the
photograph that had recorded this event, and so many other
equally precious ones. I chuckled out loud and my
daughters looked up, startled. I flipped the pictures over
and dated them carefully. This was my job. I was the one
who compiled and maintained photographic records. Not
that I was particularly good or efficient at it. It was just that
nobody else wanted to do it. This was one of my 'mother'
duties—custodian of family albums. That's what made me
laugh. All of us are in those photographs, but I'm the one
keeping track. Just like with everything else in our lives.

I turned around to look at the girls and noticed
Arundhati's long, bare legs as if for the first time. Her
'teenage limbs'. The denim shorts she was wearing were
way too short. I said so. She tugged at them absently as a
reflex action, like it would extend the length.

I went back to filing the photographs and putting them away in the chest-of-drawers. That's when I found the letters. A few written by me to the children on their birthdays or at important turning points in their lives, a few written by them to me— childish notes, baby doodles, but each one of them saying something strongly and transparently. I noticed how the hand- writing had altered with the years—from a higgledy- piggledy scrawl riddled with spelling mistakes to better formed, more rounded letters, then entire, grammatically correct sentences. Progress! How precious these letters were—are. And how much they tell me—about the children, about us.

Five years ago I had jauntily promised to write individual books for each of my children. This is a compromise. This is my way of saying, 'It's a start. I may never write the others, but I am doing this one with all my heart. For all six of you. To make up for the lost moments, not fully enjoyed or appreciated. As the cliché goes, it's never too late. I figured this was the perfect time to reach out, as we ready ourselves for the next century, as we pause to review the one just ended, as we hesitantly inch towards new beginnings, unsure of what awaits us . . . We as parents know nothing is going to be the way we've experienced it. I feel afraid. At times, I think I won't be up to the task of providing the sort of guidance changed circumstances demand. We, in India, have witnessed more sweeping changes taking place in the last decade than over the past hundred years. Think of it. Satellite TV. The internet. Foreign labels. Snazzy cars. Designer this, designer that. Anything and everything that can be conveniently clumped under the 'global lifestyle' umbrella. Enough to overwhelm us all. But what the hell, I'm going to take a shot at it anyway. I have to. I'm going to say it as it is, speak my mind, tell a few home truths, and keep my fingers crossed.

We've grown together in so many ways. I've learned from you; I hope you've learned from me too. I've tried, you've tried. I've sulked, you've sulked. We've both argued, disagreed, stormed and relented. It's been an ongoing process of adapting, readapting, caring, withdrawing, rewarding and punishing. But at the end of it all we've been in this thing called 'parenting' together. Which is the reason for this book—open letters affectionately and sincerely addressed to each of you. But before you pounce on them, beware. A warning. I have revealed a few of your secrets, but only a few. Nothing that will cause you too much embarrassment in front of your friends. I have revealed a few of my own as well. I thought you should know them, so we can understand one another better. We've travelled quite a distance together and there's still a long way to go. You guys are the future, but we have a shared past. These letters are a reminder of that—good times, fun times, angry times, sentimental times. *Speedpost* is about memory and love, confusion and uncertainty. A record of our dilemmas and moral choices as we struggled to come to terms with our respective expectations and identities, you as children, I as a parent.

The new millennium is upon us. Are we ready for it? I've asked questions—so many, too many perhaps. I don't expect answers. But I do want you to think about them—quietly, seriously. If even half of them make sense to you, if even a few make you pause and reflect, perhaps even change, every bit of the effort that has gone into the writing of this volume would have been worth it. At this point in my life, it is the only gift I can offer . . . . Or even value.

Trust me. As I trust you.

My mother
is an alien!

ANANDITA

Dear Girls,

Yes, all of you. For some time now, I have been trying to ask you a question. The reason I haven't asked earlier is that I wasn't ready for it myself. Finally, the moment all but hit me in the face. It happened when I was invited to address a group of ladies at a local club. Amongst them was a bright, talented, good-looking woman I have known for over twenty-five years. She has a daughter about your age, Radhika. So I guess she had a special reason for asking me that particular question. After reading out a short passage from *Selective Memory* to the assembled ladies, I had said I would be happy to respond to any queries they might have about the book or me. My old friend had raised her hand. 'Tell me Shobha,' she started off, 'how do your children feel about being your children, particularly your daughters? Don't you think it must exert an enormous pressure on them? Surely, people regard the girls differently from their contemporaries? They must have to deal with the inevitable comparisons. You are so high-profile. You also happen to be good-looking. Maybe they resent it.'

Well, daughters, here's my question: Do you? Do you resent being my kids? Do you think it's unfair pressure? Are you constantly compared to me? To each other?

Don't answer just yet. Think about it, as I've been doing ever since that morning. I'm sure you're curious to know how I responded to the question. Did I avoid it? Was I evasive? Diplomatic? Insincere? Perhaps a little of each. I answered briskly, 'I think all my daughters are very secure in their individual identities. I don't think they're weighed down by any sort of pressure. Generally, it's parents who create the pressure in the first place. And I've tried my best to bring them up without throwing comparisons at them. They know they're not in any kind of competition with me. Neither are they competing with one another.'

At the time, I believed what I was saying. I still do. But, in all honesty, is it possible for five very individualistic women to grow up without comparing attributes? No way. I've seen evidence of it in each one of you. And I think it's perfectly healthy to feel that way, provided you don't let negative feelings creep in and destroy a relationship. Each one of you is so different, so unique. There is barely any overlap. I am not surprised by this—it was so in my own family.

My sisters—your aunts, Mandakini and Kunda—were very different from me and from each other. Our mother was a strong, opinionated lady, a very no-nonsense person who had a distinct personality of her own. Our values matched as a family, but not our appearance. It was pretty hard to tell we were sisters or even that we were related. In later years, we acquired what is described as a 'family resemblance', but that was it. Our mannerisms were frequently compared and commented on. This may have bugged us but not too much. We dressed differently—I'll always picture Mandakini clad in magnificent Handloom House silks. We reacted differently to situations. And our tastes were radically different—in books, music, movies and food. Yet, we spoke the same language. Our vocabulary included several words and phrases that had been coined by one of us. And we all enjoyed a good joke. But there it ended.

Did we grow up tormented over the obvious differences? I don't think so. We were aware of them, occasionally irritated by them, but we didn't exactly cry ourselves to sleep each night. As you don't either. Mercifully, so far at least, all of you seem comfortable about yourselves. Of course, I get the occasional barbs and overhear a stray comment or two. But that's fine. Sibling rivalry is normal, natural. It's also okay to pit yourself against Mother from time to time, provided the mixed emotions arising out of that don't eat into you.

I'm sure there have been times when you've not enjoyed being my daughters. When you've been embarrassed, or even angry. There must have been incidents at school or college or at the workplace when you've wished you were someone else's children. But, as they say, it hasn't been such a bum trip either, has it? HAS IT? Come on. Tell me girls. I can handle it.

Jauntily,
Mother

....

Mumbai
April '99

Dear Anandita,

Last night you cried for an hour—maybe longer. I could still hear your sobs as the car pulled out and we arranged our expressions suitably for the party ahead. My evening was ruined. As was yours. I should have stayed home and comforted you. Something was obviously wrong, for you (of all the children) to have staged that tantrum. It was so unlike your 'normal' behaviour when you watch me dress and then cheerfully wave 'bye bye'. I didn't get the chance to find out what was bothering you—the moment was then, while the tears were fresh, while your face was flushed, while you pleaded and begged with me not to go. By the time we got home, you were fast asleep—in your own room, not ours. It was the only form of protest left open to you, the only way to express your rage and hurt. I felt completely wretched, and selfish. I should have followed my instincts and stayed by your side—even if you had nothing significant to say. Your tears told me more than anything words might have conveyed.

And yet, I went. To a party where I wouldn't have been missed at all. You were right when you screamed 'Who cares?' when I tried to explain why it was important for me and Daddy to go, that it was a special anniversary for our special friends. Who cares? You were right, baby. Nobody does. It was just another party with the same cast of over a hundred people. My presence hardly mattered. But my staying home would definitely have—to you and me.

So why did I leave you in tears and go? Because we adults are cowards. We get our priorities wrong. We give undue importance to unimportant things. Basically, we are fools. Last night was your night, or should have been. You needed me, plain and simple. Coming from any other child, I would have dismissed the tears as a fit of petulance. But not from you. I tried explaining, while your father paced up and down saying what men the world over say to wives who dawdle, 'We're already late.' Of course we were. But then, how could I leave you in that state?

But I did. And I'm sorry. I ought to have put my foot down but I didn't. Instead, I went along to a frivolous evening of false mirth and fake conversation, imagining you going to bed without dinner. 'I'm not hungry,' you had sobbed when I told you to eat. But I knew that you'd eaten your last meal six hours earlier.

'You're very tired,' I had pleaded, 'finish your food and then go to bed.'

'I don't want to sleep,' you had protested, your eyes swollen and nearly shutting with fatigue.

'I'll be back in an hour,' I had promised, knowing full well I wouldn't be able to keep my word. 'I don't care,' you had sobbed, 'just don't go.'

But go I did.

And suffer I did.

Just as you must have.

When I got back after midnight, I went to our bedroom eagerly. Had I found you there, I'd have known you'd forgiven me. But you were missing. I felt wretched and guilty. I told Daddy, 'See. She isn't here.' He replied, 'It's all right. She'll be fine tomorrow. She'll cool down.' He was right, but also wrong. As both of us had been about our decision to leave you last night.

There was anxiety in your nine-year-old mind. You hadn't been able to articulate it. All you knew was that you didn't want to be left alone—for whatever reason. I so desperately wanted to stay back and comfort you. Point is, I didn't. Even as your crying became more insistent, I wore my saree, took a final look in the mirror, and left. You shut your eyes and I shut my mind. I know it sounds cruel, but parents can be cruel sometimes. You may have forgotten that night (thank God for children's attention spans). You may even have forgiven me. But I will remember your expression—hurt mixed with disappointment and anger—and I won't be able to forgive myself. Not just yet. I had a miserable time at the dinner. It was obvious to all how out of sorts I was. I kept asking myself, 'What the hell am I doing here? I should have been home cuddling my baby.'

When we got home, you were in bed. Your own bed. The maid mentioned you'd skipped dinner and cried yourself to sleep. I felt wretched. I deserved to. When I saw you the next morning, I was still feeling awful. But you'd forgotten and greeted me cheerfully with a big hug and kiss. You know what? That was the worst moment. It stung more than a slap. I winced. And made you a peace offering—pancakes. That was pretty sly of me, because you were so unsuspecting. But that's how mothers operate. Any little trick that asssures peace. It doesn't always work, but who says we have to stop trying?

Yours in anguish,
Mama

....

Calcutta
May '99

Dear Children,

How are mothers supposed to deal with bouts of periodic depression, anger, hostility, rage? Bury it all 'in the interest of peace and harmony within the family'? That's how it usually works, at least in our culture. Women are not encouraged to display overt emotions, especially if these happen to be 'negative'—never mind their validity or context. I find that an awful strain sometimes. These days, I resent the idea that I have to be calm, composed, an angel of good humour at all times. It's far too demanding physically. It's also unrealistic. Each one of you is a distinct individual with well defined character traits. That's how it was in my own family as well. I know how trying it was for my parents to deal with four highly opinionated people of strong temperament. I also know how my mother had to draw upon superhuman reserves to cope with so many different personality-types, and smile through it all. She did have a temper, a quick one. And she took her time to cool down, often lapsing into extended periods of withdrawal, her face pinched and tense, deep frown lines between her brows. That was our signal to leave her alone.

My mother had an excellent rapport with her own mother and surviving sister (the youngest one died young). Perhaps they offered her the much-needed safety valve we, as children, couldn't provide. I know how much she needed to talk to them and they to her. Women require these sort of support systems to help them cope. Unfortunately, both your aunts live overseas, long-distance calls are expensive, and your grandmother passed away a bit too early, leaving our communication incomplete. When I hit a low, I don't know whom to turn to. In a city like ours, friends, even good ones, have their own frenetic lives to deal with, their own schedules and priorities. I hate imposing on any of them and feel guilty whenever I call to moan and groan about what, in retrospect, appear trivial irritants. It's not them. It's urban culture. Each of us has to look out for ourselves—no soft landings, no buffers. This can be tough, very tough.

So, what does a modern mom do when she gets the blues? I'll tell you what some of my far younger friends do. They take off on their own. They join a fitness centre and sweat off the stress. Play tennis or ride obsessively. Do reiki, shop, indulge in pedicures and facials, cut their hair, splurge, travel. Yes, they do. I don't really know whether any of this helps, but at least the girls imagine they're feeling better. Am I sounding nauseatingly martyred? I guess it's one of those days.

Last night, as I lay awake watching your sleeping forms, Arundhati and Anandita, it occurred to me all of a sudden that I hadn't had a good cry in years. I wondered why. Not that I was ever a weepie-sniffly person (even if I do shed tears unabashedly during sentimental movies), but it seemed unnatural not to activate those dried-up tear ducts from time to time if only to check if they were still in working order. Would I be able to squeeze at least a few honest-to-goodness, big, fat, salty drops out of those dry, constantly watchful eyes if I tried? You know the kind I mean? The really satisfying ones that threaten never to stop, that pour out and roll down depositing wet tracks on the cheeks? That leave the eyes prettily bloodshot and cloudy and distort the vision for a few seconds? That make one feel cleansed, almost purified? No, sorry, I haven't experienced that in a long, long time. Mainly because I don't want to upset any of you. My tears seem to scare the family, maybe because they're so unaccustomed to seeing me cry. Nobody knows how to deal with my down-in-the-dumps phase. Sometimes Arundhati does reach out, but even she looks scared. Radhika senses something amiss and hovers around sympathetically. The boys are never around. Avantika is unconditionally supportive but even she prefers me to snap out of it, and fast. As for little Anandita, I see her eyes wide with anxiety, tears threatening to spill out, and I promptly hide my own. The question is—what do I do when I'm feeling awful? Do I pretend everything is hunky-dory out of consideration for all of you? Or do I express my anguish, even if it appears irrational? Must I suppress my true feelings at all times out of fear that it would affect or alarm you? But how about the effect of long-term suppression on me? God. I can't believe I'm actually saying this. Maybe it's a mistake. Oh hell, there I go again. Even if it is a mistake—so what? Mothers can make mistakes too.

The sky outside reflects my mood perfectly. It's a pre-monsoon horizon with banks of black clouds approaching the waiting, watchful city menacingly. The air is humid and moist. The light is a sombre filtered grey. Wet crows sit miserably on leafless trees. The house itself is quiet—very quiet. The phone hasn't rung for twenty minutes—a record. I have oil in my hair, lots of it. I refuse to get out of my faded caftan. I haven't made my routine morning call to Baba to check on him. I feel strangely switched off and isolated. Perhaps you sense it and stay away. I don't want to brood. I don't want to remain switched off. I desperately want to talk. But to whom? I want to articulate the reasons for my anger. I want to be able to express this anger selfishly, without thinking of anybody else. But will I? Unlikely. I know what I will do. I'll say 'later'. I'll deal with it later (which translates to 'never'). I'll cop out, I'll bottle up my resentment, I'll work furiously and achieve very little. I'll turn productive with a vengeance, reply to letters that don't need to be replied to, send faxes with little content. I'll punish my body during the daily work-out and feel virtuous, but still angry. By evening I'll start wondering what it was about (knowing the answer full well all along). As usual, my anger will get short-changed only because it is not expected of me to show it, especially if it appears 'unjustified' or 'out of proportion' (who decides?). No, I'll bottle it up (and market it?) as I have for years. Eventually, it will evaporate (like perfume or whiskey). And I'll laugh easily, so easily, while I listen attentively to your breathless accounts of assorted adventures—at school, at work, and contribute a few jokes. While within, I will be choking. And wondering why mothers aren't allowed to be angry when the rest of the world is.

Grrrrrr,
Mama

....

Mumbai
June '99

Dear Aditya,

For the past fortnight, we have been following the fortunes of various teams playing in the World Cup. Cricket was your old passion, just as golf is your current one. Yet, I've never watched you play either game. Come to think of it, I haven't really watched you doing too many things. When you were growing up, I wasn't there. I mean, yes, I was here, but away from you, in my own home. It can be argued, 'But . . . what about kids in boarding schools? Don't their parents also see them just twice a year?' Unfortunately so. For all those of us, who, for any reason, are deprived of the full-time company of our young children, it is a loss. A mutual loss. I have always felt strongly about sending young children away to school. No matter which school. Children and parents are meant to live together, even if the future prospects of the child appear that much brighter in a distant school.

I often hear parents exclaiming, 'Oh . . . But my son had no adjustment problems at all. He didn't cry once when we went to drop him at the boarding.' He didn't, huh? Maybe he was afraid to, for I honestly cannot believe that a seven- or eight-year-old experiences no fear, no anxiety at being separated from his family. Some kids conceal it better, that's all. But the scars remain. In our case, it was different. We lived in the same city, occupied the same physical space. Yet, we were worlds apart. You grew up as the cherished grandson in an extended family, while I sought to come to terms with my new life and new family. Of course, we saw each other frequently, spoke on the phone, met at school functions, and generally co-ordinated schedules and activities. At the time, I didn't think of it as being strange. But now I do. The most natural thing would have been to stay together—after all, mothers aren't supposed to live down the road in some other house. Unfortunately, our lives were not destined to be lived 'naturally'. It's too late to reverse any of that, or regret the choices. Yet, even today, when we are closer than ever before—emotionally and otherwise—it seems bizarre to be discussing cricket scores, strokes, performances, points, wins and losses over the phone.

It's artificial. But we console ourselves that it's the next best option to enjoying something together. Not that it would be impossible if we really tried. You could come on over and we could be in the TV room watching the action, ball-by-ball, together. But that again would require special effort. It would mean your getting out of your home and driving eight kilometres to mine, only to share a few hours of cricket together. How sad. There is no room for anything impromptu in our lives. And that's been the situation for the larger part of yours. All your triumphs and glories on the playing field (or even off it) were enjoyed by me vicariously—when you told me about them later. Always later. Your activities were 'conveyed' to me, and I listened intently, with pride and joy. But why wasn't I there?

For years and years, we led parallel lives, our only 'connection' being the telephone. It can again be argued that thousands of mothers live even more isolated lives, separated from their children physically and emotionally for whatever reason. And the world still goes on. The children grow up, the mothers grow old. Soon, they stop thinking of those long, lonely years of separation. As I had, for far too long. It has only been in the last couple of years that the question has started to haunt me. There are far too many gaps that I fear may never be filled, far too many details I shall never know. Little things—how exactly did you sleep when you were eight years old, or twelve, or fourteen? Curled up? On your back? Hugging a pillow? What was the expression on your face? Why can't I visualize it? Why is it all such a blur? I wasn't there when you used your first cuss word. Nor when you looked in the mirror and noticed your freshly-sprouted whiskers. I wasn't around when you studied late into the night for your dreaded ICSE exams. I didn't sign your report cards. Or pick up your dirty socks. I don't recall the day you decided you were too old for 'half-pants', or too 'cool' for haircuts given by the regular barber at home. I do remember holding your hand while crossing the road. But no memory of sitting nervously by your side at your first driving lesson. I've never looked in on you as you pored over textbooks, nor offered to brew you a mug of coffee at midnight. My strongest memories are those of you as a little boy, a child of five, no, even younger, flying kites on the terrace during Sankranti: serious faced, curious, clingy. After that, it's a blank. Till suddenly, one day, you stood before me, a man: thick dark hair covering your legs, an impressive stubble, a deep voice, and God help us, an adam's apple, too. Where had all the intervening years gone? You looked so handsome, your head cocked characteristically to one side, your eyes faraway and dreamy—the same eyes. Yes, those hadn't changed. My heart and head could barely contain the joy that was pouring forth.

From then on, we've shifted to another plane. We are friends now, and equals. Almost. There is nothing we can't or don't discuss. I value your opinion, as I hope you value mine. Yet, I can't help but experience a twinge of deep regret each time I see old photographs. The ones that have you as a toddler in my lap. Or later, as a four-year-old, looking trustingly up at me as I hang up balloons for your birthday party. You look wistful and a little sad even there—as if you sense an imminent separation. As if your young mind knows there is going to be turbulence in your life soon. All too soon. And you are preparing for it. Maybe this is all in my imagination, but I can see the sadness, recognize it. I can feel the pain, even now, so many years later. A constant, dull ache that reminds me of that distant day when I took a plane—not just to a destination, but straight into a new destiny—and left you sleeping soundly, trustingly in the bed. You lay curled up tightly, your hair mussed up, a bit of drool on the corner of your mouth, clad in a white muslin kurta-pajama, lightly covered with a razai, smelling of talcum powder and toothpaste.

There is no better or more touching a sight in the world than that of a child in deep sleep. Which is what you were in when I tiptoed out of the room, out of the house, out of your life, never to return. It is a sight that is imprinted on my soul and will follow me into my next life—if there is one. Aditya asleep. Aditya ignorantly asleep. Aditya betrayed. I won't even ask you if you've forgiven me. I think I know the answer.

Yours sadly,
Mama

....

Mumbai
August' 99

Dear Arundhati,

Do you remember asking, 'What will you leave for me when you die?' It was a spontaneous, innocent question triggered off by your liking for a piece of jewellery I'd bought. I was most amused. Not distressed, amused. And I was happy that you'd expressed yourself so candidly. After that little outburst, you got into an even more serious discussion on the subject. You mentioned particular sarees from my wardrobe that you fancied. And you urged me, 'Keep them on my name.' You were around twelve at the time, and deeply interested in the contents of my cupboard (an interest since outgrown).

Perhaps you'd taken me seriously when I'd half joked about my will. 'What's a will?' you had wanted to know. I had said flippantly, 'It's a list of things I'll leave for each of you when I die.' Maybe from that moment on, you'd thought about what happens to possessions when the person to whom they belong is no more. Maybe you'd started making your own mental list. That particular afternoon you came with a pretty exhaustive one. 'Do you remember those small ruby earrings? They are for me. And I also want your green saree with the gold border. Please note that down.' I had laughingly asked you, 'What else? What else?' and you'd supplied the names of all the items on your wish-list most unselfconsciously.

I admire you for that. A cunning, shrewd child would have disguised that basic desire, perhaps camouflaged it with fake sentimentality. 'Oh Mama. How can you talk about dying? Please don't say those awful words. I don't want anything. Not a thing. I only want your love—promise. I want you to live forever.' Rubbish. Nobody wants anybody to live forever. Speaking for myself, let me tell you, I'd like to go before I become either a burden or an embarrassment to any of you. I don't see the point of longevity unless the person is fit in body and mind. I don't want to live the life of an invalid. I don't want to carry on merely 'existing'. I want to depart when I'm still in the pink of health, and all of you still value my existence. Even the most loved of parents eventually become a bit of a bother to their children, outliving their validity. I never want that to happen to me.

It's perfectly natural for a child to think in selfish terms. Your fancy is caught by something and you covet it. That 'something' doesn't need to be valuable at all, merely an object that has attracted you. I laugh when I think of that conversation. You'd very systematically listed out the most unexpected of my belongings—old worn-out high-heeled sandals, a buckled handbag, a wooden bracelet, even discarded lipsticks in your favourite shades. I found that very sweet. Through your 'wish list' I got to know you still better. I hadn't realized how much you fancied antique pieces of jewellery, for example. I'd have thought you'd have gone for something more modern, something flashier. Your choice of sarees was a revelation too—you preferred the more traditional ones. The colours you picked were subdued and understated. And as you spoke about those things, your animated face was a joy to watch

Someone else may have found this conversation morbid or insensitive. For me, it was neither. I'm sure you'll be embarrassed if you read this when you're older. 'How could I have said something so crass?' you might say. Well, please don't. Don't regret this moment. It was unique and special. I've noted all your requests carefully. You were more particular about a few specific pieces coming to you since you were aware of the fact that your other sisters admired them too. You reminded me about that as well and added, 'Remember . . . I asked first. They have to come to me.'

They will. And I hope when they do, you'll cherish them as much as I did during my lifetime. And maybe, just maybe, you'll think of me when you wear what was once my favourite ring. Just as I remember your Aji when I look at her mangalsutra nestling in a velvet box inside my cupboard. I rarely wear it myself. But just knowing that something that was such a big part of her life has now become an invaluable part of mine is a wonderfully reassuring feeling. I hope you experience it too, someday, and smile at the memory of our funny 'treasure hunt' afternoon.

Yours affectionately,
Mama

....

Mumbai
February '99

Dear Children,

From time to time I suffer from severe panic attacks, which, once they pass, remind me of how much I need you in my life. The panic attacks, of course, revolve around the question: do you really need me in yours? Silly, I know. But, I guess mothers the world over go through the same insecurity. Till the age of seven or so women feel entirely reassured in the knowledge that their kids can't do without them. Not true. But it's a safe delusion since kids that age are hardly likely to argue the issue. When you were adolescents I used to believe I was indispensable to your young lives. It was a good feeling, a smug feeling. Then, as one by one you grew out of that phase and flew your own way, I comforted myself with the thought that though I was no longer needed physically, I still had a very, very important psychological role to play. Rubbish. If anything, that was the time when you were looking to your peer group for answers, and a mother's viewpoint was just that—a mother's viewpoint. To be tolerated, but not necessarily accepted or even taken seriously.

I remember lamenting one day, around two years ago, to Aditya over the phone, 'I don't think Avantika needs me any more . . . she doesn't seem to value my opinions, and rarely asks for my advice.' Aditya was silent for a a moment, then laughed. 'Relax, Mother. It's just a phase.' I retreated into a sullen silence. It was true, I repeated to myself. Nobody was asking for my help now that the four of you were all grown up and on your own. Avantika, who used to consult me on the smallest problems, had suddenly withdrawn. She had her set of girlfriends fulfilling those needs and we barely talked beyond niceties. Rana was rarely at home. Radhika was busy finding her feet in the workplace. Both worked long hours, coming home very late in the night and frequently leaving early.

'Aren't you relieved?' asked an English friend. 'At least four of them are off your back . . . now two to go.' I joined in the joke but inside me my heart was breaking a little. Aditya was right about Avantika, though. Her 'independent' phase lasted no more than four months. Four very long months for me. Four months during which I'd often wonder, 'Will it never be the same again? Has she really moved that far away from me?' Aditya had offered me sage advice. 'Leave her alone. Let her be. You chill. And allow her to chill. She'll be okay. Don't try and lead her life for her. She's twenty years old, not two.' That was true, only I couldn't accept it. I'd lecture her constantly. Nag frequently. Disapprove of everything—her friends, her appearance, her conduct, her grades, her preoccupations, her habits, even the expression in her eyes. I'd weep to a close friend, 'Where has that Vanti gone? My precious little girl, the one I used to think I knew so well. Has she really changed so much? Or have I been fooling myself all these years?'

Bhawna (my friend) would make soothing noises and then burst out laughing. 'Really, Shobha. I think you're crazy. Avantika has not changed beyond recognition as you seem to think. The poor girl is only trying to grow up without you breathing down her neck constantly.' At some point I let go. Not because I wanted to. I felt it was the only way to deal with the hurt and frustration (entirely self-inflicted). I think it was one of my better decisions. Gradually all the older children started to respond differently. The younger ones seemed relieved that Mother was not all tense-neck-muscles-and-guarded-expression. Communication channels were re-established. And everybody relaxed.

That summer your aunts Kunda and Mandakini were down for their annual vacation in Mumbai. Each time I visited them at Ajoba's home, the phone would ring within ten minutes or so of my getting there. It would be one of you calling to check on something or the other. My sisters showed their irritation. 'Why can't your children leave you alone? This is absurd. They keep phoning every few minutes. You must not encourage this.' I smiled but didn't say much. I couldn't get myself to tell them how desperately I had missed those calls over the short months when the communication lines were down. Or even how much the calls meant to me even if they did intrude, even if I felt irritated at times. Even if I complained that my children gave me no space to breathe each time I left the house. Yes, even then . . . I'd still wanted those 'intrusive' calls 'disturbing' me, rather than no calls at all.

Each time we travel I pack my phone into my handbag and wait for it to ring. Only you children have the number and are allowed to call. I'm told this is an absurd, crazy and frightfully expensive way of staying in touch. 'In any case you're only gone for a week. Surely, if there's an emergency they can reach you at the hotel,' my friends point out. Do children's calls have to deal only with emergencies? Can they not be about sharing a small moment, a thought, a feeling? Yes, it's extravagant, but for me it's essential to stay in touch and any price is worth that electric charge I get when, in a strange city at an odd hour in an unfamiliar setting, the shrill ring of a cellphone nestling in my handbag galvanizes me into action. I dive for the instrument, pick it up eagerly and hear one of you say, 'Mama . . . how are you?' Believe me, I'd pay anything for the pure pleasure of listening to those sweet, simple words wherever I may be in the world. How often have I excused myself from a meeting to take a call and then carried on the conversation sotto-voce, furtively, feeling a lot like the guy in the 'Happy Birthday to You' commercials. Outsiders suppress smiles when they hear me instructing Anandita across 10,000 miles, 'No, no, no. Don't wear the black shoes with the pink dress. Wear the other ones—white will match better.' Or telling Arundhati, 'It's okay, forget it. Don't take such remarks to heart. But tell me, did you finish that crossword on pollution for your social studies journal?'

Those who overhear these long-distance conversations say, 'Are you nuts? Your kids are calling to discuss homework, or to talk about what happened in the office. Surely that can wait. Air time costs money—what a waste.' To an indifferent stranger, it must appear like a waste of both time and money. But it isn't. Not to me. Not at all. The sound of a child's voice coming through clearly over thousands of miles is the sound of love. I long to hear their laughter, the childish jokes, the excited recounting of the day's events, little snippets of city gossip, quick advice on something personal. All the small exchanges that add up to a big, golden glow that fills a cold impersonal hotel room with its warmth. I can't think of a more comforting, more satisfying, more precious human exchange. Extravagant? Nonsense. Necessary? Yes. At least for me.

You agree?

Lovingly,
Mother

....

Mumbai
February '99

Dear Avantika,

I have just finished combing Anandita's hair. It's fairly late in the night, and we are in Alibag. The monsoons have yet to arrive in Mumbai, but the pre-monsoon showers have transformed the garden outside. The water in the shower was cold—too cold for Anandita's comfort—as I bathed her. You know how much I enjoy doing that. I love the expression on her face as she waits passively for me to soap her, rinse off the suds and rub her dry with a fluffy towel. It must be a lovely feeling for a child to be lovingly bathed—there is such communion in the act.

I do recall Aji bathing me when I was a child, but the memory isn't distinct enough. I've forgotten how her hands felt on my body—were they soft or slightly calloused? Did she bathe me out of a brass bucket or a plastic one? I know the concept of showers was alien back then. In fact, I don't remember showering till we came to Mumbai. What sort of soap did Aji use? It was definitely not an expensive one. And there were no shower gels in the market in the '50s, '60s, '70s, or even '80s. I feel frustrated that I cannot recall the specific fragrance of that soap, or feel the exact temperature of the bath water on my skin. I don't remember the bathroom either—what sort of tiles did it have, and doors? Did Aji use a thin Turkish towel or an even thinner, desi version of it? Somehow, I can vaguely recreate just one image if I try really hard—standing in front of an electric heater in Delhi winters, my body like a well-done toast, while Aji powdered me carefully, briskly, and helped me into my clothes.

Every child in the world is entitled to such memories. I wonder what yours are, and I weep. I stopped bathing you when you were no more than five years old. After that, our lives were led in different homes, and you had your 'Gangabai' to perform the duties that I had abandoned to follow my own course. It was she who combed your beautiful long hair, tied colourful ribbons into double bows, found matching clips to go with your dresses, located your socks and shoes, got you ready for school and birthday parties. It was her hands that soaped and scrubbed you, her voice that soothed you when soap stung your eyes and you cried. It was her voice you heard last before drifting off to sleep, her smell that you recognized as the most familiar one. Her fingers untangled your hair when it got hopelessly knotted, her saree pallav wiped your tears when you fell off a bike and scraped your knee. Her palm soothed your fevered brow when you ran a temperature. And yet, not once did you complain. Not once did you cry out, 'Where is my mother? Why isn't she here?' Not even when you occasionally spent weekends with me, and we luxuriated in each other's company, knowing that we had only so much time together before you'd be gone, leaving me alone to savour your brief presence in my isolated life.

It was only during these infrequent visits that I could indulge myself, indulge you. But you never ever made me feel wretched, or guilty. Your love was as steadfast and as true as it had always been. No accusations, no questions. Just a cheerful acceptance of the cruel trick that had been played on you, through no fault of yours. Today, I yearn for those lost moments. I can see you now—your ready smile and childish prattle as I slide the wide-toothed comb through your waist-length, honey-brown hair, both of us in front of the dressing-table mirror. Just as minutes ago, I had been with Anandita right here. Her hair is different, so is her smile. And yet, she could be you—my beloved little girl. Trusting, innocent, sleepy, her surrender complete ('Do with me as you please. I know you'll never hurt me').

If I shut my eyes, I can see you in her place. But I don't do that, I can't. It's too painful. I can never make up for the loss. Never. All I can do is console myself that we've had other moments, other memories over time, that are equally precious, equally beautiful. But those? Those are irretrievably lost. I can only mourn their loss quietly and seek your forgiveness, my precious one.

Yours,
Mama

....

Calcutta
January '99

Dear Children,
  I don't know precisely when the transformation takes place, but there's no doubt that it does. I'm referring to role-reversal. There are situations in which I feel so much younger than any of you and I ask to be mothered. The beauty of this is that you sense my need instinctively and slip into your temporary role without the slightest self-consciousness. I notice how smoothly the transition takes place. I even call you 'mama', my voice a few decibels higher than my normal, authoritative tone, my body language more pliable.
  Generally, this happens when I'm feeling unwell. You can see it on my face—sunken eyes, listless expression, droopy smiles. You encourage me to behave like a baby at such times. Which is all the push I need to do just that. We go to the bedroom, one of you leading me by the hand. There, with great tenderness, you draw the curtains, plump up my pillows, tuck me into bed, and relax next to me. We watch TV for a while . . . I doze off . . . when I wake I can see your eyes widen with concern. 'Are you all right? Fever? Want something? Water? Tea? Shall we phone the doctor?' Often you pat your lap and say sweetly, 'Go to sleep . . .' while I rest my head on your knees, your fingers running gently through my hair. For those precious, silent moments, I feel loved and taken care of in a way that's so delicate and true. I become a child and regress to the days when in an exact replica of this scenario, I would lie with my own mother in a darkened room, her hands caressing my face. In her later years, she was the one who needed similar ministrations. I confess mine were inadequate and I often felt disoriented

and resentful, even angry that she wasn't behaving like a mother, like an adult, a take-charge person I could rely on. It was only later that I realized that at that stage of her illness, she was in no position to play the Rock of Gibraltar. She needed to be taken care of herself, after spending the major portion of her fragile life taking care of all of us. When I switch characters with you from time to time, I do so because at that moment, I need mothering. I need my mother. And when you respond to this need I feel safe. I feel myself. I feel cherished. And oh, so wonderful.

There are other occasions, too, when I am the helpless one, unable to deal with a problem. And I turn to you for a solution. Without the slightest hesitation, it is provided. Always sincerely. Always truthfully. It could involve professional decisions, or personal dilemmas. But even when it is complicated stuff about contracts, time-frames or travel schedules that are causing confusion in my mind, I know that when I seek your advice, you will tell me what's in my best interests. Funny thing is, your inexperience in matters you have never had to think about, leave aside deal with in real life, does not stop me from asking you for your take on the subject. Nor does it prevent you from discussing it. Eventually, I consider all your opinions and then do what I think best. But the fact remains, your feedback is very important to me. Do you know why? I'm sure you do. Because it is unbiased and straight from the heart. You aren't doing a number on me—you don't have to. You aren't telling me what I want to hear, you don't have to. You aren't misleading me, you don't have to. Sometimes, the bluntness of your assessment takes me by surprise and I recoil at its impact. I argue with you vehemently and say, 'I don't agree.' But you hold your ground. You shrug and comment, 'It's up to you, Mother. But since you asked . . .'

Strange, how these bonds of trust develop. I know from the depths of my heart that whatever it is you convey to me, it's one hundred per cent genuine, regardless of whether I agree or not. In fact, it's when we disagree the most that the scenario gets interesting. Generally it's over people. You feel I'm a sucker for certain types (which I am, I confess). You see through these types much before I do. But when I am under their spell, I refuse to pay heed to your warnings, only to regret it later. I pride myself on being pretty good at sizing up people. I have been proved wrong several times. You laugh when I come back from somewhere raving over someone, 'Tell us about it a few months from now, Mother.' I gush and gush (not that I'm pretending) for days on end, till something happens to make me change my opinion. That's when you guys get your kicks by gloating, 'We told you so.'

I don't mind being taken for a ride or two. Life would be so predictable and boring if each of us could figure everything out well in advance. Sometimes a betrayal can really hurt, but even through the hurt, a lesson is being learnt. I have no major regrets about having been taken in by someone—even someone you've 'warned' me against. So what? That's my childish, stubborn self. If you think I'm being foolish, say so. Not that I have to squeeze it out of you—you're only too willing to comply. I know Arundhati occasionally feels embarrassed by my kiddish outbursts. But it's okay, I tell her. Even mamas can be babies sometimes.

Trustingly yours,
Mama

....

Mumbai
March '99

Dear Girls,

One day, you girls asked me about my teenage crushes. Innocently you said, 'But did people actually have them in your time?' I chuckled inwardly. How remote my girlhood must seem to you. Yet, when I recall it, it's as if those incredibly wonderful things happened only last week. Do you know, I can still remember my first pair of high heels, bought at age fifteen to impress a rugby-playing seventeen-year-old who lived across the street? My very first crush. Yes, girls, people did have crushes in my time. Aah, the shoes. They stayed well after the crush disappeared. Soft, white calf leather, pointed toes, a two-and-a-half-inch tapered heel. I remember them so well because such purchases were rare and precious, events that needed careful planning and much debate. 'You are too young for all this,' my mother, your Aji, said a little nervously. She'd never slipped her foot into anything other than one-toed leather chappals bought from 'Navyug', a reliable footwear store in Girgaum. Since she rarely went out (especially in her later years) her chappals remained in their original cardboard box on the lowest rack of the wooden shelf in her bedroom. She had two or three pairs of these sturdily crafted chappals. Not particularly attractive, but functional.

Everything in Aji and Ajoba's life was functional. Anything that didn't fall into that category was termed 'useless', which I suppose it was. But sometimes 'useless' possessions can provide so much delicious pleasure. More, far more than useful, functional ones. In her mind my high heels were not just 'useless', they were a symbol of defiance—my way of saying 'I've grown up, I can make my own decisions.' But beyond that, the high heels represented my new-found independence. I'm sure my mother sensed it—and it scared her. Till then, I had absolutely no jurisdiction over what I wore. I certainly had strong opinions on the subject, but more often than not, they were overruled. I wore whatever was thought appropriate by my parents, whatever they bought for me. Those purchases rarely took my own pre-adolescent views into consideration, even though, unlike my siblings, I voiced them, holding back nothing.

For example, as a child, I was a part of the nylon generation. Yes, I know. Ugh is the right word. But nylon was the miracle fabric of the late '50s and early '60s, till polyester stole an equally smelly march over it. I wanted a pink nylon dress for my eleventh birthday. I wanted it so badly, I was prepared to stage a satyagraha. The sort of party frock I coveted was worn by wealthy Parsee girls in my class. I had no idea where they got theirs from. All I knew was that it looked fabulous—layers of cellophane-like nylon, combined with lace, frills, buttons and bows. The skirt of their dresses never clung to their legs limply. It fluffed out into a tea-cosy like shape, making the wearer resemble a doll—a walkie-talkie doll imported from England. I wanted my dress to be the same. After all, I'd be wearing it to school on my big day, and everybody's eyes would be on it.

I put in my request well in advance. To his credit, my father went in search of it most diligently—given the fact that we lived in a transit flat in distant Ghatkoper at the time, and the additional fact that we were new to Mumbai after having spent eight years in Delhi. Plus, Ajoba was on a fresh assignment on a limited salary, with a large family to raise. Yet he took valuable time off to locate my dream dress. He found it in a large store at Dadar and took me along for the first time to 'approve' his choice. I did. A bit cautiously, though. The dress was nylon. And it was pink. It even had lace. But it didn't fluff up. I felt a little disheartened but didn't show it. I tried to figure out what it was that made those other dresses stand out so prettily. I asked a couple of my friends casually so as not to display my own ignorance. 'Oh,' they said knowingly, 'you need a buckram underneath.' Now what on earth was buckram?

I found out quickly. It was nothing more than a stiff petticoat in layers—something like a ballerina's tutu. For the necessary effect, it had to be starched with enough starch for it to fall rigidly at an angle from the waist down. And how would anybody sit down wearing what was no softer than cardboard underneath the yielding nylon of the dress? Simple. You didn't. Fashion conscious little girls spent long afternoons prancing around the place without ever letting their bottoms touch a chair. I thought that was brilliant. And worth every bit the discomfort.

Now all I had to do was acquire the requisite buckram, starch it as per my requirements, and stun the school with the birthday frock. Plans went slightly awry despite my best efforts. No buckram. No teacosy-skirt. I wore the dress with less enthusiasm. Perhaps I wouldn't have worn it at all, but I was afraid of my father's temper. I'm certain he'd have lost it (and who wouldn't?) had I refused to wear the dress he'd taken so much trouble to organize. I got my 'buckrams' later. And while the craze lasted, I mastered the art of making the stiffest starch solution at home (with rice paste), thereby becoming the proud wearer of the flounciest dresses in school. Till, overnight, buckram was replaced by hooped petticoats. Out went the aluminium starch solution pot. It was goodbye to messy kitchen sinks filled with sticky petticoats. But while the buckram phase lasted, I was a dedicated starch-freak.

My white high-heels at fifteen can be compared to your designers trainers, except that they cost a fraction of what modern-day sneakers sell for. Today, I cannot understand your mania for Air Reeboks, just as my mother couldn't have understood my passion for high-heeled pumps. All those style statements from my pre-teen years are back as retro fashions. I wish I'd kept those pumps. They were more than mere shoes, you know. They represented freedom. And listen, don't you dare pick up my line and throw it back at me when you put in your demand for the next pair of Nikes.

Yours,
Mama

....

Mumbai
May '99

Dear Arundhati,

Do you remember the Sunday night of your first term as a senior in school when we were discussing the contents of your lunch box? I'd looked at some leftover roast chicken from dinner and suggested it be made into sandwiches the next day. You'd turned up your nose at that and said, 'No thanks. No chicken. No non-veg in my box, please.' I had been rather surprised. You? Saying no to chicken? You, whose natural preference was chicken for breakfast, chicken for lunch and chicken for dinner?

'What's the matter?' I had asked, 'since when have you started disliking chicken?' And you had explained sweetly, 'It's not fair, taking non-vegetarian items to school when so many children are vegetarians. The sight and smell of our snacks must be putting them off.' I was touched by that comment. It displayed so much consideration on your part. How many of us are that sensitive to the feelings of others? You were absolutely right in respecting the sentiments of other students. In the bargain you were prepared to give up something you liked and enjoyed a great deal yourself. I thought of all the times I must have made several queasy stomachs churn while biting into a fish fillet or relishing a leg of mutton. That night you also mentioned how you had refrained from digging into a huge portion of lamb curry brought by one of your friends. 'I could see the expressions on the faces of the other girls. I couldn't possibly have enjoyed the curry. So I went away to play basketball.' These are lessons adults can learn from kids. You also told me not to pack anything terribly different from the sort of snacks everybody else brought to school. This was such a change from kids I've observed, the ones who pester their parents to put imported chocolates into their bread-boxes, or insist smugly, 'Our tuck comes from abroad. We hate Indian cheese. It has such a lousy taste.'

Thank God you don't want to prove a cheap point with such acts. Time and again you've told me to give you 'what everybody else eats'. When I asked, 'But don't you want to take something different for a change?' you replied, 'No. Because we share our food. And I don't want anybody to feel I get something they can't get at their own home. It would make them feel so bad.' I don't know where you get this quality from; I can't claim any credit for it. But I admire it in you. I love the fact that you've arrived at it on your own without any goading, prompting or brain-washing from my side.

I agree, personal food habits can, and often do impinge on the rights of others. But I needed you to form my thoughts on the subject. I remembered my own lunch box, the contents of which rarely varied. I'd leave for school at eight, running to catch a bus from outside Churchgate station. My round dabba, always aluminium, never stainless steel, in case I lost it, would contain two toasted egg sandwiches. These would keep me going till I got home at around six o'clock. For someone who is passionate about food, it amazes me now that I never tired of the monotonous menu. For years, this formed my 'dry lunch'. It's another matter that I often ended up in the school dining hall where other, more privileged students got their hot lunches from home, and helped myself to freshly baked chappatis, spicy dals and mutton gravies.

Our dining hall was divided into vegetarian and non-vegetarian sections. I'd nonchalantly run between both, nibbling scrumptious titbits from the plates of my friends. Strange, but I never envied them for eating their lunch in such style, waited on by attentive servants who laid out their lunch in such a posh way, complete with placemats, coasters, chilled colas, coordinated crockery and expensive cutlery. I'd only be interested in the contents of their tiffin boxes—and not at all embarrassed about raiding them before running off for netball practice.

Often, I'd forget my lunch box at home. This would lead to a bit of a panic. For one, it would irritate my mother a great deal. It would irritate your poor Manda mavshi even more, for she'd be instructed to drop the box off at school on her way to work. I can imagine her mood. Poor girl, rushing to her bank job, driving herself in a smart little white Standard car, clad in a gorgeously coloured handloom saree, her hair perfectly groomed, her face immaculately made-up, her nails neatly manicured. And a ragamuffin of a kid sister waiting impatiently at the school entrance for the lunch box to arrive. In her place, I wouldn't have taken the trouble. I'd have told Aji, 'Let her starve. That's the only way she'll learn a lesson.' My sister was kinder, even if she did grumble.

I wonder today how I didn't get sick of those toasted sandwiches which tasted like damp cardboard so many hours later. Maybe my revulsion to eggs these days is a throwback to my school days. For you kids, it's been so much easier. It helps that your school is nearby. Initially, I'd agonized over the contents of your tiffins. I'd heard glorious stories about a former navy chief's wife who was greatly admired by the other wives for filling her children's boxes with innovative, scrumptious, imaginative snacks. Her sandwiches were minor works of art, it was said. I began to feel more and more guilty. Maybe I wasn't involved enough. Maybe you kids were being deprived in some way. Maybe I needed to cut back on my work and pay more attention to what was packed for you. I agonized for nights. And then it suddenly occurred to me—did the super-mom's unique sandwiches appeal to her kids? Were they even eaten by them? Or did her children raid other people's boxes to eat regular food with relish? Was their mother's effort an enormous waste? Worse, was she doing it only to impress other women and give them a complex? I felt better after this piece of neat rationalization. I even convinced myself I was right. In fact, I was ready to bet on it.

So, children, the next time you pull a face when you look at your lunch, be kind to your mother. I'm only following in Marie Antoinette's footsteps but in reverse. If you can't have cake every day, eat bread. And don't crib. I can't do too badly on an unvarying diet of egg sandwiches, did I?

Yours hungrily,
Mama

....

Mumbai
June '99

Dear Rana and Radhika,
Last night, I went to see *Stepmom* with your father. My feelings were pretty mixed. I had heard conflicting reports about the film. Aditya had already seen it and had told me to look out for two specific scenes—the one in the car when Julia Roberts and the two kids start singing *Ain't no mountain high enough*, and another in which he wanted me to focus on Julia's watch (you know how Aditya is about watches). I knew Avantika would be there with her friends. I was also aware of the fact that the film was being pitched as a five-hanky weepie. And I do weep at most films—even corny Hindi tear-jerkers (especially corny Hindi t.j.s). I was hooked from minute one, scene one. Even though my own circumstances had been different, I could understand and empathize with Julia Roberts as she struggled to win over two confused kids—children of the love of her life, separated from their biological mother and deeply resentful

of the presence of a stranger—their father's girlfriend—in their lives. It was a tough role to pull off. Pitted against Julia in the role of the nurturing 'earth mother' was another powerful actress, Susan Sarandon. As the story unfolded, my thoughts were more on you than on the characters in the film. Arundhati had wanted to accompany us. For some reason, that hadn't worked out. I could see Avantika's head in silhouette as she leaned to her right to speak to her friends. I wondered how she was relating to the film, whether it had a special significance for her—as it surely must have.

We found each other during the interval. Her eyes were as moist as mine. We held hands, but didn't exchange a word. There was no need to. The men in the group went off to fetch coffee and popcorn. When the film resumed, Avantika and I watched it silently, our fingers linked. I thought of you, Arundhati, since the little girl in the film reminded both Avantika and me so strongly of you. I wondered what your reaction to the film would have been, had you come with us. I was glad you'd stayed back. The movie was getting unbearable. I could hear strangled sobs and loud snorts all around me. Rivers were flowing down my own cheeks. This was crazy. I was clearly out of control, being manipulated by a shrewd script-writer and weeping buckets unashamedly. It was only a movie, dammit. Yet, how close to the bone it had cut.

I recalled my early years with your father, before Arundhati and Anandita were born. Even though I hadn't encountered the slightest resistance outwardly, I had been acutely aware of the conflict in the minds of Radhika and Rana. Perfectly valid, perfectly natural, but hard to confront. If that period had been awkward or hard for me, it must have been doubly so for the children who were trying desperately to cope with the death of their mother. I really don't know how I acquitted myself during those early months—I may have been preoccupied with my own emotions. A new life was beginning for me, an entirely unfamiliar life with no reference points. Your father was a virtual stranger, a man I'd instantly admired and been drawn to. What if our marriage hadn't worked out the way we had hoped it would? What then? So much mutual adjustment, so many uncertainties. One major decision of my life (marriage) hurriedly, impulsively, instinctively taken. Another (career) still pending. Then there were the two sets of kids—participants all, but with no decision-making options.

In the movie, the little girl accuses her parents of just that—keeping her out of the one big decision that's going to change her life forever—her parent's divorce and her father's remarriage. We'd done the same too. Unknowingly. Foolishly, we'd merely informed the four of you of our plans to marry. How did you feel about the whole thing? I know how you reacted (passively, positively). But how did you actually feel? I guess I'll never really know. I wish I'd invested more time then to probe, find out, perhaps reassure. Maybe I was equally uncertain, equally scared. Maybe I wasn't ready to dig, afraid of what I'd come up against. Situations like these aren't 'normal'. Nobody can prepare you for them. Whom does one turn to for advice? Or even a frank airing of views? All you're armed with are your instincts and good intentions.

So, there we were, Dilip and I, quite thrilled with ourselves, our marriage celebrations, our new life. And there you were, four little kids with God knows what anxieties. We didn't ask; you didn't tell. We said, 'Let's give it a little time. They'll settle down, get used to the idea.

These things require patience.' Of course they do. Maybe they require something more—communication. And that was one area I failed in. I can rationalize my reticence and say I tried to compensate in other ways. I truly did. But now I feel the sincere effort was fine, but not enough. I should have talked more, got you to articulate what you were going through. I didn't. I made the same dumb mistakes millions of adults frequently make—I underestimated your right to know. Your right to express your opinion. Your right to debate, disagree, dissent, damn.

I sought comfort in your silence. I said to myself, 'They're young, they'll accept the situation. They'll accept us. They'll accept me.' All of which you did, most ungrudgingly at that. Even so, I'd give anything to rewind the years, go back to the summer of '84, and replay those frenetic months when everything was happening in fast forward, when I didn't have time to press 'pause', or think. When I should have sent a special probe into your hearts and found out what was going on in there even as my own heart was beating wildly at the prospect of an exciting future. I wonder now what you might have told me then—how much? How little? Whether you'd have suppressed your true feelings to protect yourselves rather than me. Whether you even knew or realized fully what exactly was taking place. Whether the turbulence got to you with a force you found hard to handle. Whether you withdrew, play-acted, cried silent tears into your pillow. I guess I'll never know. Strange, how life develops sometimes for some of us. And we fall into familiar traps like idiots.

It's only now, as adults, as equals, that we are in any position to assess, judge, accuse or forgive. But already, the past seems so remote, almost irrelevant. Several years have passed. We've learnt to co-exist and accept one another's quirks.

While watching what was after all, only another Hollywood weepie from the dream factory, I felt hot tears coursing down my cheeks at unexpected moments. I knew they had nothing to do with the film. Nothing at all. They were about me. My feelings. My failures. My disappointments. They were about those early years when I may not have been one hundred per cent sensitive to the fears and anxieties of two very young children who'd lost their mother. When I may have missed the signals altogether, and perhaps mistaken good behaviour for the absence of internal pain. Maybe it had been more convenient for me to do so. Maybe I already had far too much to deal with. I know I was very thankful that I didn't have the additional burden of coping with tantrums and tears. That to all outward appearances, everything was calm and controlled. Who knows how I might have handled all our lives had there been ugly outbursts? Constant demands? Unrelenting competition? I didn't face any of it—not for your father's time, nor for his attention. You children were consistently well-behaved. Exemplary, even. Fortunately, I was not required to 'test' myself under adverse circumstances.

As adults, our equation has altered. We can watch a film like *Stepmom* together, and discuss its effect on us openly and without embarrassment. Remember the impromptu dinner that followed the movie? The rest of you kids joined us at the Bombay Gymkhana where Daddy ordered a huge meal. My face was still tear-streaked. I was unusually quiet, the spell the film had cast not yet broken. I couldn't concentrate on the roomali roti or the chicken tikkas. I kept thinking about us. And then cutting to the film.

The film reaffirmed my belief that it is possible to make our kind of situation work for everybody involved in it, provided the intentions are positive and sincere. The stereotype of the wicked stepmother saddled with rebellious, resentful, monster stepchildren needs to be thrown out of the window without delay. As I watched your faces that night, I felt strangely comforted. The conversation around the table was lively, everybody was relaxed. I reached for the tadka dal and dipped a roti into it. Someone laughed, was it you, Rana? I'd dropped a blob of dal on my new jacket. I looked down at the stain. Clumsy, clumsy. You, Rana, then reached over with a napkin and helped me get the mess off my lapel. At the end of the meal, we parted. You had a date. We needed to get some sleep. It was all so reassuringly 'normal'. I promised myself I'd see the film again. And weep some more.

Emotionally yours,
Mama

....

Mumbai
May '99

Dear Girls,

Don't groan. I want to talk to you about a topic you detest (as most kids do). Duties. But before I do that, I want to tell you a little—just a little—about my teenage years.

And what my own mother expected from me. Actually, not very much. I wasn't around all that much—as you aren't any longer. I had several extra-curricular activities that kept me busy and out of the house for hours. Even so, there were a few things that my mother wanted me to help out with. These became my special 'duties'. Like rolling out chappatis, frying fish on weekends, or frying puris during festivals. Making omelettes for the family for Sunday morning breakfasts, shopping for weekly vegetables, running grocery errands, ironing my school uniforms, polishing my shoes, keeping my cupboard (the one I shared with my sister Kunda) reasonably clean.

Today, I know how my mother got me to 'cooperate'—she used praise. She always told me (and meant it too) that nobody could roll out better chappatis—mine didn't resemble a wonky map of India, she said. They were perfect, even circles, without lumps or thick edges. My fish fry, she informed everyone, couldn't be better. Thick Pomfret slices done to golden brown perfection. As for the omelettes—why, they looked professional. Fluffy, neatly folded over, well done on the outside, slightly runny inside and with the most amazing fillings. With that sort of build-up and encouragement, I took a great deal of pride in my weekend chores. She also convinced me that nobody could flat iron the pleats of my thick, drill school uniform as efficiently as I could. It was true. But it was also a pain. Especially during exam-time or in the rainy season when the box-pleated tunics took more than three days to dry after washing and had to be ironed while still heavy with moisture and very damp.

I didn't mind vegetable shopping, especially since I loved the old Dhobi Talao market and was on first-name terms with the vendors. I still enjoy buying plump, fresh vegetables and bantering with the sellers. I picked the veggies with utmost care, making sure the brinjals were not too soft or spotted, the bhindis were firm and green, the palak crisp and alert. Looking for groceries was another matter. My parents preferred to patronize just one store—the government-controlled Sahakari Bhandar. Nothing wrong with that—or the store. But being government controlled meant just one thing—long queues for every little item, and dozens of little bills. I'd spend more time paying for a bar of soap than I would have if I was buying half the store.

I tried to circumvent the problem by sneakily making similar small purchases from a privately owned shop closer to home. I got caught each time. I tried arguing. 'But what difference does it make? It's the same bar of soap, the same toothpaste, the same talcum powder.' My mother told me quietly, 'Yes. But you've paid much more for the items, only to save a few minutes.' In my mind, I thought angrily, 'What about the value of time—isn't there a price on that?' Sensing my resentment, my mother tried not to force this particular 'duty' on me. I know my sisters hated it equally, but someone had to do it. Finally, we tried to combine forces—Kunda would wait in one line and I in another. It didn't halve our time exactly, but it was better than being the fifty-fifth person in a serpentine queue, waiting to pay rupees nine, paise thirty-five only, for a packet of jeera from the masala counter.

I've tried taking you along on a few shopping trips, and noticed your complete disinterest. I've tried getting you into the kitchen to help me cook on special occasions and seen the faces you've pulled. Okay, it's not a priority for you. It wasn't one for me either. But unlike you, I didn't have much of a choice. And thank God for that. A few months ago, I bragged to you, 'There is nothing, absolutely nothing around the house that I can't or won't do.' I meant that. I can cook, clean, swab, scrub, iron and wash if and when I have to. And make a reasonably good job of all these chores. Because my mother made sure I was not just exposed to them indirectly but that I actually performed them to her satisfaction. I thank her for that. When I point this out to you, you laugh and giggle saying, 'Don't worry, we'll learn when we have to. Besides, in India there are always other people to do all that for you.' Think again, kids. Ten years from now, the social situation may change altogether. Everything that you take so much for granted now might disappear—the institution of domestics included. As it is, it's harder and harder to find full-time help these days. Reliable full-time help. Ten, fifteen years from now, even part-time workers may be difficult to come by. What then? 'Everybody copes when there's no choice,' you tell me airily. I certainly hope so. I've seen plenty of young people crack up when they travel abroad and are compelled to deal with cooking, cleaning and scrubbing toilets. Either they live like complete pigs, or they pick it all up in a great big hurry. Which will it be for you? Tomorrow your own words, 'Chill . . . and watch', might apply to you. Meanwhile, I guess I'll have to fix my own omelettes. Right, girls?

Yours resignedly,
Mama

....

Circle of
love

RADHIKA

Dear Children,

If you were to ask me to name one single, strong memory of food I recall from my childhood, I'd take no time at all to say aamti. Mother's aamti—a humble dal, eaten on a daily basis with rice or chappatis, nothing more than a staple in any Maharashtrian home. Yet, I can recall its special flavour so many year later. And each time I do, I can actually taste it. What was so special about her aamti, you'll ask. I'll tell you. Mother's aamti stood for something very deep and moving for me. It stood for her commitment to all of us. It revealed her love and duty towards the family. Your Aji was not the world's greatest cook, but she excelled in the few dishes she cooked. Aamti (even on a daily basis) was obviously one of them.

Since my school was at quite a distance—more than five kilometres from home—the hours were long and tiring. Given all my extra-curricular involvements, I was rarely home before 6 p.m. and when I'd get to the small dining table with its formica laminated surface, I'd be ravenously hungry. What did I look forward to wolfing down? Two slices of hot, buttered toast dunked into the tasty aamti. I rarely varied this pre-dinner snack. And I certainly never tired of it. Toast and aamti. I relished the combination for years and years (through school, college, my first job and till the day I got married).

What I regret is that you don't have an aamti in your life. A dish that you associate exclusively with me. A dish that you'll remember with as much fondness and love when you are older. There is no aamti in my cooking repertoire, alas. Besides, I don't cook regularly, so, no matter what I prepare sporadically, no matter how good it tastes, it can never mean the same thing to you. We live in times when snacks come pre-packaged. In our home, we have cooks and maids to produce them instantly for you. Our meals are eclectic—Chinese one day, Continental occasionally, but mostly Bengali. I cannot imagine which dish will leave its mark on your palate and memory. Which dish will you associate with warmth, love and security? Sometimes I feel a little sad when I think of this. I feel even worse that I didn't think of asking Mother for the recipe when I had the chance. Today, the aamti has gone with her. Your aunts don't know exactly what went into it, your uncle Ashok (who's now a competent cook) doesn't know either. Besides, I'm not sure they were aamti fanatics in quite the same way as I. I feel sad that I'll never be able to taste it again. Or experience the same sense of anticipation while walking home from the bus stop.

Someone recently asked me in an interview whether I was always picky and fastidious about food. The interviewer wanted to know when and where I was introduced to the great foods of the world. How did I develop a taste for foie gras or caviar? Were they served in our home? I smiled to myself and once again thought of the simple aamti, visualized my mother making it in the old, dimly lit but spacious kitchen. I can see her now breaking the coconut with a firm 'thwack' (or getting Tulsi, the mannish maid to do it). Then carefully preserving the coconut water in the fridge, saving one half of the fruit for later, scraping out the required portion for the day's aamti, and wet-grinding it roughly on a traditional black stone platform, after combining the right spices. Later she'd add the pre-soaked tamarind pulp and finally pour the tadka over the simmering dal, mustard seeds popping impatiently out of the smoking oil. That's all I know about what actually went into the aamti—and I'm only guessing. It always, but always, came together with an even consistency. The taste rarely varied. And I think it was that which I found most comforting. I knew what I was coming home to. I knew it would be there. I knew it would taste good. I knew my mother would be around to serve it, I knew she'd be smiling. I knew what she'd be wearing (a soft, printed voile saree), I knew what she'd say ('so . . . how many matches did you win today?'), I knew her smell (Hazeline snow, Cuticura talc), I knew her smile. I knew her touch.

What pattern can I offer you? What predictability? None. Yes, I'm always home when you get back. But the food that is put on the table has not been made by me. Sometimes I have visitors and you have to wait to share your day's events till the person leaves. Often I'm preoccupied, either writing or on the phone. Once again, you have to wait while I look up rather absently and greet you. I see but I don't see. I hear but I don't hear. I'm there but I'm not there. This is not fair. You don't have aamti in your life, and you don't know what you're missing.

Regretfully yours,
Mama

....

Mumbai
August '99

Dear Arundhati,
Remember the trip you never took, and which, in the end, never happened? I do. It was to Lakshadweep. You were in

the seventh grade. All your friends had signed up—including far younger girls from the building. I knew you were dying to go. You'd put in your request months before the forms were to be submitted. Unfortunately, your timing had been seriously off—you'd caught me on a bad day when I was way behind schedule and nursing a headache. I'd barely looked up from my writing pad before snapping, 'Forget it, you're much too young for such long trips.' Your eyes had brimmed over, and you'd argued. The usual pitch. 'But . . . all my friends are going. They've been allowed. How can you be so mean?' It was that line, 'All my friends are going,' that had made me see red. You had overused it. Tried that tactic once too often to bully me into agreeing to something I had mixed feelings about. Now you were doing it again. I snarled, 'I don't care if "all your friends" are going. Or whether their parents have allowed them. You aren't going. And that's final.' You had left me to continue writing (it took my blood pressure a few minutes to recover) while you sulked in your room. I forgot all about Lakshadweep and the trip. Till your winter break began and you said to me cheerfully one morning, 'I'm going to say goodbye to my friends.'

'Why, where are they going?' I asked absently.

'On that school trip to Lakshadweep,' you replied.

'Really? What fun. How come you didn't want to go?'

Your face registered complete shock. 'What do you mean how come I didn't want to go? Of course I did. I was dying to. But you didn't allow me.'

'What?' I asked in genuine puzzlement. 'I don't remember any such thing.' You reminded me of our conversation . . . and I shrivelled up with shame. 'Oh darling, you must have caught me in an off-mood. Why didn't you ask again?' I asked, my own eyes filling with tears.

'I was scared to. You might have got angry and said, "Don't nag me." Or "No is no."' God. Had I become so snappy? So irritable? Had I stopped listening altogether? I felt truly awful.

Your friends left in a flurry of excitement. They were going to visit a wildlife sanctuary, stay in a forest rest house, take the ship for an island cruise. It sounded great. You saw them off sportingly. They promised to get back souvenirs. You displayed no resentment at all. None. I found that remarkable. In your place, I'm sure I'd have felt angry and sulked for a few days. You made no reference to your feelings about what was clearly a case of lousy timing. In fact, you were happy when your friends phoned you from Kochi to report excitedly about the trip till that point, all the fun they were having, the train pranks, the lousy food, and how they were missing you. You laughed and giggled, telling me all about it, again without the slightest envy. I thought that touching and admirable. More so, when they called two days later to say they'd had to abandon the cruise due to some technical snag. Pettily, I had gloated, 'See, I knew it. Had you gone on that trip . . .' You stopped me. 'Mom . . . don't say that, okay? Poor girls. They must be so disappointed.' Wisely, I shut up. Without your realizing it, I had learned a valuable lesson. Often, due to adult pressures and work-related tensions, we stop paying close attention to our children's conversation, because at that moment, they don't seem important—your own priorities do. You forget that what may be a trivial matter to you, may be vitally urgent to a child. Arundhati, I know that particular morning when you asked me about your trip, I was suffering from a systems overload. Maybe I was catching up with a missed deadline. Awful excuse. But that was really it. Without thinking anything through, I arbitrarily said,

'Forget it, you aren't going,' thereby closing the option. I admired you for the way you handled it—no tantrums, no demands. Just quiet acceptance with enormous grace. Yes, I had wielded my 'power' over you by denying a trip. But you, my dear, had demonstrated something far bigger to me—your largeness of heart. I felt sorry for my mistake. But also very proud of you for your generosity. And you know what? We made up for it—together—with the holiday we took the following summer. A holiday that may never have happened if . . . am I appeasing my guilty conscience? Perhaps. But we had a ball and that's all that matters. Parents do find different ways of making it up when they know they've erred. This was mine.

Yours sheepishly,
Mama

....

Mumbai
July '99

Dear Children,

I've been slightly worried about the business of complete and total honesty between parents and kids. Does it exist? Is it even needed? How honest is honest? No secrets? A few? We've discussed it several times in the past, and I haven't really found a satisfactory answer. I've talked to a few of my friends and contemporaries and they seemed equally confused. While I'm okay about kids confiding in parents, what concerns me more is when the situation gets reversed.

Parents these days increasingly seem to use their young children as confidants, even co-conspirators. Because of the high levels of stress we have to deal with, parents—mothers in particular—need an outlet for their emotions and children are often the most readily accessible ones. Is this fair—to either? I raise this question because I do have a few women friends who have bravely and devotedly raised kids as single parents. In the process, they've had no one else to depend on, especially during those turbulent adolescent years. Without buffers, they've turned to one another and fed off mutual anxieties, even neuroses, to a point I've considered unhealthy. For example, a divorcee friend based overseas was compelled to raise her only child all by herself after she split with her husband when the boy was barely two years old. Since she had to fend for herself, and lead what is described as a bohemian life, the boy grew up with a succession of 'uncles' sharing the home. Each time a new 'uncle' entered the picture, the mother would sit him down and go over the gory details of her previous break-up—why it had happened, who did what to whom, that sort of thing. I thought it unnecessary, even ugly. She said it was honest and upfront. How did it help the situation? Today, those early scars are clearly visible in the young man. He doesn't talk about his past, and has distanced himself from his mother. Maybe he was far too young, far too fragile when she forced him to be a reluctant participant in her roller-coaster life. Maybe she could have cushioned him better.

There are umpteen similar examples, of parents who over-involve their kids in the nitty-gritties of their own lives, who believe in telling it as it is, without censoring a single detail. Is it healthy? Or desirable? This is a trend that began with my generation of parents. Earlier, parents and children led fairly compartmentalized lives. Adult problems were dealt with by adults. Arguments took place outside the earshot of kids. Matters were settled behind closed doors. That's how I grew up. Some people think this was false, hypocritical and wrong. 'We have the right to know,' I've heard teenagers say, and I'm puzzled. Perhaps the right exists. But are you emotionally prepared to take what comes with the turf? Do you want to play referee in a fight? Take sides? Arbitrate? Surely, that's not what your formative years are meant to be? Why should you be dragged into situations that have nothing to do with you?

I've thought about this a lot. There have been occasions when I've involved some of you in my problems. You've been wonderful in your support, often providing solutions and insights I myself lacked. But at the end of it, I've felt wretched about burdening you—at your age, you have more than your share of matters to deal with. Degrees to acquire, jobs to seek. You don't need to lend a patient ear to my occasional cribbing. And yet, you've been there for me everytime I succumbed to the temptation of approaching you.

My friends tell me not to feel bad. 'That's what kids are there for,' they say. I'm not convinced. I've seen far too many mixed-up offspring to buy this theory. I've seen single mothers going off on extended booze binges with under-eighteen sons. I've seen them behaving like teeny-boppers themselves at local clubs and discotheques and I can swear I've observed their children squirm. I've been privy to lines like, 'I have no secret from my boys.' How has it helped anyone—the boys, girls or mums themselves? 'We believe in total transparency in our family,' fathers have boasted. 'Why play-act? Children are sensitive enough to figure things out for themselves.'

There I do agree. Kids instinctively know when storm clouds gather. My point is simple—tell them only as much as they need to know. Do not drag them into a sordid scenario while you get your act sorted out. Don't lie to your children—ever. Don't tell them everything is perfect even as your world is collapsing around your ears. At the same time, speak with responsibility when you have to clarify a tricky situation. Often, young minds are unable to handle the messy intricacies of adult arguments. Why let kids get caught in the cross-fire? Why convert them into convenient pawns to settle scores or to get even?

As for 'complete honesty' from your side, frankly, I don't expect it. Not after a certain age. I believe I know enough. The rest doesn't concern me—or at any rate, ought not to. You are young adults capable of running your own lives. It would be intrusive and insulting on my part to probe and pry after a point. I assume you tell me what is valid and important. The rest is your affair. I'd love to know it all, be one hundred per cent involved in each and every aspect of your daily life. But I'm realistic enough to accept that this is not possible. There are bound to be enormous tracts with a sign reading, 'out of bounds', 'no trespassers'. So long as I'm assured of two things—your physical safety and good health—the rest is inconsequential.

I may not approve of a lot of things. I may not like your friends, or even how you spend your spare time. Well, that's too bad—for me. But before you think I'm letting you off the hook entirely, let me ask you a specific question, to which I expect an honest reply. Don't bullshit me—I always find out. If for some reason you cannot answer truthfully, just say so. Tell me, 'Mother, I'd prefer not to reply to that one, at least for now. I'll tell you what you need to know at a later point.' I think that's fair. Try me. But for heaven's sake, don't mislead me, as I wouldn't mislead you. By now, you guys know that you get a straight answer from me no matter how tricky the question. In the end it saves time. I may have fibbed now and again, but over completely insignificant things. The major stuff is sacred. Not to be trifled with. I don't concoct, invent or cover up. That much I can say with—yes, complete honesty.

Yours trustingly,
Mama

....

Mumbai
May '99

Dear Girls,

Last evening happened to be a very special day for your great-aunt Nimatai, Aji's youngest sister, a lady you hardly know. (I'm certain you wouldn't even recognize her if you were to meet her 'out of context', say on a busy street.) Well, it was Nimatai's special day because her children had planned a celebration to mark fifty years of their parents' marriage. I'd received a warm invitation from my cousin Rekha to attend the function at a suburban venue. 'Bring all the children,' she'd urged.

I had agreed, knowing the lot of you would pull faces and opt out. After all, you don't know Rekha either. You've probable met her two or three times in all these years, generally on a family occasion crowded with distant (and close) relatives—most of them indistinguishable to you. Not your fault. I'm looking for scapegoats here. Whom or what shall I blame? Life in a busy, busy, metro? No, the truth is, I blame myself. There are really no excuses. My relatives and I live in the same city, yet we hardly know one another. We meet once in two years, if that.

When Aji was alive, it was different. She was the link, the glue. It was through her that we got news about her side of the family. She'd keep us informed about births, job switches, marriages, changed address and sundry gossip. Her grapevine worked effectively, thanks to regular phone calls and occasional visits. Cousins with spouses and children would converge on Aji during festivals, or to convey some 'good news' (a baby, a promotion, an engagement, or high marks in an exam), always with a box of sweetmeats and fresh temple flowers. She in turn would excitedly phone all of us to share the information. That's how the system worked. With her passing away the family experienced a serious systems failure. Our link was gone. There was no 'central news distribution agency' any more. Gradually, we lost touch.

Which is why I was determined to make it to Nimatai's 'golden wedding' anniversary. I remembered with what enthusiasm all of us had organized Aji and Ajoba's in 1985. Most of you were far too young to either enjoy or remember the occasion. Anandita wasn't even born. But for the rest of us, it was a momentous and solemn occasion. We'd been lucky in that we'd managed to hire the very same wedding hall, 'Laxmi Baug' in central Mumbai, where your grandparents had taken their marriage vows fifty years ago. We'd also managed to track down at least a few of the friends who'd attended the ceremony.

Five decades later, so much had changed—and yet, so little. As family and other guests began congregating in the modest-sized hall, I watched Nimatai enter, holding a large package. As the two sisters embraced, my eyes filled with tears. Mother was sixty-eight then, and Nimatai sixty-two. They didn't really resemble each other physically, yet their mannerisms were achingly similar. Nimatai, younger by six years, had never failed to maintain the proper hierarchical distance by showing respect to her eldest sister—your grandmother. She kept up the tradition that night, when with great dignity and grace she opened her package to reveal its contents. Nimatai had come armed with all the paraphernalia required for an aarti—she placed the prepared diyas in a silver thali, adjusted the paan leaves and betel (symbols of prosperity), dipped her finger lightly into a tiny haldi-kumkum container and anointed Aji, after sprinkling a few grains of rice over her head. In Aji's lap, and into her extended saree pallav, she offered a coconut, a blouse piece, a saree, and a gift, along with a gajra strung with fragrant mogra blossoms. All these represented auspicious symbols associated with a married woman's continued well-being, long life for her husband, health, wealth and happiness—an age-old ritual that was being lovingly adhered to. I found it touching and beautiful. I watched the other guests, some followed the same tradition on a smaller scale, others skipped it in favour of a more modern, and I guess, a more convenient expression of congratulations: flowers, cash, recycled gifts.

Nimatai sat by your Aji throughout the ceremony. It was easy to sense their closeness—just watching their body language was enough. From time to time, between receiving guests, they'd lean towards each other, whisper softly, exchange conspiratorial looks, even giggle. It was a moving sight, and I felt happy for Mother that at least one of her two sisters was there to share this moment with her. Unfortunately for Baba, both his brothers were dead. I'm certain he missed Anna, his doctor brother, that night. But their sons and daughters and grandchildren were present in good numbers. Later, when we looked at the photographs and the home video, we chuckled over some candid camera shots and commented on how much we'd all changed—cousins, aunts and uncles.

What happened last evening was slightly different. I had far too many things on my mind as I drove to the suburban hall with Baba to attend Nimatai's function. I also had to rush back within the hour to make it for a dinner I'd previously committed to be present at. I was tense and preoccupied. It was peak-hour traffic stress, combined with other worries. When I entered, I got the impression that our slightly late arrival had delayed proceedings, even though nothing was said. Nimatai greeted us warmly and I noticed how much older and smaller she looked—almost like she had shrunk.

I thought of Aji as she was before her death. She had also become smaller. Like she too had shrunk. Now, finally, I could spot a resemblance between the sisters. It was the expression in their eyes—slightly guarded, almost like a deer's when caught in the glare of strong lights. I hugged Nimatai, as we both remembered Mother. She struggled to her feet from an enormous throne-like chair she'd been made to occupy. I had to bend really low to embrace her. My only surviving aunt. My last real connection to Mother's immediate family. Yes, there was also her brother, but it wasn't the same thing. I cursed myself for wearing high heels (for the 'other' dinner).

The video cameras were on us. I gave her the envelope with cash that I was carrying and bent down to touch her feet. It seemed like such an inadequate gesture. My mother, had she been alive, would have been aghast. And disappointed. Why hadn't I thought of arranging all the paraphernalia for the ceremonial aarti, as Mother surely would have done had she been there?' After all, I was there as her representative. I felt awful. Especially as I watched other women pull out their coconuts, haldi-kumkum and flowers from their handbags and perform the aarti for my aunt. How business-like and impersonal I must have seemed. Like I was performing a duty—nothing more. I had let my mother down.

Driving back with Ajoba (in time to attend the 'other' dinner) I felt pretty wretched. It was too late to make amends. My aunt hadn't said anything to indicate she had noticed. That was her graciousness. She'd asked about all of you—why you weren't present. I had made up some hollow excuses. She knew and I knew the real reason was different—her golden wedding meant little to any of you because she meant very little, too. Again, not your fault. It was up to me to have made the effort, to have insisted on your presence.

My cousin Rekha had glowed with pride as her parents received the guests, all of whom had been personally invited by her. Nimatai had reported joyfully that two of her wishes had come true that night—her children had given her a cordless phone (so she didn't have to hobble to pick up the phone each time it rang), and a beautiful diamond ring—her first. 'I've always wanted to wear a glittering diamond on my finger,' she confessed to Ajoba. Well, now she had one—a stone that stood for so much—her children's prosperity and affection. Also, her children's desire and ability to fulfil their mother's dream. I was glad for Nimatai and wondered how Mother would have reacted had she been present. One thing I do know—she would have sent me right back home to get the aarti. And then I would have been forced to skip the 'other' dinner—which turned out to be awful, by the way. I got the feeling I was being punished as I deserved to be.

It was only on the way back, as we drove through incredibly crowded streets, trying in vain to beat the rush, that I actually squirmed in my seat. I had slipped up. I had let my mother down. But what of you—the third generation? What legacy was I passing down to you? I had vivid, real memories of my mother and other relatives actively following certain well-established, well-loved traditions. You children have hardly any memories of your mother doing the same. Soon, it will all be gone. You may never know the meaning of that lovely word 'savashin', or what it means for one happily married woman to be blessed by five other happily married women (yes, the 'savashins'), who reaffirm through ritual, song and gesture, the values of wedded life. In these jaded times, how desperately we need such ceremonies.

You may also never witness a traditional 'autti-bharaney', when a married woman is honoured by other ladies of the community who fill her aanchal with symbols of fertility, prosperity and good health. None of these mean anything to you. With each passing generation, we are losing a little more. And that 'little more' keeps adding up till there will be nothing left. In my anxiety to keep up with your world, I took the trouble to get hooked on to MTV, your movies, your music, your fads. Fine. But I should have invested the same amount of time and energy drawing you into our world, your grandmother's and mine. Then, we could have participated in each other's worlds more fully, more completely.

It isn't too late even now. So here's the good news, girls. I intend to find out more about these rituals. My guesses so far have been on track, but may not be accurate enough. They are my own clumsy interpretations. Surely, there has to be more. These are traditions that have been practised for centuries—with good reason. It's time for me to conduct some serious research. Once I'm through, I shall sit you down and pass on what I have learned. You may get impatient (as I used to with my mother), bored or feign indifference. But I'm confident the knowledge you glean will stay with you, so that when you have children of your own, or better still, when we celebrate our big occasion, you won't make the mistakes I did. Oh no. You will come, dressed for the occasion, bearing a thali with diyas, haldi-kumkum, rice grains and fresh flowers. Yes, you will.

Yours in embarrassment,
Mama

....

Mumbai
June '99

Bachchas,

Sometimes I feel like writing letters to King Tuts. He is one of the family, after all. So what if he's a dog? This month marks his sixth birthday. He came to us travelling all the way from Bangalore in a Kashmiri picnic basket. We were just about coming to terms with the death of our first pet, our boxer Marciano. Mentally, I had decided never to bring a pet into the house again. The loss generated far too much heartbreak. I'd thought to myself that maybe we weren't equipped to look after dogs. I didn't come from a doggy-family. And your father hadn't kept a dog at his home either. I'd told you kids that getting a pet was a huge responsibility. It wasn't like acquiring a new toy. A Mumbai flat didn't seem like the ideal habitat for a dog—who would walk him four times a day? Bathe him once a week, twice in summer? Train him not to mess up the house? Keep track of his various immunization shots? Take him to the vet regularly? At the time, all of you volunteered most enthusiastically: 'I'll do it,' 'I'll do it.' But I knew exactly where the buck would stop. And I wasn't wrong.

Tuts turned out to be a lovable, non-demanding chap from the word go. He accepted us all unconditionally and demanded nothing in return. All he wanted was company. He obviously had a horror of being alone (one of those!). By any standard, today he is possibly the best-adjusted member of our family. No tantrums, no ego, regular habits, an affable nature, no late nights, no food fetishes. And heaven help me—no wardrobe requirements. Give him his two meals a day, talk to him from time to time, and he's deliriously happy, wagging his stub of a tail to show it. Visitors adore him, even those who say they detest dogs. He greets every person with wild enthusiasm. If his exuberance seems slightly over-the-top and excessive, that's okay. It's better than growls and aggression.

I take Tuts for granted. He is my constant companion while I write, sitting over my bare feet. He's the one who alerts me to your homecoming—getting to the door seconds before you ring the bell. He knows and likes my friends. They in turn, love him. I often wonder—what, if anything, goes on in that head of his? What would he say to me, if he could speak? I often find his face far more expressive than most human faces. His body language is also easy to read. But it's really his eyes that make me wonder about his world. If he could articulate a few things to me, what would they be? Would he pout and accuse me of not spending enough time with him? (Not fair; I spend more time with him than any of you care to.) Would he complain that I take him far too much for granted? (I do.) Would he be brutally honest and shout,'I hate the food in this joint!'

I know you guys love him. Unfortunately, the love is not linked to responsibility. This is something I do feel bad about. Tuts is my seventh child—and the hardest one to raise, since he can't tell me what he wants. I have to guess. If, for any reason, I happen to be preoccupied, or not around, it's left to the domestics to handle him to the best of their abilities. To me it's a major concern. It's like leaving an infant in the care of a person who can't summon help in an emergency. Since Tuts is exceptionally accommodating and far from fastidious, looking after his needs has not caused too much of a problem. But your attitude has. If Tuts could write a diary, I'm sure he'd have a few things to crib about—how nobody takes him for a walk or drive. Or plays with him for more than five minutes, or accompanies him to the vet for his regular visits. I have seen other dogs in other homes and noted how the entire family is involved in looking after them. Thank God Tuts isn't one of these canines who lapse into depression if the family is away. I hear horror stories from my friends about their pets losing their appetite, even starving for days on account of the master's (or mistress's) absence. Not our Tuts, who sees us off cheerfully and is invariably there to greet us with gay abandon when we return. There is so much we can learn from Tuts. About loyalty and love. And a complete absence of selfishness. Tuts seems to exist to give us happiness. I know that when I'm stressed out, all I need to do is summon him for a back-scratch. While I run my toes over his arched spine, I actually feel my tension easing and my bunched up muscles relaxing. I imagine (as most dog owners invariably do) that he 'understands' me, understands what I'm saying to him. Maybe he does. Or maybe he doesn't. It hardly matters.

One thing I do know—he senses things in his own extraordinary way, and he's there when I need him. Which is more than I can say about a lot of human friends. If only he could speak, I'd start believing in an intelligence other than the limited one we humans feel so superior about. Right, Tuts?

Bow Wow,
Mother

....

Mumbai
24 March

Dear Children,

I'm sure you've realized by now that I am entirely addicted to certain rituals. Simple, everyday acts, but they provide a meaning to my life. Unless of course I'm investing far more into clipping your toe-nails than the chore warrants. I like rituals and hate the thought that some of you may be outgrowing them. When Aditya and Avantika were toddlers, I enjoyed cutting their hair. I became quite adept with a pair of barber's scissors. For years, their regular haircuts were my exclusive responsibility, along with fortnightly nail-cutting, ear-cleaning and daily oil massages.

Today, it's the turn of the younger children. I no longer cut Rana's hair—he prefers to have it shaved off periodically. Radhika's trims happen now and again though her latest 'shaggy look' cut by yours truly has been much appreciated by her colleagues. That leaves Arundhati and Anandita, who, I fear, will no longer settle for my ministrations now that they've discovered the hedonistic pleasure of having their hair cut and blow-dried by professionals at a nearby beauty salon. Even so, I shall persist because I love to perform these little tasks. At fourteen, Arundhati has never cut her own nails even if she gives herself a pretty competent manicure complete with buffing and polishing. Ever so often, she presents herself to me and lies flat on my bed while I set to work with baby nail scissors—blue with blunt tips. Then there are the ear-bud sessions (the buds dipped in a favourite cologne). Sometimes, I picture myself hard at work on your obstinate toe-nails even when you girls are married with kids of your own ('Oh my God! Look at those nails. Let's call Mother!').

None of you enjoyed the oil baths I so loved giving. Nobody lets me rub creamy moisturizer on rough knees and elbows. I wonder why. I'd love to be pampered in this manner. I'd definitely lie back and enjoy it. Gone are your hot oil hair massages too ('gross'). With each ritual disappearing, I feel a little less 'needed'. These days I rack my brains to think of things to do with you . . . for you. A vigorous back rub, for example. Or a go at a new hair-style. Avantika used to approve of what I did with her extra long tresses when she was around five. I'd dress up her braids with brightly-coloured ribbons or pin back stray locks with barrettes matching her dresses. These days only Anandita permits me to run a brush through her hair. My own mother didn't give me a choice. She'd comb mine exactly in the manner she thought appropriate, till such time as I developed exceedingly strong views on the subject.

Another ritual that's vital to me these days is eating together. Arundhati and Anandita get home from school at 2.30 p.m. I watch the hands of the clock impatiently from around 1 p.m. when I am hungry. Yet, I cannot bear to eat by myself. So, I get busy attending to correspondence, waiting for the doorbell to ring. Once the girls get home, lunch is served. At night, it's a repeat, only I don't eat with you girls. I make sure I sit at the table chatting while you tuck into dinner. I rarely accept lunch invitations, because it's important for me to be home when you come back from school. Instead, I invite people over to share our meal. Sometimes, I see the impatience on your faces when you come running in and spot one of my friends. They see it too, nod understandingly and whisper, 'Go ahead. Bond. We'll wait.'

Then comes a brief afternoon nap with Anandita. It's a moment I love. She wraps her right arm tightly around my neck, nearly choking me; the room is dark and cool. She has finished narrating her adventures at school; I'm taking a much-needed break from writing. She falls asleep, still mumbling. I drift off for twenty minutes. We both awake fresh and ready to tackle the world, and I half wonder—how many days do I have left of this togetherness? Soon Anandita's life will get very busy. She won't need a siesta. She'll prefer to spend time on the phone or computer. There'll be far too much homework for her to deal with. Nap? Forget it. What a waste of precious time.

How rapidly these magical years go by. I can't believe it's been twenty since the time I used to force Aditya to lie down beside me during muggy afternoons and keep his eyes shut. He'd feign deep sleep just long enough for me to sneak out of the room to check on some work. Then he'd run straight out of the house to play 'gali' cricket with the gurkha's sons. Then there was Arundhati, who needed her 'doodoo' bottle every afternoon, till she was seven years old. Precious memories of physical closeness and warmth. Yes, rituals do have a place in our busy lives. You'll realize that too, someday, when you cradle your own babies close to your heart and remember being held with the same tenderness and love when you were little and dependent.

Nostalgically,
Mother

....

Mumbai
August '99

Dear All,

Birthdays! I think every single one is special and ought to be celebrated, maybe not with a party, but with even a small gesture that marks the passing of a year. In our family, we are big on birthdays. Being such a large family, we seem to have a celebration at least once a month, if not twice. Besides, we celebrate Ajoba's birthday, as we used to Aji's when she was alive. We also celebrate anniversaries and other significant days. I'm asked whether I don't tire of planning these occasions. After all, one knows exactly what's involved—gifts, surprises, cake, candles, decorations. Sometimes, when I'm especially stressed out, I do feel drained at the thought of coming up with new ideas and executing them (with your help, of course). But when I see the expression on the face of the recipient, it makes every bit of the effort worthwhile.

Celebrating birthdays runs in families. There are so many that give this special day no importance at all. I know people who forget not only other people's birthdays but their own as well. 'What's there to celebrate?' they ask, sounding genuinely puzzled. Well, it's a point of view. For any child, it is the one day of the year for feeling extra special, the day that is looked forward to eagerly. It means new clothes, the class singing 'Happy Birthday', distributing sweets to teachers, and perhaps having a party for friends too.

We've done it all—big parties and small lunches, picnics, movies, sleepovers, slumber parties, and for Arundhati's thirteenth ('I am a teenager now, Mother'), an improvised disco party at home—girls only and nine-thirty the cut-off time. I thought it was a lot of fun, I hope all of you felt the same.

There have been marvellous surprise parties planned for me by all of you, and 'family only' outings that turned out to be the most fun. With different children, we've established different traditions. Arundhati's birthday has always been associated with a Satyanarain Puja—something she resented as a child ('Why do you have to spoil only my birthday with this boring thing?'). Now, she appreciates its significance slightly better. Anandita, being the perennial baby, has so far opted for the works—balloons, streamers, cakes and candles. Last year, we also threw in an 'adult' Chinese lunch. Radhika has shunned a big fuss ever since she was little, preferring a special dinner with just the family. Rana has had some rowdy, noisy affairs in the past (remember the 'naughty' cake he cut for his twenty-first birthday?). As has Aditya. A mariachi band played as we brought in his twenty-second birthday gift. Avantika and I have shared a special lunch ritual which remains unchanged regardless of what else she chooses to do. Then there are the birthday letters I often write—sentimental, mushy missives that manage to say on paper what I often fail to in person. Both Aditya and Avantika have a sizeable collection by now.

I believe gifts should be hand-picked and thoughtful. I try my best with mine. You kids help me fill baskets of goodies for those very special ones (eighteenth, twenty-first), when we go to town finding the exact number of objects to fill the hamper. Believe me, it isn't always easy finding eighteen or twenty-one appropriate gifts. I remember sending Aditya a bag full of gags for his twenty-first birthday celebrated on campus in Boston, including a plastic sports car to represent the real one I'd have loved to give but couldn't afford. Avantika on hers got a battery-operated toy cellphone (which actually rings) to remind her of the one she'd overused and therefore forfeited. We work hard on birthdays, don't we? Hand painted posters, complicated collages, jumbo-sized cards with funny messages and pictures, greetings scrawled across mirrors with old lipsticks, personalized T-shirts, rangoli with flowers on the bedspread. Yup. Elaborate stuff all right.

Aji always looked forward to her birthday, which we, the children, celebrated with early morning phone calls, flowers, gifts, sweets and a restaurant dinner which was eagerly looked forward to. I try and ensure we visit a temple at least on that one day of the year, because I believe the visit provides a few enforced moments of solemnity in our celebrations. We've all shared some birthdays together—and that's important. Years from now, while flipping though family albums, we will recreate some of these moments and feel enveloped in a warm glow. Personally, I'm all for birthday bashes, even on the smallest scale. By remembering one another on that day, throughout our lives, a certain vital link is created and maintained. God knows we live in fragile times, with so much—too much—on our plates. Birthdays are a reaffirmation of family bonds and feelings. They provide a legitimate reason to come together for a few hours to make that annual phone call, mail a card, a message, a token, anything that says, 'We remember you. We care.' As I grow older I find myself getting increasingly sentimental. I look back at my own birthdays and some stand out for having been more special than the rest. In our family, we do tend to go overboard and make a big production out of the day—why not?

We plan, we conspire, we plot, we scheme, we ambush, we take by surprise—all with good intentions, of course. Our cards are frequently hand-crafted, our posters mark milestones, our presents are never standard issue, off-the-shelf purchases. A great deal of time and money are invested in ensuring that the birthday person feels on top of the world. That's how it should be. When you guys get to be my age, you too will look back on these occasions and get misty-eyed as I do now. But more than that, you will carry on the tradition with your own children, and they in turn will learn from you. I suppress a secret smile these days each time Ajoba's birthday approaches. He says, 'Why celebrate an old man's birthday? I'm ninety-two . . . forget it. You must be tired of buying me gifts year after year. I don't need anything now. I have more than my requirements.'

Perhaps. But try forgetting the flowers, cake, candles and outings, and watch him sulk. That's what I mean about birthdays. They spoil you—for life. But isn't that why we celebrate them in the first place?

Happy Birthdays,
Mama

....

Mumbai
April '99

Dear Anandita and Arundhati,
  During the past few months, some of your friends have been experiencing a specific trauma—their parents have 'threatened' to send them away to boarding school. The threat has been issued as a 'final warning'. The provocation? Defiance and disobedience at home, complaints of the same from school authorities, and a general 'switching off' that has resulted in non-communication. You've discussed your friends' problem with me and asked, 'Is boarding school really all that terrible? Why do parents send their children away?' I've answered truthfully that I am not an advocate for boarding schools, never having been enrolled in one. And I'm certainly not an advocate for sending children away, no matter what the provocation. I believe parents are best equipped to deal with kids' problems, and that by threatening a confused child with banishment nothing is achieved. Different kids respond differently to the prospect of boarding school. I know some who regard it as an adventure (too many Enid Blytons?) and enjoy every

moment. It helps if parents create a conducive atmosphere in preparation for the big move. But for a majority of very young children, the idea of being separated from the family for extended periods of time is terrifying.

Of course, I have met several extremely well-adjusted children who've come out of boarding schools. But in my experience there has inevitably been a pay-off. For all their grooming and good manners, the children have exhibited signs of maladjustment, either within the family or vis-à-vis outsiders. You asked me once whether I had even considered sending you away, and I said, 'Never'. 'Even if we behaved really naughtily?' you persisted. 'Not even then,' I said. You exchanged delighted glances. 'But that doesn't give you the licence to misbehave,' I had warned in my sternest voice.

A few days after that conversation, one of you came to me with a really sad story. You told me about a friend whose parents were fighting all the time. The word 'divorce' had been overheard by the child, who had been devastated. I told you to be gentle with her since she was your best friend and had nobody else to confide in. Over the next month, I'd inadvertently eavesdropped on some of your conversations. I'd listen to your sincere 'advice' to the little girl. 'I have a plan for you. Why don't you organize a picnic for your parents? Or bake them a cake?' you'd suggest solemnly. Sometimes the other child would cry. 'Then tell them to go on a holiday together. You can come and live at our home.' I'd wonder where you were getting your ideas from. The movies?

Then one day, you came home from school crestfallen and depressed. 'I think it's going to happen very soon,' you announced glumly. 'What?' I asked. 'The divorce,' you answered. Over lunch you mentioned the other bit of bad news. 'They're sending her to a boarding school. I'll never see her again.' I thought about the difficult decision made by the feuding parents. I'm sure they'd considered all the options and decided this was the best one. Perhaps it was. At least the child would be spared the daily spats, which recently had started turning violent. I felt very sorry for your friend—a beautiful, sensitive, cheerful child, who over a period of just six months had transformed into an overweight, awkward, withdrawn girl. You said she'd turned moody, her grades were down and she no longer smiled.

After a fortnight of uncertainty the decision was taken. She was to go. You cried and I tried in vain to console you. 'It isn't fair,' you said. 'Just because her mother and father hate each other, she has to go away. It's not her fault.' I tried explaining that it was better this way, and that your friend may even enjoy boarding school, meet new girls, acquire another life. 'But this is her home. Why should she leave? They can go if they want. Or they can stay and stop fighting.' How easy it sounded. If only real life worked that way.

So, the little girl was readied for her long trip. Once again, we were back to discussing boarding schools vs day schools. 'She won't be able to meet her mama or papa for months and months,' you pointed out. 'Imagine seeing your parents just twice a year. It's so weird.'

I told you thousands of children did it without crying or complaining. 'That's because they have to—there's no choice,' you countered. By now the atmosphere in the strife-ridden home had reached a flash point. Your friend was relieved to be escaping. In a short span of a few months she'd grown up practically in front of our eyes. Her speech had changed. So had her demeanour. More than anything else, it was the look in her eyes—that of a wounded sparrow. I knew just how much you were going to miss each other. 'See you during my winter break,' your friend said, her eyes glistening with tears. You broke down and wept uncontrollably. 'We'll never be best friends again,' you cried, 'I know you'll find other people in your new school.' Two little girls with two entirely different sets of anxieties and insecurities. You were selfishly thinking of your own emotional need, whereas she was contemplating a total upheaval in her young life.

From that day on, you began to detest the idea of boarding school. Once or twice I joked about it. 'Do you want to go? You can be with your friend again.' You didn't find that funny. I guess most children don't. Once or twice, when I was really upset with you about something, I'd say, 'Do you think maybe you'll be happier in another school? Maybe the same one your friend goes to?' Your eyes would dilate with fear at the thought and I'd feel instantly ashamed of my cheap trick. Of course I had no intention of sending you away, even when you drove me up the wall. No matter what proponents of the system have to say for it, I still believe children are better off at home. I have seen far too many dysfunctional products of these fancy schools. After years of living away, they find it difficult to adjust to life within a family. The loss goes both ways—parents are deprived of being a part of some of the best years of a child's life, and the child in turn is deprived of being raised within the comfort and security of a home. Each time I heard you 'counselling' your friend, I'd wanted to hug both of you. There you were, two innocent little girls believing you could solve ugly adult problems. It was just too heart-breaking, just too sad. Well, your friend's in a new school now, and her parents have split. Who knows? Maybe the boarding school experience was just the therapy she needed.

Yours shudderingly,
Mama

....

Mumbai
April '99

Dear Children,

You look at me in complete amazement when I describe my growing-up years. 'You mean there were three of you in one room? My God! How did you manage?' As a matter of fact, very well. Not for a moment did I feel my sisters were in the way. And I hope they felt likewise. I rather liked our bedroom with its attached bathroom and balcony. It might have been slightly cramped in there, what with three beds, two cupboards and a writing desk, but we were far from inconvenienced.

Today, when I see all of you, locked into your individual rooms (except Arundhati and Anandita who share one), I wonder if you aren't missing out on something vital—sharing. Your rooms are your private havens. You've made them so self-contained, there is no need to emerge, unless you choose to. All four of you spend hours behind closed doors (in our home, we weren't allowed to do that, except when we were changing). Your room is your world. You have your cordless phones, your computers, your television sets, your books, your music, your 'zone'—what else do you need? Nobody walks in without knocking first.

Everybody looks for the right signal—oh, is the light on? Okay, then it's safe to knock. Oops, the light's off, I'll try later. With all that space—metaphorical and literal—there is no real need to reach out. Clothes are stacked neatly in individual cupboards. The bathroom's pretty exclusive too. Personal style statements abound. Framed pictures, perfumed candles, a doodles' gallery, naughty posters, cacti, wind chimes, pet rocks. It is understood that these are strictly 'no entry' zones. 'By invitation only' is the unspoken rule. 'My bed', 'my room', 'my chair', 'my shower', 'my soap', 'my music', 'my book'—so many 'my's. It's all very alien to me.

I shared a sturdy Godrej almirah with my sister Kunda. Two shelves for her stuff, two for mine, and one for common things. It worked. There was no territorial hysteria if occasionally my shirts crept onto her shelf and vice-versa. Your other mavshi, being the eldest in the family, had her very own almirah—and I was fascinated by its contents. On the few occasions when Mandakini forgot to take the key to her cupboard to office with her, I'd throw open the doors and pry shamelessly. Her 'adult' and sophisticated world intrigued me. I loved the way her cupboard smelled—of expensive French perfume and assorted creamy lotions and potions. I loved its neatness, the one-of-a kind handloom sarees hanging in a row. I loved her lipsticks and trinkets. But above all, I loved being inquisitive. I went to the extent of reading stray letters and devouring old postcards. Sneaky of me, I agree. My sister invariably knew I'd rifled through her cupboard. Don't ask me how. I used to think I'd done it without disturbing a thing. I'd make doubly sure to restore each object exactly where I'd found it. But Mandakini would immediately realize her lipsticks had shifted by a millimetre and pounce on me on her return.

These were healthy moments between siblings, an essential part of growing up. Getting into trouble with older sisters toughens a child and teaches a few lessons too. Since Kunda was studying to be a doctor those days, her nose was permanently buried in fat tomes. Her medical books weighed several kilos and were nearly impossible to shift around on the desk that was meant to be shared by both of us. Consequently, I had to study on my bed, spreading journals and notebooks all over the bedspread . . . for her to pick up later (I thought that was only fair). Kunda would study late into the night, often getting only three hours of sleep. The reading lamp would be on till four in the morning. I'd wake up at around 6.30 a.m. But I don't recall a single occasion when we argued over timings that refused to overlap. It's hard to imagine that three young women shared a bathroom without getting hysterical. You know how women feel about bathrooms, and how much time we spend in them. And yet.

We had worked out a system (Mandakini always got priority) where we managed to do what had to be done without the third world war ensuing. My careless bathroom etiquette may have driven my sisters mad, but I guess there wasn't sufficient time to even fight—what with my school timings, Kunda's college schedules and Mandakini's banking hours. Crazy. When Kunda would take a coffee break, I'd join her on the balcony. We'd chat for a while and I'd crawl right back into bed, leaving her hunched over those intimidating tomes. We shared everything: shampoo, soap, towels, toothpaste. She generally gave me whatever I fancied from her side of the cupboard, and in turn, she was welcome to help herself to my stuff. Unfortunately, our tastes were entirely different. So were our shoe sizes

(Kunda's feet are smaller). Or else I would gladly have 'borrowed' her smart shoes.

We grew up helping one another. There was no real distance between us. Our room was accessible to all the members of the family (we really had no choice there), and Father's footfalls at night made sure we behaved ourselves after hours. The radio was in the drawing room. It was much later that we got a transistor of our own. The television set too remained in a public area, as did the telephone. Yet, I never felt my privacy was being invaded. On the contrary, I loved the idea that I had someone to turn to at night if I woke up after a nightmare. Someone understanding and sympathetic, who'd pat me back to sleep, saying, 'It's okay. It was only a bad dream. Don't worry. Have some water.' It was a good feeling to have as a child. It was an even better one to know secrets could be shared on a day-and-night basis, that a trusted confidante was right there in the same room, ready to put her books aside and listen attentively to my kiddish concerns.

Kunda was my sister, yes, but she was also my friend and surrogate mother. A steady, loving figure I could talk to about everything and anything, without fear or self-consciousness. The sort of bonds that were forged then have lasted us thus far. We continue to feel as close and as comfortable with each other now, as we did so many decades ago. That kind of trust is hard to come by. All three sisters can count on one another today, because of the foundation that was laid in our youth. We instinctively understand one another, we care about one another's feelings and moods. We are sensitive to personal upheavals, we talk. Yes, we talk and communicate as only sisters who've been raised in such close proximity can. Into this female world, Ashok, your mama, is allowed entry too, as an honorary member. We have our own language and private jokes. It's such a warm, comforting thought that there are at least three individuals in the world who know you inside out and, what's more, accept you exactly the way you are. They've seen you at your worst, without your guard up, with tears streaming down your face, or plain making an idiot of yourself. Nobody has judged you harshly. Nobody has held anything against you. You slipped up? You've been insensitive? Uncaring? Oh well, these things happen, they've said philosophically. And we've gone on from there.

I would like you to have the same security nets when you grow up, grow old . . . but don't grow away. I'd like all of you to be able to pick up the phone and speak your mind freely. Seek each other's advice, derive comfort, offer support. That's what siblings are for. And I do believe these sort of feelings come through shared experiences.

The next time I hear you girls squabbling over someone having invaded your 'space', or taken a favourite T-shirt without as much as a by-your-leave (not that I endorse such a thing), I swear I shall make you sit down and re-read this letter. If that isn't threat enough . . .!

Love,
Mama

Mumbai
May '99

Dear Arundhati and Anandita,

It is something of a long-standing family joke, your khit-pitty relationship with each other. It has always been this way, and I often used to wonder whether it could ever change. There's a healthy three-and-a-half year difference between you. Yet, there are times when I feel you could happily disown one another. I often hear one of you say, 'I wish I didn't have you as a sister.' In the past the harshness of the comment used to disturb me. It no longer does. Not because you don't mean what you say. Oh God, no. I know that you do . . . when you're squabbling. But I also recognize the other side—the one that's protective and loving, and which both of you take such pains to disguise.

Some months ago, you, Arundhati, were down with a viral fever. Nothing serious. But you did look miserable as you lay in bed with a high temperature, your bright eyes droopy, your body limp. Anandita, who'd come rushing back from school, took one look at you and her expression changed. 'What's wrong, Mama?' she asked me with genuine concern. I explained it was nothing more than a bad throat accompanied by fever. Anandita shook her head and tip-toed around the room so as not to disturb her half-asleep sister. What a change from the daily arguments after school, the throwing down of heavy bags, the banging of bathroom doors and the general noisy homecoming which I'm accustomed to.

Hours later, I saw you, Anandita, hard at work. You covered the paper with your hands when I came over to your desk. Soon, you were through. When I walked into your room in the evening I saw a beautiful get-well card propped against Arundhati's pillow. It was colourful, cheerful and pretty. But it was your signature that caught my attention. 'Friends forever', it said at the bottom of the card. My eyes filled with tears. You saw me looking and felt a little embarrassed. 'That's so sweet, Anandita,' I said giving you a kiss. You smiled shyly, and we left it at that.

I thought of the innumerable occasions when I'd been forced to intervene and arbitrate in your fights. I thought of the many times I'd despaired: will these girls never get along? What will happen to their relationship later? I'd worried about your reluctance to share your things; your different personality traits. Sometimes, it was hard to believe you were sisters. I'd wonder about your diametrically opposed views and tastes. Wasn't there anything you two had in common? It used to upset me a great deal. I'd talk to you girls separately and feel defeated. I could never really understand why you quarrelled so much or so frequently—was it sibling rivalry, or something more? How come you didn't seem to have any shared interests? Why did you rejoice in putting each other down? The get-well card came as a very pleasant surprise to me. I could tell from your involvement that you were really and truly worried.

Just as these days, I can tell from Arundhati's attitude that she's genuinely bothered when you, Anandita, are feeling low, or someone's been horrid to you at school. She takes a lot more interest in your well-being, your appearance, your food habits, your overall development. I can't really say you girls are great friends even now. But you're getting there. Why, occasionally you even tolerate each other's presence at the computer, or watch the same television show without battling over the remote control panel. I'd call that progress, wouldn't you? It certainly gives me hope. Ten years later, you might even love each other's company—not as a duty, not because you're sisters, but because you genuinely enjoy it and respect each other as individuals. I'm praying, and keeping my fingers crossed as extra insurance.

Your puzzled
Mother

....

Mumbai
June '99

Dear Children,

How much praise is too much praise? Frankly, I'm never sure. I was raised with very little myself—it just wasn't done to compliment one's own children. Therefore, compliments were strictly rationed. It's possible that parents of that generation believed in old superstitions like *'bachchon ko nazar lag jayegi'*. Does that sound absurd? But I encounter it even today. Mothers who touch wood or bite their tongues after saying something as innocent as 'My Mitalee has done very well in her terminals'.

Perhaps because I was so starved of praise as a child, I tend to go overboard with it. I've always believed in the power of positive reinforcement and I've seen it work. I know you children feel awfully embarrassed when I go on and on about something I like or admire about you. Arundhati in particular actually covers her face and groans, 'Ma-a-a-a, stop it please.' She runs as far away from me as she can, blushing furiously all the way. It has become something of a game. I tease her; she flees. On the other hand, Anandita all but glows when the spotlight's turned on her. She adores attention even while pretending she's embarrassed by it. I know Aditya is very upfront in this department, often encouraging me to shower some more extravagant compliments. Radhika looks sceptical, Rana matter-of-fact, Avantika slightly wary.

I know that I behave atrociously when someone says something nice about me. I cannot handle compliments with grace. I've never learned to say a simple 'thank you'. Praise often makes me suspicious. That's because it used to be dinned into me by Ajoba that the world is full of hypocrites and sycophants. Insincere people, he said, preyed on one's vulnerabilities through shameless, blatant flattery. 'You, my dear,' he'd thunder, 'must not fall prey to such types. Women have a weakness—they cannot resist men with a sweet tongue.' He was right, if only partially, and his words have stayed with me. As a teenager, I did tend to lap up exaggerated praise, while at the back of my mind loomed the formidable image of Ajoba wagging a finger and saying, 'Watch out'. Praise felt good, very good, and I have to confess I was fooled by it. Ajoba would look up irritably from his newspaper and growl in the general direction of the person piling on compliments. Given his intimidating personality, it's a wonder anybody dared to say anything at all within his earshot. But thank God for those early warnings, or else I might have believed every bit of the mush that came my way.

When I praise you, it's with complete sincerity. I'm sure you know that. I know from experience that young children crave praise. To them even their most careless doodle is a great work of art. And so long as parents themselves know why they're praising a child, it's fine. The problem starts when parents self-delude. I've been aghast to hear words like, 'Oh, my child is a genius, a genius I tell you. Do you know what Akshay did in class today . . . ?' or 'My Raakhee is a child prodigy. She is so gifted. You have to hear her sing/play the piano/strum her guitar.' When children grow up listening to such nonsense, they lose perspective and start believing that they are indeed superior to their classmates. Often, this misleading image is carried forward into adulthood without reality checks of any kind. Such individuals grow up to discover that the rest of the world does not necessarily agree with their parents' assessment. That's when the trouble starts. The answer is, spaced out, judicious praise—just enough to motivate a child and not so much that it will turn his or her head.

That goes for criticism, too. One keeps hearing about healthy criticism. For a very young child the concept doesn't exist. All criticism is taken to heart, taken personally, and can have a devastating long-term effect. Comments like 'You are useless. No good. Don't waste your time.' 'Forget it, you'll get nowhere in life.' 'You look terrible in those clothes. Seen yourself in the mirror?' 'My God, your hair is a disaster. That colour doesn't suit you at all.' Often these sentences are uttered without thinking. Carelessly. Adults may not mean them. Worse, they may not remember them, but they stick, sometimes forever. If it's a toss-up between too much praise and too much criticism, it's better to err on the side of praise. But listen, don't take it literally when I'm ladling it out, because there may be a catch to it. Maybe I want you to do something better, work harder . . . or just run an errand for me. Buttering up goes a long way sometimes. Don't I know it?

Gushingly yours,
Mama

....

Mumbai
July '99

Dear Children,

I have been noticing a pattern in the way very young kids react to the absence of their busy parents. More and more mothers are on the move these days—their jobs demand it. Often fathers are out of town on work at the same time. Children are left in the care of illiterate maids, or indifferent relatives. How are they supposed to cope? In our family, the situation is not as bad, since I hardly accept any travel assignments. But even so, when we are away, my mind and heart are at home, wondering what's going on and praying that nothing bad should.

A holiday without you is enjoyable only upto a point. Though Daddy and I do agree that we need a little time to ourselves occasionally, when that time actually comes, both of us suffer pangs of guilt and regret, even though all of you are so encouraging about our plans. A work-related trip is slightly, but only slightly less guilt inducing since there is some amount of 'justification' involved. Even so, I actively dread the moment I have to break it to you that I'll be away for a bit. I put it off. I try to slip it in. I even pretend it's an unavoidable chore although I might be looking forward to it and it's not even as if you mind. Yet I work myself into a tizzy, explaining why I have to go.

Sometimes, separations are unavoidable. I think emotionally secure children accept that, provided they (the separations) aren't too frequent or too extended. Arundhati often says in amazement about a friend's mother, 'She's always away, travelling on business. I feel so sorry for S——, her mom's never there.' It's tough on career women trying to make their way up. If they project anything other than a get-up-and-go attitude, their colleagues outpace them. If they stick around for their kids, they're pitied, maybe sacked. If they sugar off, their kids hate them. What does a gal do? Not have kids?

I love travelling. And I figure I have maybe another decade of hectic hurtling about ahead of me. After that, travel-without-a-care will become a fantasy. Why? Because I'll be ten years older. Maybe my energy levels will flag, maybe my enthusiasm to discover new places, people and tastes will wane, maybe my bones will protest. Who knows? As of now, I am a blithe adventurer who, given the choice, would be happy to hit the road and keep going.

The other day, a power lady came to see me. She was on her way to Russia to strike a deal. Her itinerary left me breathless. She travels the world fifteen days of the month, arriving in Stockholm one morning and rushing off to Stuttgart the next. When she came to meet me, she was dressed for an important lunch. Later, the same night, she would be on her way to Moscow. She gave me a detailed account of her travel plans and habits. I was enthralled. What an action-packed life, I thought to myself. How lucky.

Then I asked about her family. She was married, she said, but no children. That had been a joint decision taken with her husband. 'I knew what my priorities were, way back then. I was ambitious and eager to make my way up. I wanted to progress in my career without compromising on time or commitment. The only way to do that was by arriving at a "no-children" pact. Fortunately, my husband felt the same way. And here I am, at the top of my profession. It feels just great.' At that exact moment the doorbell rang and the two little ones—Arundhati and Anandita—came bursting into the room. From the door itself, we could hear their voices. 'Mama . . . guess what happened today?' We stopped talking. The girls came in, saw the lady and said 'hello' shyly. I saw her staring at me.

'Does this happen everyday?' she asked. I nodded. 'My God. How do you cope with it?' she wondered aloud. 'Cope with what?' I countered. 'All this . . .' she flapped her hands dramatically to indicate her . . . her . . . I don't know what . . disgust, impatience, annoyance . . . at the intrusion. Seeing her expression, I suddenly felt sorry for her. The meeting ended abruptly. She picked up her briefcase and left for her appointment.

After she'd gone, I thought about her insensitive reaction, and that unnecessary remark. Why had she made it? Then I reasoned, how could she possibly know the pleasure of hearing high-pitched voices coming home joyfully, knowing with certainty that their mother would be there to greet them?

That's how it was for me. I cannot recall a single day—not one—when Aji wasn't home when I got back from school or college or office. The incomparable comfort of that knowledge is something I continue to cherish. It is mainly because of that specific memory that I'd decided I would try my best to emulate her, at least in this area. Our travels are scanty. If I do go anywhere it is generally on an overnight trip. Now, thanks to modern technology, we are in constant touch over the cellphone. My restricted travels are taken very sportingly by all of you. Anandita sheds a few token tears sometimes, but she soon forgets. When she was younger, she would wave bravely and even manage to say a few cheerful words, her voice quavering. I found the effort touching. I'm not sure I would have been as brave in her place. In fact, I know I wasn't. I'm told I used to behave like an absolute brat whenever Aji and Ajoba had to go out in the evening to attend a government function. My older siblings would turn away in a rage and refuse to assume any responsibility. That would leave poor Aji in a quandary—to stay home or take me with them. Most times, I'd tag along. You've spared me that trauma, I must say. I don't remember too many tears or tantrums at the crucial hour when I had to go out. Unless there had been a specific provocation.

I'm told children get used to anything, even absentee mothers. I'm sure they do; we don't give them a choice. Yes, I could have gone to Russia. And China. And South America. And Norway. I could have hurtled around India itself. The choice was mine. I made it without a single regret because I didn't want to miss out on your young lives and kick myself later, wondering, 'My God . . . where was I when this happened or that happened?' I may have passed up a few super trips and some great experiences. No problem. Each time I have said 'no' to a jaunt, I have thought of Aji and her constant presence in my life. She may not have been the most demonstrative mother, but in her own way, she conveyed her caring. It was evident in small things—the fact that she remembered every day of her life what each person in the family enjoyed eating, for example, and took the trouble to make it. Till she became physically incapacitated, it was she who cooked all the meals for Ajoba, and she served them herself—simple but tasty Maharashtrian fare that was never placed on the table indifferently. It amazed me that for nearly sixty years this one woman had made sure that her children and husband never went without a home-cooked meal. Yet, as Kunda mavshi and I were saying just the other day, towards the end of her life Aji felt she hadn't achieved a thing in all those years. She said with some longing, 'I wish I had done something with my time . . . and now it's too late.'

I never want to be in a situation filled with such regret. At the same time I don't want to hear any of you say, 'Where was she when I needed her? She wasn't around. She wasn't there.' Sigh. It isn't easy, is it? I thought of Aditya's trip to Pune last fortnight. His hours had been erratic, his location unknown. His only contact, a school friend's residence. I had tried calling him several times but with no success. On his return, he had yelled, 'Thanks a lot. You didn't phone. It's a disgrace. Nothing but a disgrace.' Suddenly, I had been made to feel like a naughty, irresponsible schoolgirl who had failed her duty. I'd found myself stammering explanations and apologies. It was he who'd been away. Even if he believed I hadn't bothered to call, what had stopped him from calling? I wondered whether I had ever accused my mother of neglect or carelessness. I honestly couldn't recall any such instance. And it certainly wasn't because she had been flawless. She had her faults (a short temper being one of them) and she made no attempt to hide them. But one thing she wasn't, and that was apologetic. Sometimes I wonder if we, the so-called modern parents, try a bit too hard. Whether we are so unsure of ourselves and our roles that we need to prove our love constantly, afraid that our children may reject us. In a way, the pressure is way too much. For all that we push ourselves to do, I sometimes wonder what the kids actually believe or feel. All I know is that we must continue to try, continue to strive, and not feel discouraged. Children always demand more than it's possible to give. Today's children, that is. We rarely asked for anything and we didn't feel deprived or unhappy.

Yesterday, I read about a young boy staying in a hostel who kidnapped a thirteen-year-old kid and smashed his face with a stone. Why did he do something so horrific? Because the pocket money his parents gave him was insufficient. He didn't have enough to keep up with his friends who smoked, drank and dated 'Bombay girls'. I couldn't get over the news report. Is this what the world is coming to, I asked myself. I felt sorry for the boy's parents. Maybe they were blaming themselves for sending him to 'sin city' without adequate funds to take care of his extra-curricular activities.

Oh dear. I have meandered again. Letter-writing gets like that. One starts by wishing to say something specific and a thousand unrelated images crowd the mind. Last night, I dreamt of Aji again. But that's another letter. Or more—a series of letters.

Exhaustedly,
Mama

....

Mumbai
May '99

Dear Kids,
The other day I was being interviewed on a radio show. The man interviewing me asked what single piece of advice I'd offer to stressed out, busy urban families that would help them to bond better. One single image came to mind—the dining-table. I consider the dining-table the single most important piece of furniture in a home. In the old days families made it a point to eat at least one (if not all) of the day's meals together. Usually it was dinner. Often members belonging to three generations sat down in an informal

setting and discussed the day's happenings. This taught youngsters social skills like communicating respectfully with elders, as well as kept them in close touch with family developments—births, deaths, marriages, funerals. Through this little ritual, people came closer to one another since they were necessarily made to participate in the lives of all the others.

Unfortunately, this charming yet crucial moment of togetherness has been replaced by TV dinners or snacks eaten on the run. Children have their own schedules, their own timings. Parents follow their own—that is, if they're staying home in the first place. Ever since eating out became a national craze, people have abandoned the practice of sitting down for meals together. At our own home, I have frequently expended my frustration over the crazy hours you keep, the careless way you eat (often standing up and shovelling food into your mouths, while someone's buzzing you impatiently from downstairs). This is crazy. It's unhealthy and it's anti-social. You tell me I'm over-reacting. No, I'm not. I like long and chatty dinners. I like to catch up on all the news. I like to keep abreast of your age group's shifting interests. Why? Because it's important to me to know what the hell is going on in your lives. Does that sound unreasonable or unnatural?

We often argue about timings, since all of us lead busy lives. The only constant during school days is the little ones' dinner time, since they have to get to bed at a reasonable hour. My point is simply this: if adult children decide that eating at least one meal together with their parents is important, they can do it. One clear hour a day should be kept aside for this. Sunday lunches can be converted into an occasion that doesn't allow for absenteeism. Unfortunately, in your jobs and with the erratic hours you keep, even that doesn't work out as regularly as we'd like it to. With the result that the kitchen is run like a canteen with hungry people ordering meals at different hours or helping themselves directly from the refrigerator. The one thing I have succeeded in putting my foot down on is 'room service' à la five-star hotels. It seems to be the trend at a certain level for kids to hang around in their rooms and ask domestics to bring in food trays at odd hours. Well, dears, this certainly hasn't happened in our home and never will.

I have wonderful memories of sitting around the dining-table in animated conversation with my sisters. At our home, too, I love it when all of you are at the table, teasing one another, cracking jokes and wolfing down meals. Sometimes we have your friends joining us and adding to the decibel levels. I look forward to such impromptu dinners where everybody is relaxed and communicative. The two activities that are totally banned at meal-time are reading while eating, and leaving the table to take calls. I find both habits rude and inconsiderate. I never accept calls during meals. I don't think anybody would be offended if politely requested to phone back. I hate disturbing people while they're enjoying a good meal and I expect them to react the same way. My good friends can always tell I'm eating by the tone of my voice (to say nothing about muffled speech).

Arundhati sometimes pleads with me to allow her to finish an Archie comic while eating dinner. 'But Mama, I get very little time to read,' she wails. It's true. With the amount of homework the kids get these days there is very little free time to catch up on light reading. But I still insist on her putting the comic away. As I also insist on all your friends phoning back. That is, if I pick up the call. Given a choice, I know you'd prefer to chat away on a cordless phone while digging into dinner. But hey, if that's all dinner with the family means to you—shovelling dal chawal down your gullet—then the whole exercise is meaningless.

Meal times are family times. And families that eat together stay together. Take a look around you. See the stressed-out faces of some of our neighbours. The ones who get into the elevator with half-eaten toast in one hand and a mug of half-drunk coffee in the other. Watch them as they rush in from a work-out at the gym downstairs and rush out after microwaving some improvised mishmash that passes for dinner. Their kids do the same, charging around like zombies, eating at irregular hours. I feel like telling them, get a grip, get a life, get a proper meal, and then see the difference in the quality of your communication.

And yes, I find round tables most democratic. That way, one avoids fixed places and hierarchies. Tried playing musical chairs lately? No? Don't knock it till you do. Builds up an appetite, too. Just kidding, okay? Another thing—no gloomy faces and preoccupied expressions at the table. The one thing you have to bring to a meal is good cheer. Nothing kills an appetite like grumpy sullen diners growling into their plates. So smile, okay?

Cheerfully yours,
Mama

....

Dear Anandita,

I'll never call you 'Anu' like your friends and their mothers do. I happen to like your name. It has a happy musical ring to it. And now that you are ten years old, I'm more determined than ever to address you by your given name and to encourage you to behave your age. Yes, I know it's all my doing. But that's what happens to the youngest child. Ask me. Aji was so reluctant to let me grow up. Of course, it suited me just fine. Despite the other children pointing it out to her, she continued to baby me till the end of her days (when I was in my forties). It sounds crazy, but it worked for us. It certainly worked for me. There is a baby in all of us. And it's a shame that we abandon it so early in our lives. We are in such a hurry to grow up, we leave our babyhood behind too quickly, never to regain it.

Before your tenth birthday, we held several summits—what was it to be? A nice, grown-up lunch with a few friends in Alibag or an outing with the girls from the building? Perhaps yet another rowdy party with the entire class in attendance? You weren't sure. While the idea of a pre-teen lunch appealed to you, you weren't ready to say goodbye to a traditional kiddy-party complete with balloons, hooters, cake and candles. So we compromised and decided to combine both ideas. A high-tea was arranged in a newly-opened coffee shop.

Arundhati didn't much approve of this. Naturally we consulted her each step of the way. I know how much her opinion matters to you. The arguments started with the presents. You wanted a doll and Arundhati scoffed at the idea. 'Doll? Aren't you too old for dolls? How babyish can you get? I stopped playing with dolls when I was five . . . maybe three.' You looked crestfallen. I tried to make you feel better by saying (truthfully), 'There's no age limit for dolls. I used to play with them till very late in life. In fact, I still love dolls, and if you girls allowed me to, I'd want to join in the fun when you're playing with your doll's house.' You giggled uncertainly. Arundhati glared. The matter was dropped, or so I thought.

Arundhati brought it up a few days later. 'Don't you think you are treating Anandita like a real baby? She'll never grow up. Imagine, she's ten years old and you still feed her. It's embarrassing.' I thought about her words. She'd said it was embarrassing. For whom? Not for me, and not for Anandita. But obviously, something was troubling Arundhati. I decided to find out. The next time we sat down at the dinner table, I refused to pick up the spoon or mix your food for you. You didn't say a thing. But you made it perfectly clear you weren't going to feed yourself either.

Arundhati pounced triumphantly, 'See. She isn't eating. God, it's disgusting. A ten-year-old who can't eat by herself.' At which point, you rolled your eyes and reluctantly picked up a fork and began pushing the food around in the plate. Arundhati kept up a steady barrage of critical comments. 'Behaving like a brat. All because Mother doesn't know how to handle her. She'll still be like this when she's twenty.' That night, you starved and I was upset. Really upset. The simple act of feeding a child is such a fulfilling one. I have always loved it, and joked about how much better food tastes because of my 'yummy yummy' fingers. I explained to Arundhati that it was a mutually satisfying arrangement, that it shouldn't affect her so much.

'But it does,' she spluttered. 'You stopped doing that for me when I was two or three.' I said, 'You were a different child. Your needs were different. You were far more self-sufficient. You preferred to eat by yourself. Had you wanted me to continue feeding you I'd have been happy to oblige.' Arundhati continued to glower. After some time, she said, 'You also help her much more with her projects and homework.' 'She needs assistance,' I explained a little lamely. 'Aren't you proud you did it all on your own?' 'No,' snapped Arundhati, 'I did it on my own because you didn't offer to do it for me—or with me.' She was right. And that was the real crux of the problem.

Now what?

I couldn't abruptly stop a ritual that was so important to both of us. But Arundhati had made me realize it was time to wean you away from the dependence. I made up my mind to start the process, but slowly, gently. I began by encouraging you to pick up your food yourself, rather than my piling it on your plate. After resisting initially, you actually began to exercise choice. All these years you had left it entirely to me to organize your meals, using my own preferences in the matter. Now, gradually, I began to notice a pattern. You clearly preferred chappatis to rice, masoor dal to toor dal, chicken legs to bhindi. And dahi with sugar over caramel custard. Jelly continued to rule, though.

Today, I still feed you from time to time. But it's more of an 'in' joke that everybody laughs over—even Arundhati. I encourage you to complete your homework by yourself, barely supervising it once you're done. You've suddenly grown up during the past six months, though I'm glad to see you still play with dolls and kitchen sets. Your school work has improved and there's a new confidence evident in your behaviour. All this is thanks to Arundhati. Without that outburst on the eve of your birthday, I might never have let go, let you be, let you grow. I still miss our baby talk—the special language we had devised, with concocted words and gestures. I'm glad we are still able to slip into those old roles occasionally without self-consciousness. It would be such a pity to leave them behind and become like everybody else. That was our special world, created by us, inhabited by us. But it was time to join the rest before we got left behind. Fortunately, we did that before it was too late.

By the way, I love it when you cuddle up kitten-like, close to me, and mew contentedly. It's the best de-stresser in the world. Don't ever stop. Not even when you're twenty. And don't worry about Arundhati. I'll handle her scorn. I'm getting better and better at doing that. But I seriously doubt she'll notice. She'll be far too busy with her own life by then, and mature enough to realize it had been a harmless little game between us all along.

Your loving
Mama

....

Mumbai
August '99

Dear Arundhati,

Do you remember the day you decided you didn't need me to take you shopping any more? It was more than two years ago. You were barely eleven. Yet, even at that tender age, you knew your mind. Not just about what you wanted to wear but also where you wanted to buy it from. You knew your mind about other things as well—your preferences were clearly defined. Not that you were obstinate—just sure. Very sure. Take food, for instance. You'd refuse to even sample something you'd decided was 'yucky'. I'd ask you in frustration, 'But how can you decide it's yucky if you haven't tasted it?' You'd stare me down and say firmly, 'I can tell.' And you wouldn't budge.

Initially, I tried to persuade you to at least give the 'good stuff' a chance. You'd oblige me by eating a morsel. Often, I'd catch you taking even that little bit out of your mouth when you thought I wasn't looking. After some time, I gave up, as mothers the world over do. You hated milk? Fine, you didn't have to drink it. You detested vegetables? Okay. You only ate chicken? No problem. Fruits were a no-no? Leave them. You were growing fine—shooting up by the second, as it were. Obviously, you were eating right by your body's requirements. Often, I'd drive myself up the wall watching you fussily remove all traces of onions or tomatoes from any preparation—pizzas included. I'd turn away my eyes, unable to handle your pained expression as you swallowed something the rest of us loved. Instead of converting the dining room into a battleground, I called a truce by leaving you alone.

By the time you were twelve, you'd become increasingly weight-conscious. I attributed it to peer pressure. All your friends seemed to obsess over a few milligrams gained or lost. I called it a sickness. You preferred the term 'smart eating'. I watched the body fat (not much of it to begin with) whittle away. You told me you felt better about yourself, now that your waist was well-defined and your legs wonderfully toned. At thirteen? I asked myself. Aren't these kids a bit too young to worry so much about their silhouettes? I talked to other mothers. They had a similar story to tell.

We passed the buck and blamed television. 'It's all those anorexic pop singers and models, you know,' we clucked. 'These silly girls are trying to look like them.' We were partially right. But only partially. These kids had their role models—as every generation does. The only problem was, we disagreed with their idea of idols—as every generation also does. I watched you, Arundhati, as you gazed at the hardboard stomachs grinding away on various channels and lamented the extra centimetre or two around your own. 'Don't be absurd,' I admonished, 'you are still a kid.' That line was clearly a mistake. 'I'm not a kid,' you protested. Just as I remember protesting at your age. No, I was slightly older—all of fifteen. But it was too late. Those awful words were already out of my mouth and hurting inside your heart.

With your new, improved, streamlined frame, you naturally wanted a wardrobe to match. 'I hate all my baby clothes,' you declared vehemently, even as I stared in utter bafflement at all the T-shirts and shorts you'd worn with what I thought was pride till then. 'Only babies wear such silly prints,' you snorted. I held my tongue for once and asked patiently, 'Well—what would you rather wear in that case? Leopard skin?' 'Stuff,' you answered laconically. Right. Stuff. That was helpful. I noticed you'd changed your walk, and the way you wore your school uniform—all low-slung belt and rolled up sleeves. Oh well. If it was slink you were after, sorry, thirteen was way too young for it. 'Let's go shopping for a few things then,' I suggested brightly. You looked at me steadily and said, 'Why don't you give me the money and I'll go shopping.' I remember feeling hurt, almost indignant. 'Why? Do you think my taste isn't good enough?' You grinned, 'It's not that. It may be good for you. But mine is different.' It could have led to an argument but wisely, I backed off. We haggled over the budget, and I handed you the money. 'I'll go with my friends,' you announced cheerily before zooming off.

Those couple of hours that you were away, I agonized over the big change I felt had come over you. At one level, it was a question of ego. Mine was dented. ('So, she doesn't trust my taste. She thinks I'm out of it. Old-fashioned and antiquated.') On the other, I worried about your attempt to break loose this early. ('Just thirteen—and already so set in her views.') Mainly, I agonized over your bid for independence. I thought it premature. It wasn't the clothes; it was something more. If you'd asserted yourself this early in that area, how much longer before you pushed for full and final sovereignty? Had I done the right thing by handing over the money? Had it been cowardice or discretion? I wasn't sure. On one level, I felt proud of you. There you were, a thirteen-year-old who knew her mind and wasn't afraid to speak it. There was no rudeness or defiance, just quiet self-assertion. Far more scary. 'If I give in to her now, will I have to compromise on bigger issues later?' I kept asking myself as I waited for you to come back.

As it turned out, my fears were exaggerated (aren't they always?). You'd picked your clothes wisely and well. Simple, sporty, casual things that suited you far better than anything I had bought in the past. I asked you to model your latest acquisitions for me. When you emerged, even I was taken aback. You were a different girl—a teenager with great poise. Gone were the awkward angles and gawky strides. I felt very proud of you as you twirled around, doing a comic version of the typical 'model walk'. 'What do you think?' you asked. 'I think you look smashing,' I replied. You really did. My spontaneous compliment made you glow. You stared at yourself in a full-length mirror. You pirouetted some more, you preened as a joke—and you looked really, really happy. Suddenly you stopped, stared at your reflection in the mirror and announced, 'My hair . . . oh my God.' I was startled. Was something wrong? 'Yes . . . yes. Look at it. Horrible. Awful. It has to go.' 'What?' I nearly cried, 'Go?' At that time, your beautiful, glossy hair was nearly waist-length. 'Yes,' you said determinedly. 'Like, I have to cut it. It doesn't go with my new clothes.' I knew it. The clothes were just the beginning. It was time for me to get used to several new 'you's.

And you know what? It took me a while to adjust to the rapid and dramatic changes, but once I did, I loved them. Absolutely loved them. Today, you have short, sensible hair and smart, trendy clothes. Nothing frilly, nothing fussy. Everything is practical and sporty. Just like you. Know something else? I couldn't have improved on it. This is your 'look'. You found it. You created it. It suits you. You look great. And that's what matters, isn't it?

Admiringly,
Mama

....

Mumbai
May '99

Dear Arundhati,

You will be fourteen a few months from now. A difficult age but also a very exciting one. We've had our rows during the past two years. Nothing major—the usual mother-daughter tiffs about never-ending telephone calls, and rising hemlines. I have in front of me a card you had painstakingly designed. It's bright pink in colour and carries one bold word on the cover. 'Sorry' says your card, the yellow letters of the word nearly jumping out of the small space. It's pretty. It must have taken you quite a while to make. Each letter is individually cut out and stuck on the pink background. The edges are finished with your favourite zig-zag scissors. You've even used your prized silver pen to draw squiggles all over your handiwork. What you said inside is really touching. It's touching because it is meant sincerely.

You were apologizing for your lack of responsibility. I had given you a small errand to run, but in your excitement over getting cinema tickets for yourself you'd forgotten my little job. This wasn't the first time. And I was angry, very angry. I gave you a mouthful, using harsh words to underline my visible rage. I lectured you on your 'duties'. I asked you, 'Is this how low priority my requests are? How would you feel if I consistently "forgot" to do something you had asked me to?' Then I took off on your facial expression. I told you I couldn't stand it. That you should change it immediately. I saw your face crumple. You took the offending finger out of your mouth, and readjusted the look in your eyes. 'That's better,' I barked, before turning away and resuming my writing. You didn't cry, you didn't argue (thank God). Nor did you try and 'justify' your conduct. You knew you had slipped up. In a small voice you said, 'But . . . I have been trying to be responsible these days.' I snapped, 'You'll have to try much harder. I'm afraid the effort isn't good enough.'

I watched your retreating figure. Those long, well-toned legs, the straight back, the shining hair. My God. You had grown up. And yet, what a baby you were in so many ways.

In your sweet pink card you had underlined the words, 'I promise to improve myself.' And I thought, 'Did I ever say that to my own mother?' No. Never. I had resolved to do so on several occasions. But I never ever articulated the thought. You'd also added a P.S. which said, 'Please forgive me. But I don't know what to do about my face which you can't stand.' Reading these words, I was so sad. It isn't your sweet face I can't stand, darling. It's your expression that bothers me, especially when I'm furious. Maybe you aren't aware of it, but it looks stony. As if nothing I'm saying is actually getting through to you.

It wasn't easy being fourteen for me either. I must have got on my mother's nerves equally. I remember being withdrawn and defiant by turn, rarely attentive to whatever she was saying. I must have been pretty indifferent, too, and switched off. And yet, I cannot recall her reprimanding me so strongly. I often feel I'm hard on you. Harder than I am on the other children. Maybe it's a reflection of my expectations. You appear far more 'sensible' than the rest. You are a generous, giving girl by temperament. I therefore assume you are far more 'responsible' too; how can you forget something important you've been asked to do? Often I set you tasks only to 'test' you. This is unfair since I don't 'test' the others in the same way. Maybe I know I won't be wasting my time with you. I seek reaffirmation of my own assessment of your personality. This is an awful thing to subject you to, especially at this delicate stage in your life, when you are seeking reaffirmation yourself. I constantly refer to my own teenage years which were pretty turbulent, far more rocky than yours so far. The big difference is this: you and I can talk about our fears and anxieties. I couldn't do that with my mother. She responded to my mixed-up condition intuitively, but we never actually discussed it. I had to remind myself that she was barely out of her teens when she married. She had not been allowed the luxury of experiencing teenage angst. Yet, with all my experience, insights and hindsight, I often end up screaming at you. Of course, I make up for it with extra love. Later. But that's no excuse.

I remember I used to be on the phone for hours, and the family would get mad. My mother often wondered what there was left to be said after a long day at school. I'd say, like millions of teenagers the world over, 'Forget it. You won't understand.' Today, I hear the same words from you. I couldn't have imagined it would ever reach the stage when my own daughter would say my lines back to me. The thing is, I do understand. And I am sensitive to what you're going through. Some children seem to negotiate the adolescent hump effortlessly. One day they're babies and the next they're young ladies full of poise. It didn't go that way for me. And it's not going that way for you.

I watch you peering into the mirror looking for imaginary spots. You obsess over your hair, you worry about your height . . . your weight . . . your proportions. You love dancing, you learn dancing, and yet, you're too shy to dance for us. You are one girl in your class who's consistently helpful to the others. You became a class representative with a thumping majority. You were the girl who wrote a 'get well soon' card to a neighbour's son when he came out of hospital after a nasty accident you were a witness to. You are well liked and popular . . . teachers appreciate your positive attitude. So do your peers. And you were the one who taught me to be computer literate. I see all this and feel proud of you. Now, if only I could get you to run the odd errand. Just kidding, darling. When it comes to the bigger stuff, you never let me down. But I want you to focus equally on the minor stuff. Mothers hand out chores only to instill a sense of responsibility in children. I could so easily entrust them to others in the house—anybody could pick up the odd package for me. When I request you to do so, it's because I want to involve you in the tedious routine of running a home, so that you know the little things that go into making this place function efficiently. One day when you run your own home, you'll be able to remember these experiences and put them to good use. Sounds like a dreary exercise mothers invent to torture their children, right? H'mm. Maybe you have a point.

Naggingly yours,
Mama

....

Mumbai
July '99

To All the Older Children,

This is, ahem, a touchy topic. Very touchy. But I'm going to tackle it head-on. Smoking. You know how strongly I feel about it. We've had arguments galore, but never quite resolved what you see as a contradiction. I entirely believe in the adage that parents shouldn't preach if they cannot practise what they're sermonizing about. You have seen me smoke and you've seen your father smoke. That does not make it all right. Let me clarify. I smoke one solitary cigarette a day, just before dinner. I have done so for years. Agreed, it's an awful habit, one that I ought to have abandoned years ago. I know I sound silly—like

Clinton—when I point out that I hardly inhale even from that one cigarette. 'Then why do you smoke it? Why can't you give it up?' you demand, while I say, a trifle too defensively, 'Because it makes me feel relaxed after a hard day's work. Because I'm used to it. Because I look forward to it. Oh hell—because I happen to like it. Okay?'

No, it isn't okay. And you are absolutely right in saying so. I have thought about it and what I want to tell you is this: mine was a foolish and ignorant generation. Those of us who grew up in the '60s, thought of ourselves in rather grandiose terms. We were different. We were the true rebels. We didn't believe in rules. We did our own thing. We were the '60s generation. Special. We forgot one important aspect—some of us paid a huge price for all that. Cigarette smoking became *de rigueur* on college campuses in the '60s. If you didn't smoke, you were square. A jerk. Totally out of it. There was enormous pressure—even to be a bonafide non-conformist, one had to conform. Smoking became a part of that awful non-conformism. Being an athlete and therefore health conscious, I never really took to it. At my 'peak', I couldn't go beyond two cigarettes a day. But somewhere the habit stuck. I'd tell myself I could give up ciggies whenever I chose to. I really could. And did. During each of my pregnancies and for months afterwards, I'd stop totally and not miss it at all. I could sit next to a smoker and not be tempted to ask for a drag. Then one day the urge would get the better of me and I'd light up. The thing is, I know myself and my body. I know my system would reject any attempt at stepping it up. And if there's one thing I don't lack, it's self-discipline. If I were convinced that any of you could remain within such strict self-imposed limits, perhaps my attitude would be different.

I remember how horrified and upset my parents were when they 'found out'. It could hardly have remained a secret for long—I used to have my smoke in the balcony adjoining my room and given the strong sea breeze where we lived, the smoke would invariably waft into their bedroom. They spoke about it strongly to me—particularly my father. But I made no promises to give up. It was understood that none of the children would ever have the nerve to smoke in my father's presence. In fact, my brother's smoking (he quit years ago) remained a well-guarded family secret till he too was 'caught'. All those years back, the health hazard connected with smoking was not known in such detail. Cigarette packs did not carry statutory warnings and the link between smoking and lung cancer had not been established. We smoked because it was considered fashionable, rebellious, daring. It was an attitude statement; we had no idea of the consequences. Today, we know better. We know that cigarettes are killers. Besides, there is a worldwide movement against smoking, particularly targeting your generation. It's a complete no-no. In fact, a smoker risks becoming a social outcast in a place like California where smoking is strongly condemned. There must be some peer pressure for you, I am sure, but you kids are more aware of the dangers of smoking than I ever was.

So why don't I quit? Anandita and Arundhati detest the sight of that nightly cigarette, they keep nagging me about it. I haven't quit entirely because, frankly, I don't want to. I have weighed all the options and convinced myself it's a pretty harmless indulgence. I find my nightly fix most relaxing. It helps me to unwind. Corny excuse? Sure. There are definitely other, far healthier ways to relax and unwind. But there it is, my little Achilles' heel, my unfortunate weakness. But that does not give you the licence to puff away. You know better. Besides, what's left for you guys to rebel about? For us, there was plenty—a nicotine weed was one of the ways we used to assert our identity. For you, there is no such problem. There is nothing left to rebel about. Simply put, cigarettes are bad for you. But if you can stick to one as I have—here's the deal—I'll look the other way. What's fair for me is fair for you. Conversely, if I quit, you quit. Okay? Promise me that and I'll stop completely. Stop what? Smoking or preaching? Both, darlings, both. Shall we shake on it?

Deal.

Mother

....

Mumbai
June '99

Dear Daughters,
Occasionally, Arundhati has voiced her impatience when people walk up at a public place to ask, 'Oh . . . and is she the daughter who features in all your columns?' I've seen you shrinking, Arundhati, and forcing a smile. I've seen all of you exchanging looks when strangers have asked cheerily, 'So . . . which one of you has taken after the mother? Come on . . . tell us. Who's going to be the writer in the family?'

I've seen Avantika looking shy when at a glamorous event, say a fashion show, someone from my distant past has demanded, 'Why aren't you modelling like your mother, huh? Don't like it or what? You look like her . . . You should try it.'

I've also caught the embarrassed expression on your faces when first-time visitors to our home have lined you up for inspection and declared, 'Bengali. You look Bengali like your Daddy. Bengali eyes are black and long, you have Bengali eyes. Not like your mother's light ones. Never mind, Bengali eyes are also nice.' Adults can be so insensitive at times. Children detest such comments and feel horribly self-conscious under such scrutiny. Yet, very few grown-ups realize the potential hurt they may be causing young people when they focus on physical features, pass careless comments on noses ('How come yours is so long/broad/hooked/bulbous?'), hair ('Heavens! Look at your hair! So curly.'), body weight ('H'mm, you've been eating far too many chocolates, young lady. Go easy on those additional calories. Not good for the silhouette. We don't want to be fatty-bambolas, do we?'). Children loathe such remarks. They don't regard them as 'harmless jokes'. Comparisons (even flattering ones) leave a bad taste that lingers for years. Kids revel in their individuality. Yet, adults insist on boxing them into neatly labelled categories—a convenient filing system for easy reference ('Oh, that one? Of course, I remember. Buck teeth, right? And a mole on the right cheek.') Even within families, children are often given cruel pet names that zero in on their physical 'defects'—a none-too-perfect nose ('Captain Hook'), or kinky hair.

When I was a little girl, one particular aunt got a kick out of tormenting the nephews and nieces with nicknames that were nasty and sadistic. All of us had one. To this day, I can see the reaction when, at family get-togethers, a reference is made to the old tags. My aunt, who was not a bad human being, only immature, giggled when she saw young children squirming at her relentless 'teasing'. I could never understand that. Sometimes, my own mother would join in the 'fun' and all of us would be horrified by what we perceived as a betrayal.

Children who wear glasses are often singled out for taunts, as if it's their fault, somehow, that their eyesight is weak. 'Arrey, chasmis,' young boys yell, as a classmate struggles to read something written on the blackboard. It's worse when they're on a playing field and even teachers who ought to know better, ask bespectacled kids to sit out the game ('You might break your glasses, dear. And then your parents will kill me').

Growing up is all about acne and awkwardness. We know that. Yet, we haven't trained ourselves to handle adolescence with the delicacy and tact it requires. 'Pimple Face', 'Fat Slob', 'Hairy Fairy', 'Gol Matol', 'Butter Ball'. Names like that stick—sometimes for life.

When you, Arundhati, required glasses, you went off with your father to pick a pair. As in all such matters, you were very clear about the kind of frames you wanted. And you got them. Slightly expensive, but worth the extra price. You know why? They made you feel good. They suited you. When you came home with the brand new spectacles balanced on the bridge of your nose, all of us complimented the new 'look'. We weren't faking our response. Your smart, metallic oval frames changed your appearance for sure. But they also added something—an appealing seriousness. You thought they made you look 'nerdy' and 'geeky', till your friends saw you and gave their stamp of approval. I was happy that you had accepted the need to wear glasses with such naturalness from day one. Fortunately, nobody in the family (not even the domestics) made you feel self-conscious. But what if someone had? All it needs is a single careless remark. So few of us are aware of its long-term effect. Your aunts, Mandakini and Kunda, still smart at the memory of hurtful comments made during their childhood. I have to say I don't recall any, but today, I make a conscious effort not to let careless words about physical attributes slip past my lips. But of course they do. Especially when I'm angry or irritated about something. Funnily enough, you, Arundhati, react the strongest to compliments—you insist you hate them. Obviously, they make you self-conscious. Why, darling? These days, I weigh mine carefully lest you burst into tears. Aah—adolescence. So distant, in my case, and yet, how acutely I remember it all.

Yours,
Mama

....

Alibag
July '99

Dear Anandita,

Of late your dreams have begun to intrigue me. You've always had a very rich and peopled dream-life. But now at ten, the pattern of your dreams has changed. I'm a great dreamer myself. I mean that literally. I love my dreams and can recall most of them. I dream best in the morning—after 7 a.m. Which is one of the reasons I hate waking up before 9 a.m.; I find it so hard to let go of my dreams. I don't see any reason to, either. I like to lie in bed sleepily going over the ones I've enjoyed the most, discarding the scary ones and smiling to myself over the confusing few. I see the same trait in you.

Your last summer holidays were spent almost entirely in our room. For two months you and Arundhati slept on your improvised bed on the floor. Each night, I'd watch you in your sleep. Sometimes you'd laugh, at others cry out softly. You'd toss and turn restlessly, often fidgeting so energetically as to wake your sister. Once or twice you sat up and announced, 'Mama, are you there? I've been dreaming.' I held you, spoke to you softly, so as not to disturb Daddy, and stayed with you, rocking you gently back to sleep.

Your dreams are important to me. They provide a window into your mysterious world, your unique imagination. Last night, you said you didn't like to sleep facing a window or a door. When I asked you why, you said, 'Because someone could easily come in through there and take me away.' I then prodded you into identifying that 'someone'. You said sleepily, 'The hypnotist who comes to me in my dreams. I know if I look into her eyes, I won't be able to stop myself from growing wings and flying out of the window with her.' You looked at me to see if I was laughing. I never laugh at dreams. They always tell us something. So, I asked you to tell me more about the 'hypnotizing lady' (as you called her).

'The watchman downstairs told me the story,' you said. 'He said she comes to the garden and tries to make friends with the children. She seems very friendly and sweet, but she isn't that at all. She's a wicked woman. The trick is not to look into her eyes. Because if a child does that, she casts a spell and kidnaps the kid.' I listened carefully, without interrupting you. This was your story and you obviously believed it. I didn't want to dismiss it by ridiculing the watchman. So I said, 'Adults often make up such stories to control young children. They try and create fear in your heart, so that you'll obey them. That's all. Has anybody actually seen this woman?' You shook your head. 'Then?' You stared at me. 'But she exists. I know she does. I don't want to go to the bathroom by myself. I'm scared. She may fly in through the window. She is everywhere.' I understood your fear, only because I could so clearly recall my own at that age. I did not make fun of it (the fear, not you), nor did I try and convince you in a very adult fashion that such things simply did not happen. In a child's mind, anything can and does happen.

I remembered my own phobia. I was terrified of women in white sarees. I never looked at their feet for fear of discovering they had feet that faced the other way (as was popularly believed about 'ghost ladies'). I was also sure that were I to run into such women they'd kidnap me. Even today, on some half-forgotten level, I still shrink when I see a group of white-saree-clad women. I can also recall a recurrent dream that used to keep me awake night after night. In it, a man would accost me on the road and demand that I look at a framed picture in his hands. I'd resist with all my might. But he'd be most insistent. Finally, I'd be left with no choice but to stare at it. I'd be sucked into the frame, drawn by the magnetic gaze of the woman in it. The man would shout triumphantly, 'See, see. I knew it. I knew you were one of us.' He'd take me by the arm and lead me away firmly. I'd offer very little resistance because in my heart of hearts, I'd know he was right. I did belong to 'them'; I was an imposter in my family. For years I was convinced I would actually meet such a man. I was exactly your age then.

I've seen that the best way to help you go back to sleep is to talk about your fear. Sometimes, I point out how irrational it is. But that's when I myself am awfully tired. There is nothing rational or irrational about the unconscious. Imagination knows no bounds. I remember being charmed by your 'explanation' as to why you weren't afraid to sleep next to the sliding doors of our ship's cabin when we took that recent cruise from Singapore. You stated simply, 'The ship's propellor was my friend. I knew nothing would happen to me.' I asked you to elaborate. 'See . . . I looked down at the water and saw the huge propellor. I immediately liked it. And I knew it liked me, because it said, don't worry. If anything happens, I'll look after you. It made me feel very safe.' I asked you with utmost seriousness, 'Oh . . . so the propellor spoke to you, did it?' You nodded happily.

It made sense, perfect sense. You'd struck a pact with a powerful ally. You knew that with the propellor on your side no harm could possibly come to you. If that gave you a sense of security, why not? In another graphic dream you told me how a green garden snake had bitten you. 'But the bites didn't hurt at all, they turned into glittering emeralds on my arms.'

When you're older, your unique imagination is likely to disappear. You'll be conditioned to think, dream and act like everybody else. You will no longer do deals with propellors or other inanimate objects. You'll probably laugh at other little girls who do. Your special world may vanish too. And with it, your current fears. You'll discover as I did that most fears are self-inflicted. You will learn to rationalize them and then there won't be any 'hypnotizing ladies' striking terror in your heart. Instead you might encounter a scarier monster: boredom. And then what will you do, my precious?

Lots and lots and lots of love,
Mama

....

Mumbai
February '99

Hey, Big Spenders,

One day, a friend of mine complained, 'My kids are so ungrateful. I give them five thousand rupees as pocket money every month, but they keep cribbing that it isn't enough.' I was aghast. 'Do you realize that's more than the Average Joe earns by way of a salary?' I asked. 'Oh come on, Shobha. Don't be so bloody middle-class. How can you compare our children's lifestyles with those who live by paltry pay-checks?' 'Speak for yourself, dear woman,' I said. But her comment stayed with me. She's mentioned her children's 'lifestyle' more than once. 'Poor kids, going out costs so much these days. When my son takes a girl out to a club, the evening costs him two thousand bucks. And that's only because he drives his father's car and doesn't have to pay for the gas.'

'Well,' I'd argued, 'he doesn't need to go to the ritziest clubs in town. He doesn't have to date girls with such fancy tastes.' 'But if he doesn't spend lavishly on chicks, he'll be called a cheapskate and the girls will stop going out with him,' she lamented. 'I don't want my kids to get a complex. I don't want them to feel inferior.' 'Maybe they should change their friends in that case,' I suggested. It was no use. 'So, what are you going to do? Up the allowance by another five grand?' I asked. 'Do I have a choice?' 'Yes, you do,' I almost yelled. 'You can tell your kids where to get off. You can teach them to value money and work for it. Or stay home dateless.'

We've had arguments over money ourselves. I've won some, but mainly, I've lost. I didn't give any of you 'pocket money' while you were at school. If you needed to buy something, you'd ask for it, tell me the amount, and if the request was reasonable, I'd give it. I thought it was a workable arrangement; you didn't. 'All our friends get a fixed amount from their parents,' you said. 'What do they do with it?' I wanted to know. 'Oh . . . they buy things. Snacks, clothes, music cassettes, cosmetics . . . you know . . . stuff they want.' We tried it for a few months. The system didn't work. You exhausted your quota in a week and it was back to, 'May I have some more. . . I'm broke?' Children these days are permanently broke. How come?

I had a tiny wallet while I was at school. It was really, really small; no more than three inches by two inches. In it, I carefully carried between four to eight annas. This was meant for emergencies, in case I missed the train for which I had a pass, and was forced to take a bus instead. Sometimes, I spent the money on bhelpuri or an ice cream. And believe me, the money never ran out. If I needed shoes, clothes, sports gear, I asked for a specific amount which was subsequently sanctioned by Ajoba. I did not complain about the arrangement. It worked fine even through my college years. Since I walked to St. Xavier's and back, I saved my coins for a mutton-cutlet gravy from the canteen. Nobody laughed at me, as you claim your friends do at children whose wallets aren't crammed with notes. I never went hungry; nor was I ever bored.

I think mutely handing out money to young children isn't a good practice, particularly in the present environment. One hears horrific stories about drug peddlers lurking outside school gates and luring unsuspecting students with harmless-looking ice-lollies that are laced with something far more lethal. We didn't have to deal with such terrifying temptations in our days. My parents' worries stopped at my getting a sore threat by over-eating raw imli with the extra four annas in my wallet. When I was older, there were no pubs, bars or clubs to go to. Maybe that's why I wasn't frustrated over the lack of generous funds. A cup of coffee at Napoli Bistro, Volga, Venice or any of the popular cafés of the time cost five bucks, if that. We managed that through careful hoarding. And it isn't as if we didn't have fun.

These days, kids demand new clothes for every occasion. New accessories, new shoes, new everything. Plus, pocket money that adds up to a pretty tidy sum. Parents who refuse to shell out on demand are labelled 'selfish', 'chikoos', 'misers' and worse. My friends tell me they dread foreign vacations because their children terrorize them for 'shopping money' that runs into lakhs of rupees. This is absurd. When I talk to you about it, you say, 'This is life. Life today.' Perhaps it is. But guess what, children? It isn't going to be your life. And don't try and shame me into doling out the bucks because 'everybody' does it. I am not 'everybody'. You know me better than that. No? No? Hey . . . here's five bucks. And don't you dare sneer. Take it and say thank you.

Stingily yours,
Mama

Goa
July '99

Dear Radhika,

When you were a little girl, no more than twelve years old, you went through a phase that had me worried. Perhaps it had something to do with school; you were always different from the rest of your classmates. You had a very rich inner life peopled by characters from your vivid imagination. You didn't belong to the rest of the group, mainly because your interests were so completely at variance with those of your contemporaries. While the other kids listened to Michael Jackson, you preferred Mozart. While they watched cornball comedies like *Beverley Hills Cop*, you attended classical music concerts. They played tennis, you played the piano. They liked trendy clothes, you liked comfy gear. They liked outdoor sports, you liked indoor plants. They experimented with the latest make-up, you experimented with insects and reptiles (dead or alive). They spent long hours on the phone, you spent long hours drawing pictures.

It was the same at college, except that you made a few new friends and were fortunate enough to meet like-minded people. You lingered over Sylvia Plath, so did they. You watched obscure Czech movies, so did they. You discovered Hariprasad Chaurasia, so did they. You flowered during your final year and graduated with high honours, so did they. Then it was time to pick a career. Since you'd majored in English Literature, I suggested you take a crack at journalism. You pulled a face. I suggested training as a book editor. You pulled some more faces. I even suggested a master's programme at Bombay University. You insisted you'd had enough of English. Quite enough. Chaucer? Keep

him, you said. You chose to do computer graphics instead.
After completing the course, you plunged into career-mode.
You slogged long hours, commuting by bus and train to
distant studios. You earned a modest salary. Your health
seemed frail and your appearance began to worry Daddy
and me. All those days and nights spent in a freezing studio,
hunched before a terminal, had taken their toll. Your skin
was sallow, your eyes dull and glazed, your body language
listless.

'Why are you doing this to yourself?' I asked agitatedly.
'You don't need to prove anything to anyone. Why this
crazy schedule, especially since the returns are so poor?'
You were adamant. This was what you'd chosen, and this
was what you intended to pursue. Money isn't everything,
you argued. I hadn't said it was. We watched you losing
weight. You'd become paler still—the effect of no sunshine
and a poor diet. Everybody in this business works like this,
you said. That's how studios function—erratic hours and
very little sleep. We'd lie awake, sick with worry, watching
the hours ticking by. 2 a.m., 3 a.m., 4 a.m.—and no trace of
Radhika. Calls to the studio would be met with the reply,
'I'm stuck here. A last-minute edit has just come in. Don't
worry, I'll cab it home in an hour or so.' You'd rush in, only
to leave again after a quick shower. The question of talking
you out of it didn't arise. You weren't listening, anyway.

Till, one day, you collapsed. Fatigue finally caught up
with you. The signals came from your own body and you
had no choice but to wind down. That was it. You quit your
job and took enforced rest. For more than a month, you
stayed put at home, listening to music, reading, doodling,
catching up on lost sleep, eating regular meals. It was time
well spent on some much-needed introspection. You went
to visit your grandmother in Calcutta, you hung around

with your maternal cousin, you caught up with yourself. And it did you a world of good.

Today, you seem far surer of what you wish to do henceforth. You are still completely indifferent about your appearance, often borrowing mismatched clothes from your kid sisters' cupboards. You are free of most of the hang-ups that preoccupy people of your generation. You don't care a hoot about being 'in', about wearing the right labels (or any label, for that matter), about being seen at hip clubs and happening places around town. You can spend hours by yourself, playing the flute, or listening to Satyajit Ray's soundtrack from *Pather Panchali*. You have a few close friends who enjoy the same things, and are equally liberated from the burden of conforming to set norms and patterns. Your needs are few, and touchingly simple. Your habits continue to be Spartan, almost monk-like. Possessions of any kind don't interest you. It is as if you occupy another world, live on another plane. And yet, you amongst all the children are the kindest and the most considerate, especially with elderly people and little children. It is you who feel the most for the less privileged and are willing to reach out and help, whatever it might take. This is a very special quality, and a rare one in today's materialistic, grab-what-you-can times. May you never lose it.

Appreciatively yours,
Mummy

....

Mumbai
September '99

Dear Rana,

Do you know something? You may find this hard to believe, but what strikes me the most about you, is your self-sufficiency. It has been thus since you were pretty young. Remember the recent BMW case in Delhi? Remember the many discussions we had at home about the tragedy? Remember how strongly I felt about reckless, drunken driving? Well, in a slightly different context, I also felt relieved. You could have been Sanjeev Nanda. You could have been that unfortunate boy behind the wheel of a car that mowed down seven innocent people. But you weren't, and that was no coincidence. You weren't that young man because you never ever 'borrowed' any of Daddy's cars without his knowledge. Not even to impress your friends (the main reason youngsters run around in fancy cars). You could so easily have 'flicked' the keys and zoomed off (like so many underage kids we know). But you didn't. Not even when you were a restless, rebellious teenager. Just as you never asked for money after you started earning your own. Your first salary was a pittance, modest by any standards. Even so, you took pride in paying your own bills from then on. And that's how it has remained. My friends ask me, 'But don't you give him extra cash to subsidize his other expenses?' When I say no, they look at me strangely, as if to suggest there's something odd about the arrangement. Is there? I don't think so. And happily, neither do you.

Today, you earn more than you did when you started off, but it isn't a fortune. Compared to some of your buddies, your requirements are few. The other kids tease you about how frugal you are, and how carefully you guard your money. Why not? You spend sensibly on things you want. You save for the luxuries you lust after. And you make sure your accounts are in order. What's more, if occasionally your funds are low at the end of the month, and you touch either Daddy or me for a few hundred bucks, you make sure you scrupulously return the 'loan'. I think that's good training. We may wave the gesture aside, but the point is, you make it. Not many children do. It is taken for granted that parents are there to pick up the tabs. I know families where sons run up incredibly high bills, where daughters are given credit cards with no limits, where cars and chauffeurs are made available round-the-clock without any questions asked, where even very young children are encouraged to go on unsupervised shopping trips and buy whatever catches their fancy. This does not happen in our home. And mercifully, there's no debate on the subject. You've shown pride and self-control while managing your money. You may have displayed immaturity in some other areas (and which young man doesn't?), but when it comes to things that matter, you've shone.

Sometimes, you tease me about my 'antiquated' views. Last week you mentioned you've finally understood where I'm 'coming from'. Have you really. If so, I'm saved. Maybe the next time I nag you about irritants like leaving air-conditioners on in empty rooms, or not 'wasting money' on 'useless things', you won't give me 'those looks' because you've understood my neuroses. You know where I'm 'coming from'; I hope you also know where I'm 'going'. Is that a deal?

Jauntily,
Mummy

Alibag
September '99

Dear Aditya,

The hour is late. Very late. I'm in Alibag sitting at the marble-topped wrought iron table we'd both liked so much when we first spotted it in a dusty shop at Chor Bazaar (my all-time favourite hang-out). The table is now the centrepiece of the paved courtyard next to the dining room where we have shared so many al fresco meals over the years. I can see all of you if I shut my eyes. Anandita on the antique Gujarati jhoola nearby. Avantika cycling around the farm, vainly convincing herself that twenty rounds are the equivalent of an hour-long work out (the one she has skipped). Radhika, sitting by the tiny pond looking for brightly-coloured dragon flies. Rana and Arundhati playing table-tennis under the canopy provided by the fig tree. And you, sprawled out beside me on one of the planter's chairs, reading *Fortune* and dreaming of making one yourself. And, as always, there is me, grumbling away about punishing deadlines while you children laugh at my overwrought state and tease me about the new frown lines creasing my brow.

I've been thinking about you, Aditya, especially over the past few days. Do you know why? Because I sense a change is about to take place and transform your life. You seem poised on the brink of an important breakthrough in your career. And I get the feeling it's going to work out just fine for you once the initial hurdles are crossed.

I wasn't in India for your birthday this year. You'd been very sweet about my absence, saying magnanimously, 'It's okay, Mom. Go ahead. Take that trip to New York. It isn't every month that you get such a chance.' The rest of the family had made sure to make up for my non-show at the poolside party your friends had organized for you. As always, you'd picked your own birthday gift ('Please Mom, no surprises, okay? Just let me choose my own present p-l-e-a-s-e . . .'). Always the over-fastidious, hard-to-please one with definite ideas of what you like or abhor. The one who, even as a child, stated flatly, 'It has to be that, or nothing', happily setting for 'nothing' if the offer didn't match 'that'. When I'd spoken to you from Manda mavshi's Manhattan home on your birthday, you'd sounded upbeat and cheerful, and not a bit reproachful.

Just a few months earlier, we'd had an intense and somewhat heated discussion at an unlikely venue—the parking lot of the Breach Candy Hospital. Do you remember that evening? We were paying a sick call. Ashok mama had checked in for a minor health problem. I'd suggested a tea break at the snack van downstairs, and you'd decided to accompany me. God knows what had triggered it off, but the light discussion we'd started over weak tea served in thermacole cups suddenly turned into an argumentative battleground. It had to do with your job. You said you hated every minute of it since you weren't really learning anything. I said, 'Hang in there. Don't be so impatient.' You wanted to quit. I wanted you to stay. You insisted it was dumb advice. I yelled, 'What do you know about "dumb"?' The man selling sandwiches from the van started to look worried.

Twenty minutes later, we were still shouting at each other. Of course I knew you didn't like the assignments you'd been sent on—the bug-ridden beds in seedy hotels, bumpy autorickshaw rides to distant factories, dormitory-style living with colleagues in army guest houses. I accused you of being a spoilt, elitist brat who couldn't rough it out. You accused me of being harsh and judgemental. The slanging match continued for another twenty minutes. Suddenly, it was over. Something you said made me see your point of view, and I cooled down. 'Okay, fine. Quit if you want to,' I conceded. We went upstairs to say goodbye to the patient, friends again.

You put in your papers next week, and declared yourself officially out of the job market. 'I want to be on my own, Mother. I want to start something that I can call mine,' you announced. And that's exactly what you did. Today, you are a bonafide entrepreneur with ambitious plans. A future tycoon (your secret self-image). You're working hard and your head is bursting with ideas. Your golf is going good (two holes-in-one in a single year—not bad). You now have time for all the things that are important to you, that you enjoy. After many, many months, you look relaxed and enthused about the future. I'm happy for you, because you are happy about yourself. That's what parents want, really. Just basic stuff—happiness, peace, good health and prosperity for their kids.

The owls nesting in the jamun tree are squabbling again. There have been additions to their family. We now have eight owls in residence. I like that. We are a family of eight, too. But unlike the din being created by the owls, I hope our squabbles don't wake up the farmer next door.

Affectionately,
Mama

....

Mumbai
September '99

Darling Vanti,

I was flipping through old albums last night (again!) and came across a photograph of you that I know you hate. I'm not sure why you dislike it so much. Is it because you think you look 'fat' in it? Or does it remind you of the one year in school that made you miserable—your passing-out year? Perhaps it's both. The picture was taken by your 'best-est' friend Soha on the annual sports day. You were the games captain, leading the marchpast along with the head boy and head girl. It should have been a very proud moment for you. But you didn't look all that happy. The previous year you had won most of your special events. This year you were expected to win them again.

It had been a particularly rough year for you. We had battled over several decisions. You had wanted to leave school after the tenth and join junior college. We had 'persuaded' you to stay on, like your siblings had before you. I know how desperately you had wanted to join your friends studying in universities abroad. Your entire circle had gone, leaving you very alone. Resentful and isolated, you had withdrawn into a shell, barely participating in school activities. I knew that feeling very well myself. The last year of school had been traumatic for me. The worst year of my life. Nothing had gone right. My grades were dismal. My athletics record was not what I would've liked it to be. I recognized identical symptoms in you and sympathized.

After the marchpast on a blisteringly hot day—a few students had fainted in the heat—you looked dehydrated. I noticed a few of your old classmates sitting in the stands. They'd already developed 'attitude' since they were at various colleges here and abroad while you were technically still a 'schoolgirl' wearing a uniform. I could understand your self-consciousness as you took charge of juniors from your 'School House' and lined them up for their events. I had come armed with my camera, all set to record your moment of glory. Your favourite event, the 100-metre race, was scheduled to start soon, and you seemed very relaxed. I thought a bit too relaxed. Your friends wished you luck as your name was called out. I saw you at the starting line, crouching in readiness for the sharp crack of the pistol. Then you were off. I yelled and screamed along with your friends. Then suddenly, midway through the race, you fell behind. As if you'd run out of steam. The others whizzed past you. The race was over. You hadn't won.

As you walked towards us, I thought I saw your lower lip tremble just a little. But your eyes were smiling. We hugged and I whispered, 'It's okay. You did your best.' Your friends also hugged you warmly. But I knew it wasn't all that casual a defeat. A few minutes later I decided to leave the stadium (your events were over) since Arundhati and Anandita needed to be dropped back home. You walked to the car with me. And then, the minute we were out of everybody's sight, you collapsed in a flood of tears, clinging to me and sobbing like your heart was breaking. I know mine did at that moment. I would have done anything to make you feel better, anything at all. But I knew I was powerless at that point. You needed to cry and I needed just to hold you, comfort you, try and convince you it wasn't the end of the world. After a few minutes you wiped your tears. You had spotted your friends strolling up. We both beamed at them. They were considerate enough not to comment on your puffy eyes or mine.

Once again, I went into flashback. I remembered that awful year, when I had suffered similarly. I'd hated every minute of those twelve months. And especially hated the sports day when, for the first time in my life, I had run a race indifferently, without my heart being in it, not caring about losing or winning (I had lost). But I hadn't had Aji to share that sinking feeling with me. I don't remember if she was present that afternoon. I only remember feeling terribly lonely, as if a certain period of my young life was over and behind me. I walked out of that stadium, never to return. I didn't run the 100-metre dash again. That phase was finished. And a new chapter opened. A new direction beckoned. That's how it was for you too. That is how it will always be. With each fresh opportunity, you will realize your own potential. You didn't look back even once; you didn't have the time to. You found new challenges, new diversions. Hopefully, you also learnt a lesson. I know I did. There is an awful word called 'over-estimation'. And life itself is like a series of 100-metre races. Nobody can afford to take even a single stretch lightly. For if you do, you lag behind, and unless you buck up, you never catch up. But I think you already know that.

Sportingly yours,
Mama

Mumbai
March '99

Dear Arundhati,

Tomorrow is your chemistry exam. And you are all nerves. I don't know how to help you. Chemistry was never my favourite subject. You are so wound up with tension, you've developed a cold and broken out into a rash. I feel so sad seeing you like this. Of all the children, you are the only one who gets worked up over exams. Today, you panicked at the thought of your maths paper a few days away. 'I make small, silly mistakes,' you cried, yes, cried, great big tears rolling down your cheeks. I hugged you and said, 'It's all right to make mistakes. Just don't lose your concentration. Stay calm.' You shot back, 'But how do I do that? I can't stay calm when I'm so worried.' 'What are you worried about?' I asked. 'I want to do well. Very well,' you said. 'Then you have to tell yourself not to get nervous. Start your paper after taking a few deep breaths. Say a short prayer. It helps.' 'But I do all that. And I still make those errors.' Oh dear. I stroked your forehead and tried to smooth the creases. I advised you to take a break. Listen to music, watch the sea outside, chat with a friend, play with the dog. Nothing helped.

Often, when I see you at your desk frowning over tedious journals and notes, my heart goes out to students the world over. This isn't fair. This isn't fun. This isn't the way to gain knowledge or learn anything. This is torture. You have no time to relax, unwind, play games, joke, do any of the things childhood and young adulthood are meant for. I don't like the sight of you slogging. Hours and hours spent hunched over papers, files, maps and graphs. You rarely smile. You rarely eat. The pressure is obviously too much. All this for a few extra grades? That's crazy.

Then there are the extra tuitions. Last night you got back at 10 p.m. You had spent the morning writing an exam paper; your afternoon was devoted to cramming. You carried on, even though your eyes were watering and you were running a slight fever. Late in the evening, you announced you had to leave for a special class organized by your study group. I urged you not to. You looked at me like I was unhinged. 'What if I fail?' you asked, a wild expression in your eyes. 'You won't,' I assured you. 'I have to go,' you said firmly, and left. The family was at dinner when you staggered in. I saw your posture, shoulders slumped, head hanging low. You were hungry and tired. But you didn't want to waste time over food. Insane and inhuman, I thought to myself.

When I was a student, my own mother was blissfully unaware of my curriculum or exam schedule and I'm ready to bet my father would have had to scratch his head to recall which class I was studying in. We were expected to do our bit and get on with it; work hard and do well. The question of coaching classes did not arise, though out of desperation at my pathetic results in maths and physics, my father had persuaded a clever clerk from his office to help me for a modest fee during my school-leaving year. I experienced zero pressure. But that was also because I was an indifferent student. You are far more competitive and focused—as I suppose students have to be in the present scenario. Sometimes, you accuse me of living in a fool's paradise. 'Mother,' you say, 'do you have any idea how difficult it is?' Yes, darling, I do. And it worries me.

Your generation has had to face the most awful competition in all areas of your young life. You have to succeed, succeed, succeed at all costs. And this is an expectation that comes not from us, your parents, but your peer group. You make fun of losers; the worst insult your generation can hurl at someone is to label that person a 'loser'. I hardly see any happy faces around me. You girls are coiled up with anxiety most of the year. You can't even relax during vacations because you're thinking of your term exams when school reopens. I find that absurd. This summer you took a heavy load of books along on our holiday. You could hardly concentrate on any of the activities we were engaged in, because at the back of your mind, you were bothered about your homework. You tell me most other parents would feel proud of their kids if they displayed these traits. I guess, in that case, I'm different. I have unorthodox views on education. Real education.

I don't know how much you learn in your classroom, or even how relevant it is. I see you undertaking excruciatingly tedious projects. You spend hours sourcing references. The time given is so limited, you don't absorb any of it. What you end up doing is merely filling up a fat notebook with appropriate photographs and captions. When I ask you a few questions even a week later, you can't recall the answers because they have not registered. Doesn't that render the entire exercise useless? You remind me that you don't make the rules. That this is how it is. That you don't have a choice in the matter. True. But I want you to look at the bigger picture. To learn to be curious, to be alive, to absorb, to enjoy. I suppose I'm asking for too much. You are so tired merely coping with school work, there's no time for reflection. For all that the system teaches you to cram, cram, cram, swotting isn't studying, it's a memory game. And it teaches you to forget the moment the exams are over.

Each morning when you leave for school, your bag weighs between five and seven kilos. There's no time for a proper breakfast. You just about manage to make it on time after a quick shower and a hastily gulped down mug of milk. My own school days were different. I actually enjoyed myself—-yes, even in the classrooms. Winning and scoring were indeed important, and my parents expected good results from all of us. But I never reached breaking point.

So, what do we do now, little girl? Where do we go from here? You have a biggie (standard ten) coming up down the line. And we aren't even talking about college exams. How do I make it easier for you? I don't see myself joining the ranks of overwrought, hyper-tense mothers who spend sleepless nights 'studying' with their kids. Moms who talk in terms of 'our exam', 'our syllabus', 'our timetable'. I can't visualize standing outside an exam hall with a tender coconut to quench your thirst, reading out chapters feverishly while you bite into a sandwich between papers. Yes, I'll make coffee for you at night and provide whatever other support you require. But please, I'm through with exams. I've put in my time. I'm no good at any of your specialized subjects. I'd flunk arithmetic at grade IV level. I don't see the point of staying awake 'taking up lessons'. I admire mothers who do it—good for them—but I was raised differently and taught to be self-reliant as a student. It was my responsibility to do my best. The buck stopped with me. And I'm glad it did. I learned to value my time and prioritize. Also, I didn't look around for crutches or excuses. When I did badly in my senior Cambridge examination, I took it on the chin and worked slightly harder for my SSC (compulsory in my school). I appeared for that running a high fever. And yes, Aji was there just outside the centre during breaks, with my medicine bottle and tablets. Along with Ajoba and Kunda mavshi they made sure I had my doses on time so that my head didn't reel while writing those boring papers.

The thing is, even when I disappointed my parents with my lousy grades, they never humiliated me—not once. They did express their disappointment. They did get angry. And they did impose a few strictures ('No going down to the garden for a week'). But that was about it. I was naturally aghast when you told me how some of the mothers of your friends beat the kids mercilessly if they flunked a paper or came home with poor marks. I recall you telling me about an incident when your friend refused to go home with a bad report card because she was sure she'd be thrashed by her mother.

How do I convince you that there is life after studies? Here you are, a bright young person with boundless energy. You have an alert, questioning mind. Your grasp is enviable, and your desire to succeed most commendable. But at what cost, my baby, at what cost? All I want to tell you is this—do your best. Nothing else matters. Honestly, I wouldn't care if you came first or tenth in class. Not because I'm indifferent. It's because I have complete confidence in your abilities. You'll be all right. You'll do just fine. Even if you do get a quarter per cent less here or there. So, don't feel dismayed. Like I often remind you (much to your irritation), 'It's only an exam.' Life, too, is a series of exams with regular mid-term tests. And then the dreaded finals which nobody can afford to flunk. Grades? Yes, there are grades to deal with. But I wouldn't worry too much about high scores in every single subject. You 'max' some , you 'duck' some. It doesn't change a thing. Really.

Philosophically yours,
Mama

....

Mumbai
May '99

Dear Anandita and Radhika,

Sometime ago, we had a visitor at our home. A little boy of seven or so, a stranger. You, Anandita, were at the computer when he walked in with Radhika Didi. She was baby-sitting a friend's son. He headed straight for the computer and demanded time on it. Didi requested you to stop your game and give the little boy a chance. You held out saying you'd move only after the game ended. Fair enough. But once the little boy occupied your chair, your attitude changed. You made it obvious that you resented his presence and that you wanted your computer back. You were clearly annoyed that you'd been forced to abandon your game because of the boy, and you showed it. This led to an embarrassing situation which irritated Didi. She thought you were behaving like an overpossessive brat. You thought she was 'favouring' the stranger over you. Meanwhile, the little boy played on. You became vociferous about your protests, plus, Didi insists, were rude and aggressive towards the boy. Didi lost her shirt. She took you aside and scolded you severely for your 'bad' behaviour. You promptly burst into tears and phoned me to complain.

The problem was, I was thousands of miles away in London. The time was unearthly and there was little I could do from that distance besides calming you down with some cooing, soothing noises. You were in no mood to be placated. You demanded that I arbitrate in the matter and take sides. I refused to do so. I couldn't. How on earth was I supposed to play mediator under the circumstances? My one-point agenda was to re-establish peace without having to declare whose side I was on. You howled even louder. I felt helpless. This was getting out of hand. I thought desperately about my options. There were none, so I kept the phone receiver close to my ear and let you cry your heart out. You needed that. You called the boy all kinds of horrible names. You accused Didi of beating and torturing you, you insisted everybody had ganged up against you. You ordered me to come back on the next flight. A few minutes went by; I had said nothing. Soon your angry crying subsided into sniffles and sobs. You managed to calm yourself down. I asked for Arundhati. She gave me her version of the events, making it obvious her sympathies were with the little boy who had since retreated into another room, not daring to come anywhere close to the computer. The storm was over. I assured you I'd deal with the problem on my return a few days later.

I expected you to have got over the fight by the time I arrived in Mumbai. But no, you had merely suppressed your rage. At the very first opportunity you got you took me aside to say, 'Don't listen to anybody else. They'll tell you lies. You only listen to me.' And then off you went again about how 'cruelly' you had been treated. I could see your trauma was for real, even though you had exaggerated the incident in your mind. I listened attentively and told you I'd think about it and get back when I had some answers.

After a couple of days, I raised the topic at the dining table when we were eating lunch. Your eyes filled with tears as you once again launched into an account of that troubling Sunday afternoon. It was then that I realized two things that put things into perspective. One, that you felt Didi had been unfair to you, her little sister, by taking the side of the little boy. It was seen as an act of disloyalty. Two, that you had felt humiliated at being reprimanded so strongly by her. There was one more thing: your possessiveness. You had not been prepared to 'share' the computer with a child you had never met, someone who wasn't your friend. And you had probably felt ashamed of your own reaction.

Children are constantly lectured about 'sharing' their toys with other kids. Well, I believe there is a phase during which children do not wish to share their things and it's no use pushing them into doing so. Often, this is a temporary phase that disappears when a child realizes that social behaviour demands a certain amount of generosity. Different children arrive at this point at entirely different stages; some get it as early as at three, others at fifteen, still others, never at all. There is no standardized, uniform cut-off point and it's futile to try and impose one. Parents have to be sensitive to that and not make silly comparisons—'Look at your sister, see how sweetly she gives things to people. Why can't you be like her? Have you ever seen her saying "no"? And she's much younger than you.' Great, good for her. But not everybody reacts this way. We must respect that.

In your case, I've noticed you are selective about who you wish to share your things with. If you like the person, you'll give him or her your most precious objects of desire. But if you don't, you'll be mean with a stick of gum. I find that very easy to understand. But I also know it could create problems for you within your peer group. At school, teachers are constantly urging kids to 'share, share, share'. I've seen class bullies grabbing snacks out of the mouths of timid children and then taunting, 'Cry baby, cry baby. Doesn't know how to share?' making it far worse for the victim. People are generally possessive about their belongings. It depends on what's important to an individual. Some people hide their possessiveness cleverly (maybe for self-protection) and hand over their things while secretly resenting it. One has to accept that some people are more generous than others. Some give with all their hearts. It kills others to do the same. Of course it is important to inculcate feelings of goodwill towards others at a young age. But these things cannot be enforced beyond a point.

I used to be unusually possessive as a child. I'm told I even demanded that a family friend tear open his stomach and retrieve a half-pastry meant for me that he had eaten. If my siblings ever asked for a bite, I would carefully pick out the tiniest portion of the snack and hand it over. But never once did I allow anybody to sink their teeth into something I was eating. I outgrew this trait almost completely as an adult. Today, I don't feel particularly possessive about anything—except my biscuits. Since I have a strictly rationed number of a favourite biscuit, I don't like it if you kids come and grab. It used to be that way with papads (which I've stopped eating). Each time any of you casually reached for a piece, I'd glare and say sharply, 'If you'd like a papad, get one for yourself; leave mine alone.' Strangely, I don't feel that way about clothes, accessories, cosmetics, perfumes or jewellery—normally the sort of things women are paranoid about. So long as you girls promise to take good care of whatever it is you've borrowed, I don't lose sleep over it.

The little boy incident must be seen in the right light. First, you didn't know the fellow. Second, you were asked to abandon your computer game. Third, you felt displaced. Fourth, you were transferring your anger (from Didi to the kid). Since that day, you've been going out of your way to share your things. Why, you even let Arundhati use your brand new Little Prince pencil box for her exams. And it was very sweet of you. I've noticed other things as well. The way you ask, 'Would you like some?' when a plate of your favourite caramel popcorn arrives. Two months ago, you wouldn't have done that. Hanging onto stuff that you see as 'yours' exclusively is quite a natural reaction. I wouldn't worry about it too much. Already you've become conscious of the need to let go. To give. In time, you'll also discover something else, something far more important—the joy you derive in doing so.

Love,
Mama

....

Mumbai
September '99

Dear Children,
    The hour was late, peak-hour traffic at its worst. I was experiencing road-rage (even though I don't drive). We were on our way to collect Anandita from a friend's home—a friend who seemed to be rather lonely in that vast and lively classroom of forty-five children. As we were coming home, goodbyes said, water bottle and bag checked, Anandita repeated the conversation she had had with her little hostess. Apparently, her friend had turned to her rather forlornly and asked, 'Why does everybody hate me? Is it my fault that I am rich?' I was completely taken aback, and said so. Anandita continued, 'Poor thing, I feel so bad for her. She has a fantastic car, a fantastic house, fantastic toys, but no friends.' For a minute, I thought of the comic strip character Richie Rich and his unfortunate experience as the wealthiest boy in high school. It wasn't all that

different for this child, who was isolated by her classmates and teased mercilessly for the lifestyle not she, but her parents represented. It had come to a point where the kid had taken to lying about her family's possessions. 'Come on . . . tell us. How many cars do you have?' other children would ask. She'd fib and say, 'Two.' 'Lies. All lies. We know you have ten,' the children would chorus.

I'm not sure about this girl's feelings on the matter, but even by Mumbai's extravagant, over-the-top standards, she did lead an extraordinary life. At ten, she had a fleet of cars to choose from. All the chauffeurs communicated via the latest model of cellphones, and the girl had one for herself as well. She lived in a four-storey villa in the poshest locality of Mumbai and had an entire floor to herself. She holidayed abroad twice or thrice a year, was protected by armed guards, and her home resembled a fortress with sophisticated security systems screening visitors.

Unfortunately for her, she had been enrolled in a school in which most of the students came from a more modest background. Nobody seemed to know what this girl's father did. But he was obviously in a high-risk business going by all the high-tech gadgetry in their home. That's Mumbai. And it's amazing how children grow up in such a bizarre atmosphere without it getting to them. Mumbai kids are raised in a city that thinks it's a film set. It's difficult to escape Bollywood's far-reaching tentacles when you live here. Life, at some point, starts imitating the movies. Everything is exaggerated; it's hard to tell what's real and what isn't. And yet, kids grow up, go through school and then college, get married, live their lives like everybody else in the lunatic metropolis. It sounds weird to outsiders. But here in Mumbai, it's life.

The little girl's comments could so easily have been a part of a snatched dialogue she had heard on television. Maybe it was a line from a blockbuster. But it was also her reality. She actually lived in that surrealistic zone with gunmen and guard-dogs prowling around a home that resembled a mobster's den with black walls and black floors. And yet, she was a sweet if puzzled kid. She wasn't puzzled by her life, oh no, but by people's reaction to it. Very few children from her class got invited to this strange address. Those who did, rarely returned. Her mother boasted, 'Kids love coming to our bungalow because it is so beautiful, most of them have never seen anything like it.' Not true. They found the atmosphere spooky. As did Anandita. We talked about it for a while and I tried telling her that different people have different tastes. What may appear sinister to her could be considered sophisticated by the owners. She wiggled her eyebrows, shrugged and kept silent. Then once again she asked, 'How rich are they really? Too rich? Or only a little rich?' What kind of a scale could I provide? So I tried changing the subject. She kept coming back to it. 'Why do they need so much? Why does she have to show off?' I agreed there was no need for her or anybody else to show off, not just their money but anything else—talent included.

She listened thoughtfully and said, 'I feel sorry for her because she's so miserable. But I really love her car—can't we get one like it?' I burst out laughing. In one breath Anandita had displayed her mixed feelings—of sympathy and envy. I'm sure the rest of the girls in their class felt exactly the same way. I'd seen this very child change over the past three years, from a pretty cheerful kid in expensive designer clothes, to a sullen morose kid in still more expensive designer clothes. It wasn't her fault she came from such an affluent background. Yet her classmates were

making her feel guilty and wretched about it. I wondered
whether her mother knew what the girl was facing at
school.

Anandita turned serious again. 'There's another person in
our class who is in big trouble. Because she's also very rich.'
Oh God, I groaned. Not again. I was only half-listening.
'Her Daddy has been getting bad telephone calls from really
bad people. They told him they were going to kidnap his
children. They asked for five crore rupees.' I was instantly
on the alert. 'Anandita,' I said sternly, 'are you sure you
aren't making all this up?' She was most offended. 'Why
should I do that?' she asked indignantly. 'It's true. The
whole class knows about it. That's why S   hasn't been
attending school for a few days—she's so scared, poor
thing. Do you think those kidnappers will kill her?' That did
send a shiver down my spine. Is this what we've come to?
When ten-year-olds discuss kidnappings and killing? Has it
become so much a part of our daily life that we've stopped
reacting to such conversations with revulsion and horror? I
found that far more frightening than the actual threat. And I
felt it was best to discuss it upfront with Anandita, keeping
in mind her limited exposure to violence of any kind—even
the movie variety. I did not want her to talk so casually
about such a serious issue. Neither did I want her to think of
it in such a casual, conversational way—as if it's a normal,
everyday thing for a child to deal with such matters.

It's a problem peculiar to our city. How does a mother
face it without scaring the living daylights out of a child? Do
I tell Anandita not to believe a word of what she has heard
because such things don't happen? Or do I tell her truthfully
that unfortunately we are living in dangerous times.
Hopefully it's an ugly phase that'll blow over. But as things
stand, there are gangsters out there terrorizing people and

making life very difficult even for those who aren't directly involved. How much can a ten-year-old comprehend about a situation that befuddles most right-thinking adults? What do I tell her about shoot-outs and dons and ransoms and murders that occur so frequently? All I can do is inform her calmly that such awful things do happen. And that she has to be careful, very careful, about talking to strangers, accepting gifts from people she does not know, or saying 'yes' to a car-lift from a mere acquaintance.

Anandita is growing up in a very different city from the one I knew and loved as a child. The rules have changed. The people have changed. There is no innocence left. Nobody can be trusted. Nobody. I feel sorry for her. Sorry that I have to be the one to break it to her, to tell her the harsh truth. Not to do so would be to fail her. My worry is simply this: I don't want to alarm someone so young and trusting. I don't want her to keep looking over her shoulder to see whether she's being followed. I don't want her to think every person she meets is a killer. I would like to believe things will change. Soon Mumbai will rediscover itself, regain its old reputation, re-emerge as a city for people with dreams, goals and ambitions. I've always felt I got a great deal from Mumbai. It allowed me to be myself, to grow and develop as an individual. To test my limits, to put myself on the line time and again. To fall down, get up, then start from scratch. I felt safe here, I felt accepted and understood. Yes, it was always a tough city. It demanded a lot. But nobody resented paying the price. Mumbai made everything worth the effort because it was only in Mumbai that one felt free. Free in every sense of the word. Anandita's Mumbai isn't like that at all. And I feel angry about it. We've short-changed the next generation by denying them the same privileges.

I was quiet for the rest of the journey back home. So was Anandita. When we got to the lobby of our building, I saw her staring suspiciously at someone. 'Is he a kidnapper?' she asked fearfully. There was genuine anxiety in her eyes. I held her close. I couldn't even console her with any conviction. For all I knew he may well have been that—a kidnapper. That's how bad it really is. And I'm not a paranoid person.

Anandita will learn to cope, as kids do. She'll be tough and alert, knowing and savvy. Today, she doesn't know the difference between a crore and a crow. But tomorrow she will. She'll discover soon enough within her classroom itself that there are families that have enormous wealth and those that make it on very little. She'll be able to tell between the haves and have-nots by merely glancing at a classmate's pencil-box and the contents of her packed lunch. That day, I shall feel a little sad . . . for her . . . for me . . . for all of us who live in such an unequal world. And I'll tell her yet again, not to let prejudice colour her friendships. Not to hold one girl's fleet of limousines against her. In the same way she wouldn't put down another for coming to school in a public bus. Different circumstances, different lives, but beneath it all, lost little girls. Just like her.

Easier said.

Tiredly,
Mama

....

Mumbai
February '99

Dear Aditya and Anandita,

Strange that the two of you—so different in every way—should have discussed the concept of 'leadership' with me. In a particular context of course. Anandita went through a phase when she was being excluded by the other, slightly older children who play regularly in the garden downstairs. I used to wonder why. Sometimes, she'd come up crying and spend the rest of the evening sulking in her room. At other times, she'd stick around in the garden watching the others paying hide-and-seek, while I'd be watching her miserably from upstairs, unable to intervene . . . forbidden from doing so by both Arundhati and Anandita herself. 'Mother, you cannot interfere. This is between Anandita and those girls. She has to sort out her own problems,' Arundhati had warned me, while resolutely refusing to get involved in her baby sister's battles. 'Yes. I can easily go and bully the children into including her in their games. They'll have to listen to me because I'm older. But they'll take it out on Anandita in some other way later. Let's leave her alone and everything will be okay.'

Months went by. Come evening and Anandita would be playing all by herself while we could hear the happy, excited voices of all the little girls floating up to our home. I'd try and amuse Anandita, but I'd sense her indifference, see it in her eyes. Every fibre of her being was longing to join the others downstairs. But she had retired hurt and had withdrawn into her shell. Now, it had become a question of pride and priorities. 'I don't want to go,' she'd exclaim emphatically if I tried to force her to take that elevator and go where the laughter was. 'I'm happy playing upstairs. Besides, I have homework,' she'd tell me stubbornly.

Finally, the breakthrough took place a few months later. The details were unclear. But one evening, I found her dressing enthusiastically. 'I'm going to play,' she announced happily. I made no comment. A few minutes later, I looked out of the window and saw her playing chor-police with the usual group. I could also see Arundhati at a short distance playing with her friends. Things seemed to have gone back to normal. Back to the good old days when for an hour or two, the house would be comparatively quiet and I'd be left in peace for at least a few minutes, knowing the girls were having fun in the park right under my nose. When Anandita came up, she was hot and flushed and sweaty. She looked deliriously happy. 'Everybody is talking to me now,' she said triumphantly. 'Good,' I replied. After a few minutes I asked, 'How did you make up?' She sat down, sighed deeply, rolled her eyes and explained. 'See, it was like this. You know that girl with the long hair and pink clips? The one who lives on the sixth floor? She was the one who started it.' 'How?' I wanted to know. 'She had decided that she would be the leader every evening and for each game. She forced us to listen to her. She made all the rules. She also changed the rules when she got out. Was that fair?' I kept quiet and let her talk. 'I didn't like that at all. So . . . I told her that we should take turns being leaders. One day, it could be her, and the next day it could be me. I also wanted to be the leader. She refused and threw me out of the gang.'

I was very amused and in an effort to make a joke of the leadership issue, I asked, 'But if all of you want to be leaders who will be the followers? You can't have leaders without followers.' Anandita stared at me and said coldly, 'Some children like being the leader. Others like being followers. I wanted a chance to be a leader too. If the others didn't like me, I wouldn't have forced myself on them. But at least they should have given me the chance. That girl didn't want to give anybody a chance. And all the others were too scared to say anything to her. She wasn't a real leader, she was a bully.' What had changed, in that case? How come they'd accepted Anandita back into the fold? 'I decided enough was enough. I wanted to play with all of them again. So I went down and told them what I felt. I said, give me one try. At first they didn't want to listen. They told me to go away. I refused to. I told them, I have come here to be your friend. I want to be everybody's friend. We should all be friends. And whoever wants to be the leader should be allowed one chance at least.' 'So they listened to you?' I asked. 'Not at the beginning. They said, "We have our gang rules. If you don't like them, you don't have to play with us." I kept quiet and joined the game. After half-an-hour I told them to vote if they wanted that same girl or me. And they voted for me. Finished. Now we are friends. No problem.'

This was wonderful. If only our politicians thought like children.

That brings me to Aditya. It was his first job interview. I was nervous; he wasn't. 'Have you prepared for it?' I asked. 'I've read the papers. I've dressed in appropriate clothes. What else?' 'Answer properly. Take your time. It's better to think a little rather then just start blabbing,' I instructed. 'Don't worry, Mother,' Aditya said casually, 'I'll do fine.' Three hours later, the phone rang and I pounced on the instrument. 'How did it go?' I asked eagerly. 'Good. Fine,' he replied. 'Did you answer clearly? I hope you weren't nervous or anything. No mistakes, no stuttering . . . ?'

'Relax, Mother. It went fine.' Aditya sounded a little exasperated. 'What did they ask you? How many people were there on the panel? Were they tough? Give me an example . . .' He was obviously not in the mood to recreate the entire interview. But seeing my persistence, he probably thought the easiest way to get me off his back was to repeat at least one of the several questions. 'I was asked, "Are you a leader or a follower?"' Aditya informed me. I swooped instantly. 'And . . . and . . . what was your reply?' 'I said, "Depends on the situation."' I was dismayed. 'What does that mean? Oh God! How could you say something like that? Why didn't you answer directly?' 'There is no direct response to that, Mother. I told the panel, in a situation where the other person knows far more than I do, I would follow him. But if the situation were reversed, I would expect the others to follow me. See?'

I was suitably impressed. But then, I was the candidate's mother, not his future employer. A few days later he got the call we were (or at any rate, I was) waiting for. I don't know if it was Aditya's response to that one simple question that worked in his favour. But my heart was bursting with pride when he got his appointment letter. It was as if I had got the job. Like I had passed an important and difficult test. But I had also learnt another lesson from my children: two interesting perspectives, or call them rudimentary lessons, on leadership and responsibility.

Yours thoughtfully,
Mama

....

Mumbai
August '99

Darling Arundhati,

I write this on the eve of your fourteenth birthday. An important day. You've left me a short note with various instructions on the dining-table before leaving for school. At the end of it you've signed off with 'your soon-to-be-fourteen-year-old kid'. I liked the use of the word 'kid'. It was a change from your standard response when you knocked on my door and I asked, 'Who's that?' and you invariably said, 'I am your daughter.' Like you are the only daughter. Sometimes, I wonder if that is what you would have liked to be—the only one. And whether I'm depriving you of your entitled time with me. If that's so, I'm so sorry, darling. It's a signal. And I should pay attention to it. If it's only a small joke, then that's fine.

However, this birthday is going to be very special and significantly different from your last one. On the eve of your thirteenth, you had announced more to the world than to me—'Do you realize something? I am going to be a teenager. You know? A teenager.' Maybe you had expected the universe to stop spinning for at least a micro-second to acknowledge the full import of that sentence. Maybe it did stop spinning. I had been amused and a little heartbroken. You seemed so grown up, with never-ending legs and that determined little face, all serious with the silver spectacle frames resting on the bridge of your nose. I had thought to myself, 'The cuddly days are over. She won't allow me to bathe and powder her from now on.' I was right; you haven't. It marked a turning point.

A year has already gone. Too soon. You said so in the car last night as we drove through blinding rain in search of your birthday clothes. I sat exhausted, watching enormous waves crashing against the parapet on Marine Drive, and wondered how long it would take us in that slow traffic to reach a store whose location we didn't quite know. You started to cry and confessed you felt 'guilty' about forcing me to make that trip. Then I felt guilty for making you feel awful. It wasn't a pleasant ride. You also said that something or the other always made you cry before your birthday. And I snapped, 'Why do you always remember negative stuff? Why can't you recall all the happy moments instead?' You wept some more. Your body crumpled into the front seat, I felt wretched. A migraine was about to come on. There was a scary squall threatening to break over the city. This was no way to plan a birthday. Both of us were completely miserable.

I remembered your 'disco' party last year, when our drawing room had been taken over by thirty self-conscious little girls playing grown up. The only males present were two amused dj's mixing the music. It had been a good party and you'd seemed genuinely happy. I'm confident your fourteenth will go off equally well. But you're suffering from nerves. 'My birthday has come far too soon this year,' you said. 'I haven't had the time to think about it. Or even feel excited.' It's true. 1999 has gone by in a blur for most of us. We are in the eighth month already. The run-up to the millenium has begun. You will turn fourteen in a few hours. The cake's been ordered. Two bowling lanes have been booked. You want to play pool. Fine. You want to wear Capri pants. Fine. You don't want pizzas. Fine. You want samosas. Fine. It will go well, even if you seem so unsure. Thanks to the 'kid' in you. An adorable, lovable kid.

I hope, selfishly perhaps, that you will retain the 'kid' part for as long as possible. It may not reflect your need, but it does reflect my own. I like the 'kid' in you. Fourteen, huh? Big girl, huh? Making all your own decisions, huh? Mind of your own, too. But I desperately miss the little Arundhati, who refused to sleep unless her soft hands could reach my cheeks for five satisfying minutes of 'touch touch'. I know she's locked up in there somewhere. I glimpse her from time to time. My heart does a somersault each time I spot her. I know mothers stupidly say, 'Don't ever change, darling.' I'm stupid and I'm saying it too. We have our arguments and tears and guilts and hurts. But you know (or you should, if you don't) that I love you very, very dearly. And I can't bear to see you sad.

Tomorrow the world will stop spinning. Just for you. And I'll know when that happens. Our eyes will meet and lock at some point during the celebrations. You'll smile a little shyly. I'll smile back, also a little shyly. It will be very, very still for one fleeting moment. And a trusting fourteen-year-old will feel especially blessed.

All, yes, all my love,
Mama

....

Mumbai
March '99

Dear A & A,
    Yes, you two. The youngest. I am having a late lunch. A really, really late lunch. Anandita's friend from school is

over. There's something brewing. I can tell from little Tara's
mischievous eyes. She exchanges meaningful looks with
Anandita and places a finger on her lips. Anandita, I can
tell, is dying to tell me whatever it is they're giggling over. I
eat my bean sprouts hungrily, feigning indifference. But I'm
dying to know their secret. Anandita starts. 'Our teacher
was saying in class today . . .' Tara shuts her up. 'Sssh . . .
you are not supposed to tell. It's a secret.' They eat their
soup and giggle some more. 'We were discussing issues,'
Tara informs me seriously, 'and our teacher told us
whatever we talk about in this period is between her and us,
we don't have to tell our mothers.' 'Fine,' I say. 'Then don't
tell me.' I know that will be the trigger to spill the beans.
Had I said, 'How could your teacher say that? You have to
tell your mother everything. Come on, out with it. What
were you discussing in class today?' I would never have
been able to get it out of them. We continue to eat in silence.
Finally, Anandita bursts out, 'Teacher said, if your mother
is driving the car and you are in the back seat screaming . . .'
Tara promptly interrupts her. 'No. She didn't say that
exactly. What she meant was . . .' Okay. Okay. 'Teacher
basically said your mother can die of a heart attack if you
scream at her and show your anger . . . is that true?' I am
slightly taken aback. 'Depends,' I answer non-commitally.
'What was the topic anyway?'

After much prompting and prodding, I got to know that
they'd been handling 'back answering' by children. The
teacher had urged them to be honest and put up their hands
if they sometimes lost their temper and spoke rudely to their
parents. Tara and Anandita chorused, 'We never do that.' It
was true. Tara added smugly, 'And we never ever say "shut
up" to our mothers.' But thirty-five girls in the class had

said that they did. Also, they'd confessed that they used bad
words and abused their moms when they got angry when
their moms refused to buy them something in a shop. Tara's
eyes were round with surprise and outrage. 'My mother
would slap me if I ever tried that. Not hit me, exactly. But
she'd get really, really upset. I'm scared of my mother. I
never talk back to her.' Anandita widened her own eyes
further and said piously, 'I don't do that either. Do I,
Mama?'

I shook my head. It's true. You girls never ever use awful
language in my presence even when you are throwing
tantrums. You've never embarrassed me in a shop by
demanding something I didn't wish to buy and then bawling
because you weren't getting it. You didn't resort to such
obnoxious conduct even when you were toddlers. 'Some of
the girls in our class repeated the bad words they called their
mothers in anger,' Tara said virtuously. Anandita shook her
head to indicate her disapproval. 'I'd never do such a
terrible thing . . . what if my mother got a heart attack and
died because I said "shut up" to her?' Oh-oh. Maybe I
should speak to the well-meaning teacher, I made a mental
note. Kids shouldn't go around feeling this alarmed over a
'shut up'. I assured Anandita my heart was sturdier than
that. But yes, we didn't want 'shut ups' floating around the
house.

It was revealing to me that thirty-five children out of a
class of forty-five were honest enough to put up their hands
and confess they had been rude to their parents. 'But our
teacher told us to be honest. What is the use of pretending?
She was trying to help us. And she also said she wouldn't tell
our mothers what we said in class.' Smart teacher.

The apartment block where we live is full of kids. Often, while riding up in the elevator with them, I've overheard their unguarded remarks. The raw language never fails to stun me. And I remember what flew past my ears while climbing the wooden stairs up to Arundhati's class to attend her 'Open Day'. A young girl, no more than eight, was viciously calling another child a 'fucking bitch and a half'. None of the kids in the group looked particularly upset, which meant it was normal conversation. Two minutes later, I saw a child being taunted by her classmates: 'Lesbian-lesbian. We know you are a lesbian. You do dirty things in the bathroom.' The girl was in tears. A teacher strolled up to stop the fight and reassure the child. Where were these kids picking it all up from? Their homes? Television? Movies? The internet?

That afternoon I asked Anandita if she'd heard of that word (lesbian) and if she had, what did it mean? At first she played coy and pretended she didn't know what I was talking about. Then she tried to prove how savvy she was. 'Of course I know, Mama. It means boys who like boys and girls who like girls. They kiss each other on the mouth and hug all the time.'

So many 'issues'. My parents didn't have to deal with anything comparable. We sorted out our own confusions, relying on peers or older siblings. I watched Tara and Anandita playing happily after the 'shut up' discussion. Both girls were feeling very good about themselves. After all, they never said 'shut up' to their mothers. So, I wanted to know, how do they express their anger? What do they do when they can't control it?' 'I cry,' said Tara. 'I also cry,' said Anandita. How simple that sounded. It obviously worked too. Next time I'll do the same. I'll take myself off to a corner and cry quietly till I'm calmer. Who knows, the teacher may be right. I don't want to drop dead of a heart attack. Not before the new millenium at any rate.

Here's to a new tranquillity, girls.

Yours restlessly,
Mama

....

Mumbai
September '99

Dear Arundhati,

With each birthday of yours I realize how many changes have taken place without either of us noticing, in one short year. Twelve months are all it takes for some little childhood ritual to get phased out. It started with the occasional bath or oil massage I used to give you from time to time. I used to look forward to those occasions, weekends mostly, when I'd spread a narrow chatai on the floor of your room and proceed to 'ragdo' you with all the strength in my body. You'd protest and squeal and pretend you hated every minute of it. But I know it wasn't like that at all. After the massage, I'd help you tiptoe carefully into the bathroom lest your slippery feet led to a fall. And then I'd pour tumblers full of hot water over your fidgety form. You'd scream, I'd scream, and it would end with soap suds in your eyes, while I shampooed excess oil out of your hair.

That's over. These days I'm not allowed into the bathroom while you're bathing. You scream 'Eeks' if I walk in by mistake after you've carelessly forgotten to lock the door. Fine. I accept your need for privacy under the shower.

But you still come to me to get your nails cut. Even though Radhika Didi does possess an efficient nailcutter that the rest of us borrow. Every fortnight I wait for you to say, 'Mama . . . please cut my nails. The prefects at school have been complaining . . .' You come to our room and hand me the nail scissors. You've only recently progressed to an adult one. All these years, I'd used the blunt baby scissors you felt 'safe' with. Nails clipped, you reach for the jar containing ear-buds. 'Now clean my ears. And use a nice cologne,' you instruct. I place your head on my lap, dip the earbud in any light perfume and twirl it gently inside your ear. I keep my touch very, very light, making sure I don't hurt you.

Sometimes you ask me to trim your hair. But of late, you behave like you aren't confident of my ability to give you a decent enough trim. It's just that you've become more fastidious, preferring to get a professional job at a proper salon. But you still allow me to brush your tresses from time to time. When you wore your hair longer, I used to lavish more attention on it. Now it's a quick comb-through, which you don't really approve of either. I see how rapidly you are growing up. I no longer pick your clothes or toiletries for you. You have definite ideas of your own. Your preferences are strong even when it comes to soaps and face washes. You tell me, 'I know what suits my skin.' As if I wouldn't know that myself. You consult your friends—not me—when it comes to wardrobe decisions. Their approval matters to you much more than mine. I accept that, too. I never asked Aji, 'What shall I wear?' when I was going out. I would call up a classmate.

But, you know something? I miss those moments desperately. I miss doing things for you. Little things. I know my role in your life has changed. I know that henceforth, I shall be required for bigger, more 'important' things, maybe. But I miss the head massage. I miss talcum powdering you after a long bath. I miss rubbing you down with a large towel and helping you into your nightie. I miss coming home with clothes for you that I am sure you'll like. I miss shopping spontaneously for you while travelling abroad, buying fun things—Tweety bird T-shirts or Pocahontas pajamas. Now you're a big girl with a mind of your own. You don't like what I choose for you any longer. You pull faces and say in a kind but firm voice, 'I do like it, Mama. But I'd prefer something else.'

There was a time when you'd raid my cupboard. Be fascinated by the contents of my dressing table. Try on my shoes. Carry my handbags. Create costumes with my scarves and dupattas. Borrow my T-shirts. And generally feel thrilled playing 'grown up'. Today, you find my stuff 'weird'. 'It's so old-fashioned,' you remind me. 'My friends will laugh. Don't you have anything young and funky?' No darling, I don't. You see, I am not young and funky myself. But even with all your adult preening and strutting around, you are still my little girl. Once in a while, you forget your all-important teenage status and allow me to treat you as the kid you still are. I'd still like to believe I'm indispensable to your young life. Even if you refused to wear my beautiful mirror-work ghagra for 'dandiya raas' this year. I'm warning you, I'm going to redo your salon-administered French manicure tomorrow. And clean your ears. Or else, your nails will grow like Howard Hughes', and your ears will get blocked with all that accumulated wax . . . without

me. Am I being 'mean' (your favourite word)? No, darling.
I'm just being a mother who needs to be needed. Okay?

Love,
Mama

New York
June '99

Dear Kids,

I used to think saying 'I love you' to one's own children was a particularly American thing to do. I saw it happening only in the movies and it sounded awfully phoney. 'What's all this mushy talk between parents and kids? Of course I love my children. And they know it. Why do I have to make regular declarations?' I must admit the whole thing was alien to me. Nobody in my family had ever said 'I love you' to me. Shown it, yes. Demonstrated the same, several times. But nobody ever came right out and said it. One took it for granted: you loved your parents and your parents loved you.

Then I started hearing carelessly distributed 'I love you's around me. Little girls lisping it to their mothers, fathers planting kisses on sweaty foreheads after articulating the mandatory mantra. I said to myself, 'This is weird. Are these people merely aping the movies? Do they mean it? Or is it a new-age style thing?' I began to notice how children, very young children, responded to those three words. And I have to say this, the kids all but glowed. So, it worked. It obviously worked. I thought I should try it out, too.

The first time was awkward. I felt a little foolish. I must have sounded it too. Your reaction was one of puzzlement. A 'what's wrong with her?' kind of response. Naturally. Then Anandita (around three then) came upto me and gave me a great big hug. Encouraged by that, I repeated it a few more times; you got used to it some more and stopped giggling. Then I said to myself, 'You've said it. It was easy. What's more, it sounded nice. Very sweet. Maybe you should say it again and again.' So I said it again and again.

The words tripped off my tongue lightly. Soon you began to reciprocate.

What a pity, I mused, that I grew up never actually hearing my parents say either to us or to each other, the three words which have the power to change the world. They were old-fashioned, conservative and shy. And I, far too inhibited. Today, I say them frequently, warmly, often accompanying them with a hug or a kiss. And I can see the effect on you. Conversely, you've started saying them back to me, too. And I love hearing them. I kick myself for all the time lost, the years of keeping silent . . . what a waste. I know you will remember the 'three little words that say a lot' always—especially while repeating them to your own children. Such a lovely thought.

Mushily yours,
Mama

....

Mumbai
April '99

Dear Children,

I'm frequently asked by contemporaries, 'Tell me . . . when was it that you sat your kids down and discussed sex?' I stare at them blankly and say, 'Never'. They can't believe it. For the next one hour I'm given a lecture on how important it is to talk about the subject . . . This is the age of AIDS. How can you avoid the subject? It's ridiculous, come on, we're all living in the nineties. Soon we'll be in a different century. What's the problem? Don't tell us you're embarrassed?

Guess what? I am. My friends are right. I am horribly embarrassed. People find this bizarre. They say, 'But you write sexually explicit books. So . . . how can you of all people feel embarrassed by the topic?' But I am. Writing books is one thing. Discussing sex with you, quite another. I have made a few clumsy attempts to raise the subject, but failed miserably. Maybe I didn't want to succeed in this particular area. Succeed in prescribed terms, that is. I am not even sure it's such a good idea for modern parents to discuss sex in such an easy way, almost like they're discussing a new trend or fashion. In fact, that's what these so-called discussions have been reduced to—a contemporary fashion.

'We are very open with our children,' a mother told me. 'It's better that way. I've advised my daughter on how to protect herself when she's with her boyfriend.' Another said, 'We know our children are having regular sex. Why pretend otherwise?' A third shrugged. 'Look. I told my son when he was fifteen or sixteen, "Never leave home without a condom. God knows whom you might meet." I'm not making any of this up. You know that. You probably even know the people I'm talking about. Sorry, but I could never engage you in such a conversation. Call me squeamish if you like. I honestly believe that talking about such a delicate subject so clinically, takes away the mystery and romance of a healthy relationship. It diminishes sex, reduces it to yet another physical activity, an alternative to a work-out in a fancy gym. Also, by being so matter-of-fact about it, parents end up endorsing casual sex. The unconscious message is: go ahead and lead promiscuous lives. Just make sure you are protected. As if the use of condoms is all it involves. As if sex is nothing more than the scrupulous observance of certain rules. I also refuse to believe it is all that prosaic for your generation. Surely being in love has something to do with it? Or am I the only romantic fool around?

I discussed the matter with a close friend who has children your age. She thought I was behaving absurdly. 'You must speak to them, no matter how distasteful you find it,' she said. I tried. It was no good. I felt silly. Ridiculous. Self-conscious. What was I supposed to say? 'Listen son, listen daughter. I hope you know enough about birth control to not impregnate someone or get pregnant yourself.' That is the basic message, isn't it? That's what worries most parents. Well, I choose to differ. I am here to advise you if you ask for it. And I am here to guide you in case you need any clarification regarding your feelings. But I am not here to point the way to the nearest chemist's shop or suggest the best condom brands. I will never advocate birth control pills, nor will I say it's okay to sleep around. Because I believe it is wrong to do so. Regardless of gender, I'm perfectly willing to argue my case, and defend my point of view. I'm also perfectly willing to listen to you if you think otherwise. I know all of you are sufficiently clued in. While I have never pried into your lives, I am aware of exactly what's going on. My only worry has been about your emotional response during your respective involvements. I'm confident you know how to handle the physical side of it. You don't really need me to educate you.

I have seen an enormous change taking place during the past ten years. And the change has disturbed me on several levels. Sex is so easily available, so easily accessible, it has lost its value in a relationship. Often, your generation gets to know a body before finding out anything about the mind. Isn't that sad? Or am I hyper-ventilating? I have talked to you several times about respecting not just your own body but also your partner's. Sex isn't about energetic coupling with the first attractive stranger you meet. It's more than a mere 'need'.

To me, sex without commitment or feeling is an empty, sad, lonely act without any validity. I feel sorry when I see so many of your generation going from one bed to the next without stopping to even look into the partner's eyes. 'What's love got to do with it?' young people mock when the argument gets going. Sex is merely a physical necessity and ought to be treated as such. I vehemently disagree. A dialogue on the subject is possible if you are receptive to my views. As of now, I think we are out of sync. You find my attitude anti-diluvian; I find yours offensive, even revolting.

Your generation is hopelessly confused and mixed up. You'll grin and remind me that Ajoba probably said that about mine (he did!). Mine was no better, I have to confess, but in this regard there were certain rules—wonky and lopsided as they might seem to you. 'Good' girls and 'decent' boys did not indulge in random sex. It was an act invested with some sentiment and significance. Partners were not changed lightly or treated like discarded clothes.

You'll never hear me say, 'Practise safe sex, darling.' But if you were ever to seek my opinion, I would definitely tell you to behave responsibly, respect your bodies, be sensitive in your relationships. And never, ever abuse trust.

Your concerned
Mama

....

Mumbai
January '99

Dear Vanti and Radhika,

Do you remember your first heartbreak? I do. Because it broke my heart as well. No, I said to myself, my little girls don't need this, they're far too young, far too vulnerable, far too sensitive. Plus, the persons they're weeping for aren't worthy enough. It was your pain that hurt me, and I began to detest the young men who'd caused it. Avantika, you moaned for months, unable to concentrate on your studies. Your appearance changed. You seemed perennially distracted and low. Your self-worth hit rock-bottom. I wanted to kill the man responsible for your grief. You didn't. You preferred to blame yourself, your lack of experience, your immaturity (you were only eighteen at the time), and make excuses for the bounder. Now, when I look back, I realize he wasn't a villain. He was just an older person who happened to be in a hurry. He couldn't deal with what he perceived as your 'childishness'. And you were very much a kid then—a 'young' eighteen. He was not a villain. He just wasn't the right person for you.

Well, all that is behind you (and me) now. Today, if I run into him anywhere, I feel indifferent, not angry—as I know you do, too.

Radhika, you've been through a rough patch yourself. The same story—inexperience and a lack of judgement (the two generally go hand in hand). With both of you, I had to force myself not to say: I told you so. Maybe my expression conveyed the sentiment. But I can tell you it took all my self-control to prevent myself from shouting out the words. How true it is that mothers often clearly see what their children blind themselves to. The person you fancied then had 'unsuitable boy' written all over him.

Both young men were anything but 'suitable boys'. My frustration was, if I could recognize this with such clarity, why wouldn't you? Maybe I had temporarily forgotten my own youthful adventures and follies. Or maybe I didn't want to pay heed when both of you were indirectly pleading with me to 'back off'. I remember saying, 'But can't you see he's all wrong for you? This relationship can only bring grief. Why can't you listen to me? After all, I'm so much older. I've seen more of life.' These really are the last words a parent should utter to children in love. How come I was so stupid? I should have known better and realized that instead of helping you to see reason, I was pushing you towards the boys. I had done that myself as a young girl. The more my parents disapproved, the greater the attraction became. It wasn't a question of defiance alone (though it did include that). I preferred to make my own mistakes. 'Why do you want to learn the hard way,' I recall lamenting with you girls. Avantika had wept and said, 'Because I can't live my life according to your experiences. I must discover things for myself.' 'But why?' I'd despaired. 'Why can't you trust me? I know better.' Oops—wrong words again. Of course parents think they know better. And they probably do. But kids want the option to stumble along, fall down and get up again—on their own. You girls were absolutely right. Your life had to be lived on your terms—not mine.

It took years for me to get the message. It was very hard to stop myself from 'interfering', especially when I saw you struggling to come to terms with your feelings. I wanted to help . . . I wanted to lessen your pain. But I felt helpless. I still don't know the tack I should have taken. What had my own mother done? She had been a neutral observer offering advice, and that too rarely. It had worked because I had elder sisters whose judgement I relied on. I was close enough to them to not feel shy about discussing all my teenage traumas. I had friends I could talk freely to. My mother remained calm and receptive whenever I did approach her. And frankly, there were hardly any significant secrets I kept from her. She knew all about my adolescent crushes, and even met a few of the pimply-faced youths I so adored. The difference between her approach and mine was this: she didn't push the pace. She waited for me to wake up (years went by) and see reason (which I refused to). But in your case, I was suspicious and hostile because I saw through your young men much before you girls did.

Having seen through them, I found it impossible to remain a silent spectator. You were my responsibility. I felt protective. I didn't want you to get hurt. My intentions were good but the method was all wrong. I played the heavy rather clumsily. I came down on you a bit too hard. I bet you felt suffocated and resentful—as I would have in your place.

Anyway, it's history. Both of you are in a new and exciting phase of your life, and there have been other relationships. This time I'm determined to get it right. I'm trying hard not to be judgmental. I don't sneer or mock. I'm even being nice to your suitors and looking at the more positive side of the developments. You are that much older, that much surer. There are times when I'm amazed at how far you've come in such a short time. You're handling yourselves brilliantly, displaying such maturity, it astonishes me. Whether or not the current relationships lead anywhere, I feel confident you are in a position to deal with them. Of course, I'd love to 'remote control' their progress. But I'm restraining myself from doing that. You seem happy, more in control. And of course, the young men cannot be compared to the other two. About their 'suitability'—aaah, that's another question. A sore point that shouldn't be discussed.

I suppose most mothers find the young men or women picked by their children entirely unsuitable. Meanwhile, you'll agree my 'lectures' have reduced somewhat. I keep my opinions largely to myself. In my heart, I know the kind of man who'll make you happy. A mother always knows. But I'm prepared to keep mum and go along with your plans. The one criterion I will not compromise on is your happiness. A man who makes you feel lousy about yourself is simply not worth keeping. What is it they say about the 'glow of true love'? I believe in it. The day I see it reflected on your face, I'll be the first to bless you. Sorry, girls—so far, I haven't noticed it. And I don't have blinkers on.

If you were to ask me my ideas on men who constitute husband material I would tell you that they are old-fashioned and traditional. That's how I was raised. That was the sort of marriage I grew up watching at close quarters. I would like you to marry men of honour. Men who will stand by you. Men who will cherish you. Men who will respect you. I don't think that's a tall order. I believe that's the bare minimum required to build an enduring relationship on. Everything else is incidental—looks, money, glamour, lifestyle—anybody can acquire all these and more. But when it comes to character (and trust me, at a crunch, nothing else counts), that's when your own will be tested too. What choices will you make? What will you opt for? I'm confident you'll make the right decision. Meanwhile, I can't help being me—critical, watchful, on red-alert. One wrong move from any man, and guess whom they'll have to reckon with? Enough to scare the bravest heart, I hope. Whether you want it or not, whether you like it or not, your emotional well-being is my business. If I see trouble ahead, I will say so, and do something about it, even if it means war. So girls, remember, you've been warned.

Determinedly yours,
Mother

....

Mumbai
August '99

Dear Rana and Aditya,
   Don't groan. Don't make faces. Don't say, 'Mother, is this your lecture number 74 or 108?' the same way you categorize my facial expressions ('oh-oh . . . here comes number 89—disgust, scowl, disapproval'). Well, okay, go ahead and say it. Like you're going to stop because I've asked. We've discussed the girlfriend issue many times. You boys know exactly how I feel about it. The idea of switching girlfriends on a bi-monthly basis scares me, even if you do say that's how it goes these days. I watch the parade of beautiful young girls walk in and out of our home, and wonder. Is it really that easy to find and chuck human beings? Are girlfriends like trendy T-shirts one sports and discards after a few weeks? Occasionally you've surprised me by asking half-seriously, 'But tell us, Mother, what kind of a woman, according to you, will make us happy?' And I've offered my views unreservedly. Right? As a parent, I've felt   strongly   about   a   few   basic   things—like compatibility—while your focus has perhaps been on combustibility. I've seen some of your girlfriends, chatted

with them, sized them up. Nope. I didn't identify a future daughter-in-law in that lot. You'll laugh while reading this. Or maybe you won't.

I believe both you boys will eventually settle down with fairly conventional girls, and not the frisky 'babes' you date. It's such an 'Indian' thing, really. Go out with one kind, enjoy your time together, and then settle down with a 'gharelu' (albeit a modern-day version). My guess is you'll opt for career women who value family life as well. Intelligent partners whose company you'll enjoy. I've already seen a slight shift, from ultra-glamorous 'chicks' to less flamboyant (but distinctly attractive) professionals. The mating-dating game has undergone a great change since my time, as you constantly point out. These days I play full-time telephone operator to well-mannered female callers asking for you. Girls are taking all the initiatives and setting the pace for a relationship. It seems a far more equal situation, even if less romantic in many ways. There is a business-like approach I sense, which puzzles me. Almost as if a relationship is a cut-and-dried transaction with a cut-off date and a specified shelf-life. You move smoothly from phase to phase, girl to girl, with no visible scars. Girlfriends transform into just friends. Just friends suddenly become girlfriends. It appears so easy and effortless. I'm told this is 'the scene' everywhere. Well, I guess it is. You move on; the girls move on. No time for regrets. Everybody is happy, except me. Don't worry, though. I'm teaching myself to 'unlearn' old rules. One of these days I'll get there. Till then, patience, sons, patience.

Intolerantly yours,
Mother

Mumbai
September '99

Dear Aditya,

Do you remember when you turned up with an American girl on one of your early vacation breaks while studying in Boston? She was probably a very nice girl. But the fact that she'd accompanied you to India had sent shock waves through the family. Nobody had done that before. And nobody expected it from you. You were supposed to be the shy, reserved, bhola-bhola one. Yet, here you were springing a surprise without prior notice. You didn't seek your grandparents' permission. You didn't ask for mine. You coolly announced your intention to bring her along. And all of us gasped. 'What will everybody say?' your grandmother worried. 'How will we explain her presence in the home? What about the . . . er, arrangements? Where will she sleep? And her food habits? How will she eat traditional Indian food day in and day out for a month? If people ask, what explanation should we give? In India, it's not enough to say, 'She's just a friend' or, 'Mind your own business'. Everybody wants to know everything. Also, as your grandmother pointed out, there'd be the awkwardness with domestics. Why scandalize them? Or scandalize your grandaunts?

I can tell you her arrival set off a furore within the extended family. Furore and speculation. 'Are you going to marry the girl?' you were asked bluntly, even before you could unpack. Your spontaneous reply—'Don't be ridiculous. I'm still a student and she's a close friend'—didn't satisfy anybody. How can a young man and a young lady be 'close friends' without a commitment? You dealt with all the questions as patiently as was possible. Then, you stopped answering. Just like that.

It took everybody a few days to adjust to her presence in the home. And it took a great deal of tact and deft handling on your part to dissuade her from strolling around in unsuitable attire. The curiosity would have overwhelmed a lesser girl. But your friend was remarkably composed and unfazed.

Your grandmother commented that she was considerably older, and taller. You snapped, 'So what?' Grandma shut up. I mentioned her mannerisms; you gave me a withering look. I promptly shut up. 'It's only for a month,' we reasoned. 'But what if it's not? What if they decide to get married?' Ba agonized. 'We'll deal with it when that happens,' I reassured her. Frankly, I was dead sure your friendship wouldn't survive the next semester. It didn't. But trust me, it was a major turning point for the family. You signalled so many different things to us when you made up your mind to bring her to India. You told us you were now old enough and independent enough to make your own decisions. You also told us who was in charge—you. It was all much too much and much too sudden. It took us a while to accept the fact that you were now your own man—our little boy had grown up. And grown up so fast, we hadn't noticed the years whizzing by.

Soon, the vacation ended. You asked me to give her a gift, which I did. There was nothing wrong with the girl. I really couldn't fault her conduct. She was well behaved and well mannered and stayed out of everybody's way. Even so, we were relieved when she left. I told Ba confidently, 'Don't worry. This won't last.' It didn't. A dramatic chapter in all our lives came to a close, without too much turbulence.

I was surprised by all our reactions—most of all by my own. My close friends asked me, 'My God. How did you deal with it? Didn't you hate her? Could you get yourself to be polite? Were you a little jealous?' Surprisingly, I wasn't any of those things. I assessed her accurately and fairly, and accepted the fact that she belonged to an entirely different culture. I also saw your involvement in the light of your background. Yours had been an over-protected, sheltered upbringing. Then, at a comparatively young age, you had decided to go to America and get yourself a degree. She was one of the first people you ran into on campus. Her extended hand of friendship was grabbed by you gratefully. That formed the basis of your relationship. I understood the pattern perfectly.

What was harder to figure out was your unilateral decision to bring her home. Of course it's the done thing in America. Students often ask friends over for Thanksgiving weekends and Fourth of July celebrations. But in her case, she was ready to travel thousands of miles to a distant country and alien culture, just to be with you. Tough. For her, and for a family that had never envisaged such a possibility. I remember one of Ba's main concerns being, 'What will the domestics think?' These were not just servants. They were family retainers who had known you since birth. Their opinion mattered. After much deliberation, certain arrangements were made that placated all members of the family. Rules of propriety being what they are in Indian homes, it was important not to shake up the status quo. As Ba put it in her no-nonsense, practical way, 'What you do in America is your business. But what you do here is ours.' With that understood, a pleasant time was had by all. Fortunately, both of you conducted yourselves with restraint and discretion, offending nobody. After the airport goodbyes, we came home pretty sure that was the last we'd seen of the young lady. We were right.

The other day I came across a photo album containing pictures of her visit. Your hair is much longer in them. Some of the pictures are sweet. Really sweet. You look relaxed and happy. So does she. I hope when she looks back on her trip to India, it will be with affection. She got to see an aspect of it most tourists don't. She lived with a large traditional Indian family for a month, and that experience alone is worth a lot. Travel brochures never prepare you for something like that. It was the best kind of exposure to another culture, which I'm sure she'll value, if not now, then later. As for you, much has happened in your life. But for all for us, that summer of '95 will always remain special. Very special.

Fondly,
Mama

....

Mumbai
August '99
Dear Arundhati,
    A few months ago you came back from school all flushed and embarrassed. You said you had gone to the school library with your friends and come across one of my early novels. You must have been five or six at the time it was published, and therefore have no recollection of the reactions it had generated. Your friends grabbed the book innocently and started reading it. As they flipped the pages, they came across a few explicit passages, and were shocked. As any twelve- or thirteen-year-old would be. You were

more than shocked. You were embarrassed. You rushed to me and demanded an explanation. 'Mama, how could you write such things?' It was then that I decided to talk to you frankly about how I could. Why I did.

'This book is meant for adults, not your age group,' I explained. 'Maybe,' you argued, 'but how could you have written it?' I tried giving it perspective. But you didn't want to listen. I guess you were far too stunned—both by the contents, and the fact that you had stumbled on them in the company of your friends. I thought it wise to leave it for the moment. What may have seemed 'cheap' to you had to be seen in a certain context. I didn't expect you at your young age to grasp the intricacies of that. In any case, you of all the children are the most prudish when it comes to upfront discussions related to body parts or sex. It is you who find some of the paintings at home 'vulgar' because they feature nude figures. You hate clothes that cling. Your conversation is never peppered with objectionable words. And you restrict your reading to the classics or innocuous adventure books. I'm sure the unexpected stumbling upon risqué passages in your mother's books must have come as a shock. I wonder how I would have reacted at that age if something similar had occurred to me. I'm sure I would have been equally devastated.

After a week or so I raised the topic of pornography. I mentioned how in a year or two, someone or the other in your class would draw your attention to 'blue films', 'blue books' and 'blue sites' on the net. It's unavoidable, and very much a part of growing up in cities. You didn't want to pursue the subject, saying such things didn't interest you. Not now, maybe. But one day they might. You'll be curious, you'll want to know. You'll want to see. How long will your innocent lack of interest last? What then?

I thought of my adolescent years, of the first time I discovered 'naughty' books. It was a thrilling experience, mainly because it was forbidden. I don't know whether I would have enjoyed the clandestine activity as much had my mother casually picked up the 'pondies' (as we called them) and launched into a discussion on the subject. The idea that it was something I would not ever raise with her made it all the more exciting. I devoured quite a collection of those cheap books, even if I didn't understand some of the more graphic passages. After a while, I got bored. They were depressingly repetitive and lousily written. It was the same with blue films, which I found either revolting or laughable. I'm certain my responses would have been different had Aji 'found out' or 'punished' me.

The thing, Arundhati, is this. At your age, curiosity levels are at their highest. You want to know everything about everything—sex included. Yet, there is so much social conditioning that it's pretty impossible to discuss such matters openly. Most times kids get their distorted 'sex education' from ill-informed classmates. They don't have the confidence to crosscheck the information with parents. If they did, there would be less fuzziness, less ignorance, and more importantly, less misinformation and mis-understanding in what I consider a very important area of life. Since social taboos are so strong, young children feel ashamed to ask questions. They prefer to seek answers from peers. Even though most schools have introduced basic sex education, in the classroom it remains just that—basic. Very basic. Besides a factual account of how babies are made, nothing else is discussed, neither the psychological nor the emotional aspects of sexual intimacy. Most children grow up thinking sex is 'dirty'. And that prejudice sticks for

life. They also feel sex is sinful, because they are taught to
see it in isolation.

In a way, I'm glad you stumbled on my book. It seems
more natural this way, rather than my sitting you down and
saying earnestly, 'Look Arundhati. These are some of the
books your mother wrote when you were this high.' Now
that you've read a passage here and there, you've made it
easier for me to talk about why I wrote what I did, when I
did. Not now, but when you're ready for it. I want you to
grow up with a healthy, open, positive attitude to sex. You
will inevitably come across strong oppressive, hard-core
sites on the net one of these days, despite all the monitoring.
What then? I want you to feel confident enough to
approach me, rather than your equally confused friends. I'll
be able to help you deal with your mixed feelings on the
issue, because I know exactly what goes through a young
girl's mind when confronted with the subject for the first
time. Most parents are reluctant to deal with it, because
their own reactions are in a grey zone. They also feel very
embarrassed to discuss such topics freely. Our repressed
society would rather pretend sex does not exist, than cope
with the questions children ask. Sometimes teachers too
make a curious child feel guilty by labelling him or her a
'pervert'. Such strong words leave their mark. I've seen a
little girl from your school being ostracized by the others for
daring to raise uncomfortable sex-related issues. I often
wonder: why are we so scared of the subject? Dealt with
responsibly, it can be demystified. Try me.

I notice how you cover your face during kissing scenes in
Hollywood films—even those meant for your age group.
We ourselves ensure you aren't in the room when we watch
popular films like *Pretty Woman* or *There's Something
About Mary*. There are references in these which are clearly

not designed for minors. There are jokes, visual gags and ideas, which if not explained could give you wrong notions about adult relationships. I believe there is a time for everything—pornography included. You will encounter it at some point, and when you do, it's important that you recognize it for what it is: a demeaning version of sex. So long as you don't allow yourself to plunge into what is now a multi-million dollar industry, you'll be all right. It's when curiosity becomes an obsession, or a full-time preoccupation, cutting into other priorities, that parents need to worry.

Most children outgrow this phase if it's handled tactfully. It doesn't help to call a child nasty names for peeping into *Playboy*. Or to accuse the child of being a sex-maniac for lingering too long over any controversial material. Ideally, parents should take it in their stride, not make too big a fuss, not give it too much attention, and distract the child with something else. Children's attention spans are notoriously short. Show them a more interesting option and they'll grab it. Meanwhile, it's important to stress the fact that not everything one encounters that is disrobed, constitutes pornography. We have a great many paintings in our home, some of them featuring nudes. I remember the reactions of your friends (those who come from backgrounds in which they were not exposed to art). They'd look at the canvases and start giggling. A few would make comments ('Chichi—how vulgar'), and that would embarrass you. In fact, you'd often beg me to remove a painting, saying, 'Why do you and Daddy like such dirty things, why can't we put pictures of flowers on the wall?' I particularly recall one of your tutors being unable to take his eyes off a large blue nude painted by Sakti Burman, our favourite artist. You noticed it, too. 'Why don't we hang a cloth over that naked lady?' you suggested. I laughed. Your tuitions continued.

Today, you're far more comfortable with nudity, though you did correct me sharply when I tried to discuss with you the sublime beauty of the naked human figure. 'Please,' you beseeched, 'I don't care what you think. I still find it gross.' I put it down to your tender age. Soon, you'll be out of your teens and ready to view the very same paintings differently. Till such time I'll make sure I keep the picture of Michaelangelo's David well out of your sight. Okay?

Love,
Mama

....

Mumbai
August '99

Dear Radhika and Avantika,

Last night I watched *Father of the Bride* for the fourth time, and wept. Also for the fourth time. Absurd. How can a commercial, manipulative Hollywood film make me feel so sentimental? There is no explanation other than the obvious one—in every commercial, manipulative Hollywood film is buried a precious grain of truth. While watching Steve Martin and Diane Keaton planning their twenty-two-year-old daughter's wedding, I could visualize us doing just that, sitting around the table discussing mundane details while avoiding the moment of truth all parents have to confront at a time like this—the imminent departure of a beloved daughter from her parental home. So far I have not had to deal with such a situation. When the time does come, how prepared will I be?

For years and years we have discussed weddings and marriages. I have teased you about various eligible men. You've hotly denied any involvement, and a couple of times you've blushed and changed the subject. I've made my views on extravagant weddings known to all of you. It's a subject I feel pretty strongly about. Avantika, you've always said you wanted a wedding with all the frills, 'spread over eight or ten days'. Arundhati, too, confessed to me that when she gets married she'd like it to be a super-production—just like they do it in all the recent Hindi movies, five or six pre-wedding ceremonies including sangeet, mehendi, cocktails etc. I had shuddered visibly, rolled my eyes and said, 'Heaven help us. Are you nuts?' I meant it. Radhika has never expressed her views on the subject, often stating her desire to stay single forever. But I know that when she meets the right man those resolves will go straight out of the window, as they do for most young girls who are focused single-mindedly on career goals.

I believe a wedding should be simple, meaningful and aesthetically pleasing. That's all. It shouldn't be a statement about one's vanity or wealth. I like the idea of intimate weddings involving close family and friends. A few years ago, I was taken aback when I received an invitation to attend the wedding of a complete stranger—a prominent industrialist I'd never met. I asked the person who'd come to deliver the card why I'd been invited. 'Because we have been given a quota. I have to call at least ten known people. You were on my list.' At least the man was frank. Today, when I attend extravagant affairs called society weddings, I'm appalled by the waste. Such an ostentatious display. Such lavish expenditure. What for? So that hundreds of acquaintances can come to the venue to display their jewels and fine clothes, drink, dance, eat and make merry at the hosts' expense, and then go home, criticize all the arrangements, gossip about the people present, and forget the entire thing next morning. And to think people are willing to spend crores and crores for this dubious thrill! No, thank you, girls. I hope when the time comes we'll be in agreement over the scale and style of the function. Keep it simple and keep it short, is my attitude. If there is money to spare, feed the poor. They might bless you for it. If there's still more money to spare, give it to a worthy charity or sponsor a deserving child. But for heaven's sake don't throw it away on impressing anybody. For this to work, one needs to find a marriage partner who feels the same way about conspicuous consumption. I expect you girls to display discretion, good sense and good taste when the time comes. Of course, we'll have all the ceremonies you enjoy and are looking forward to—why should you lose out on your big moment? But in the midst of all the revelry, I'd like you to remember that weddings are sacred and should be regarded as such. Partying is secondary to the solemn ceremony. It is not enough to sit through it without trying to follow its significance. I'd like you to understand the vows you take and to absorb the meaning of the mantras being chanted. Otherwise, it becomes a futile, meaningless exercise. Of course, if you opt out of a religious ceremony in favour of a registered marriage, that would be fine by me too. But please, dear girls, remember my horror of loud, boisterous, showy affairs. I'd like your weddings to be memorable, yes, but for the right reasons. Instead of investing time, money and energy on an opulent two- or three-day-circus, I'd rather you spent that same amount setting up your new home.

My sympathies were with Steve Martin, the father of the bride, in the movie. But more than his panic attacks over his wife's decision to give their daughter a 'beautiful' (read: expensive) wedding, it was the private moments spent with the young bride-to-be on the eve of the big day, that moved me very much. Lovely scenes between the father and daughter as they recalled the years past when she was just a little girl growing up, with all the accompanying pleasures and pains. There was a montage of charming flashbacks showing the daughter at various stages of her young life as seen through her doting father's eyes. It was at these points that my own eyes filled with tears . . . as your faces got superimposed on hers. I asked myself, 'How will you cope?' I'm afraid of the answer. I cannot imagine life being any other way than how it is at present. I cannot visualize you in someone else's home . . . being a part of someone else's family. When that happens as it inevitably must—will I be ready to keep my chin up and smile though the tears? I guess we'll find out soon enough. Sniff, sniff.

Your 'senti'
Mama

....

Mumbai
August '99

Dear Avantika, Radhika, Rana and Aditya,
    Once or twice you girls have asked me a disturbing question: 'Is marriage worth it?' I have put the ball back in your court by countering, 'What do you think?' It has led to

long discussions on the subject . . . interesting discussions through which I got an insight into the minds of your generation, to whom this question is obviously a perplexing one. You know what I feel? Marriage is worth it only if you think so, not otherwise. You have to believe in marriage. If you don't, or if you think of it as a career option, then you're better off staying single. I hate using the word 'compromise' in any context . . . least of all marriage. It makes it sound so awful and unattractive. Who likes 'compromise'? On the other hand, I couldn't romanticize it à la *Hum Apke Hain Kaun* either. Now you girls are old enough to have figured out a few things for yourselves, the chief one being, what goes into a successful marriage.

I'd say hard work, even at the risk of making it sound like an ongoing thermal project. Your generation detests both hard work and compromise. I find most of you have very low tolerance levels. You want a marriage that moves along on well-greased wheels without a single bump ruining the ride. That's not possible. You know it, but refuse to accept it. I remember telling you about one of your contemporaries who got married to someone she claimed she was madly in love with, only to divorce him a year later. Why? Because he criticized her driving and found fault with her parking skills. Not surprisingly, the marriage broke up in a parking lot when he thought her reversing wasn't upto scratch. I mentioned this to a young friend, thinking she'd find it funny. Instead she said, 'Quite right. The girl had sense. She got out of the mess in time. If a man can crib about your driving, he can crib about practically everything else too. Who wants to live with such a guy?' Different perceptions.

Avantika wants to live a fairy tale for the rest of her life. She is romantic and sentimental. Well, I hope she's fortunate enough to find a Prince Charming who'll live it with her. Radhika is more practical. 'I won't be able to stay with someone who'll dictate terms to me,' she says. Right now, with her erratic work schedule, she values her independence far too much to let marriage enter the picture. 'If I do get married, it will be to a man who respects my commitment to my career. If he's in the same business, he'll understand my crazy timings and not make a big deal out of missed appointments.' Which made me wonder—was she looking for a husband or a working partner? She laughed. 'It's different for our age group. I could never be just a wife-wife, waiting at home for the guy to come back. If I cook, he should also cook. We should do things together. But we should also have our independent lives. I don't want to be answerable to anyone.'

We discussed a young film-maker friend of mine, whom you girls know quite well. Her marriage had recently come apart and we were analysing why that might have happened. I said, 'She was far too busy pursuing her own goals. They hardly saw each other. She was never around. Theirs was worse than a weekend marriage because most weekends she was away on shoots. He saw more of the bai who ran the home than his wife.' Avantika laughed, 'In that case he should have married the bai.'

Marriages go through rough patches. The fights could be over several things—money, children, priorities, possessiveness. Sometimes, a small irritant like fighting over the remote control can trigger off a major fallout. One has to see it coming and prepare for it. Generally it's a sign that something's wrong. When I point out these things to you, I know they do register and make you think. For those of you who're growing up in the nineties, individuality has become a big issue. Often it gets mixed up with power. Marriage is neither an ego trip nor a power trip. To use a cliché, you give some, you get some. To an extent, the all-important 'self' has to take a back seat from time to time . . . but that again depends on the role 'self' plays in your relationship. If it overwhelms and dominates the marriage, there's bound to be trouble.

'Why should I stop seeing my old friends just because I'm married?' I've heard young brides complain after a bitter fight. I've heard young bridegrooms say the same thing after a rollicking boys' night out. We've talked about it too, since both you girls feel so strongly about your territorial rights. It's a tricky thing, really. Each couple has to work out an equation that fits into their lifestyle and value system. But these sort of irritants ought to be settled before taking the plunge.

You're amused by some of the self- imposed rules in your mother's marriage. Simple things like not taking calls or fixing meetings when Daddy is around. It's not because he's asked me to. I prefer it this way because I don't think it's fair to let my professional commitments spill over into our private time together. When I'm with my husband, I want to be hundred per cent with him. Yes, we argue, fight and sulk. We have our bad days and truly terrible days. Yes, we hyperventilate and withdraw from each other. At such times, I'm non-communicative and desperately miserable. Sometimes I talk to you about it. Sometimes I don't. But soon, the sun comes out again and the smile returns to my face. That's marriage. No permanent highs and no permanent lows. The only permanent thing about it is your desire to be in a long-lasting, loving relationship. It is that commitment alone that sustains marriage through its lows. It's easy to desire marriage when everything is going great. It's equally easy to reject it when the chips are down. Finally, what counts is the depth of your feelings and how much it matters to you, how much you want to invest in it and whether or not it helps you grow as an individual. A marriage that stifles one or both individuals destroys itself. But even in a fulfilling relationship there are parameters that need to be drawn and respected. You have to sacrifice a little to gain a lot. You and I know how much Daddy has given up for us . . . for me. If I think he's a different, far better person than the guy I married, I hope he feels the same way about me too. He's changed (gone is the mercurial temper), I've changed (gone, the intimidating sarcasm). With years of close interaction, we've shaped our lives to accommodate each other's needs.

I see so much impatience these days. Twenty-somethings are attracted by the idea of marriage, sure. But once in it, they feel suffocated and depressed. If the partner happens to be a control freak, there's even more of a problem. Because stress levels are already pretty high, the relationship can't take the pressure. Though the trend these days is to marry young (alarmingly young, according to me), I see far too many wrecked marriages too. All you kids seem to have a sane, practical attitude to marriage. I'm sure you'll pick your partners with care and not jump into anything recklessly. I've told you about the upside and flip side of marriage often enough. While I don't think it should be the end-all or be-all of your lives, I have to be honest and say that I hope you do opt for it when you're ready. Too many lovely women of forty-plus (that must seem so distant to you), start wondering what they're going to do with the rest of their lives once the career thing is out of their systems. Of course, I've also met the happy-to-be-single ones who swear they wouldn't switch roles for anything in the world. But knowing both of you, I can tell you'll eventually opt for domesticity—even if it does sound like a dreadfully dull prospect to you at present. All those 'duties', all those 'married people' rituals. Years and years spent with the same person. The tiresome habits, the routine, the sameness of it all. Right? I know. I felt like that at your age. All I wanted was excitement, novelty, experience, thrills, constant stimulation, highs, surprises. That and more. And yet when the time came, I 'knew'. And so many years later, I still 'know'; there are no regrets. There have been lots of irritations, a few legitimate grouses. And the annoying compulsion to control another's life—yes, that too. I think the hiccups are well behind me now. I feel at peace, as you will someday. And when you do, you too will think of marriage as a joyful, gratifying life long experience which has seen you bloom and flower as individuals. Personal growth is of vital importance. But how much more fun it is if you're lucky to be married to someone who shares your progress with you, enjoys the journey equally and is there to hold your hand every step of the way and say 'Bravo' when you succeed and 'Don't worry' when you fail.

I'm praying. Praying really, really hard that both of you will meet such a man. And that when you do, you will recognize him and live happily ever after. Just like in fairy tales.

Wistfully,
Your mother

....

Mumbai
June '99

Dear Girls,

There are times when I feel I'm a bit too open and candid with you about matters that are far too complex or 'adult' for you to fully comprehend. Your father often corrects me when he overhears our conversations. 'Why are you discussing such topics?' he asks. I immediately react with a defensive, 'Why not? The girls are adults now. Surely they're old enough to understand what I'm saying.' He puts it into perspective immediately. 'They may understand the words. But do they also know the context? Can they arrive at any worthwhile conclusions based on their limited experience of life?' He is right, of course. But I think a lot of modern mothers fall into this trap a bit too easily. We are so free with our daughters, we sometimes forget that they're young girls who still have a lot of living ahead of them— living on their terms, unbiased and uncoloured by our views, unprejudiced by our opinions. Unfortunately, we live in complex and confusing times. I wonder whether there is anything at all that our children don't know, haven't talked about or seen on television.

There are times when I'm discussing a marital problem with a friend whose marriage is passing through stormy weather and I forget you're there, and listening. The friend may pour out sordid details about her life, instances of adultery, cheating, financial scams, lying, alcoholism, abuse and worse. You may hear some or all of it. Later, you are likely to ask me to fill in details. This becomes dangerous, since you aren't aware of the complete story. You've heard stray bits and pieces. What do I do? Go ahead and provide the gory missing links? Or tell you it's none of your business, kindly stay out of it? I don't know. I play it by ear

. . . revealing as much as I feel I need to, while not betraying my friend's confidence. Sometimes, you hear awful stories about our friends from outsiders and ask us to confirm, clarify or deny. This is also tricky territory. How much does one reveal? My fear is simply this—you girls are on the threshold of your young lives. Still single, still romantic and full of dreams and hopes. Do I have the right to destroy your ideals by narrating incidents from less-than-perfect marriages? Will it distort your views on the institution? Put you off? Or should I tell myself, 'They must learn to take it in their stride. After all, how long will it be before they find out a few ugly truths for themselves?'

By and large, I do try and protect you from the kind of cynicism which is rampant in urban middle-class society. I want you to continue to believe in the beauty of sunsets and roses. I want poetry to affect you. I want you to go weak in the knees over romantic gestures. I want you to weep while watching soppy films. I like the idea of mush myself. Yes, even now, so many years later. It would be awful for you to miss out on this phase and turn hard and practical. God knows there's time enough for that. All around us, one can see the debris of failed relationships. You and I frequently discuss the ones we know, and ask ourselves why and where they went wrong. Even at these times, I try and put a pretty face on the mess because I don't want you to think most marriages end this way.

With all the ugliness and bitterness in contemporary life, it's important to preserve one's better, finer feelings, to be in touch with the softer side of living. Not everything is harsh and forbidding, and you girls are perceptive enough to know the truth. I feel, on my part, that I must reaffirm the positive aspect of love, marriage and commitment. Not all modern marriages are rotten, no matter what the soap operas tell us. You must believe not only in the goodness of marriage but also in the goodness of human beings. Of course, even the best of relationships goes through hellishly rough patches—fights over money, property, rights, differing values, divergent viewpoints, varying moral standards. There can be arguments, hostility, and soon the marriage is in trouble, or over. This doesn't have to be the case, provided the two people can sort out the areas of conflict in a mature way and arrive at a situation where healthy respect is shown for the other's point of view. The keyword is tolerance. That comes with time. And it only comes when there is a deeper level of commitment and a genuine desire to work things out in a positive way.

I've bounced my anxieties off you girls several times, and received remarkably mature advice. I've marvelled at your 'wisdom' at such times, when you've provided me with a much-needed perspective and supported my stand, while reminding me gently of my own words and bringing me back to a calmer state. I used to be far more impatient and prickly a few years ago, taking arguments to heart and sulking for days on end. It was when I decided that such an attitude was getting me nowhere and that I should stop brooding and start doing something about a difficult situation, that real change took place. Today, when I look back on those outbursts and deep hurts, I smile at the memory and remember how wonderful you were during those troubling times. I feel so grateful. I thank you for seeing me through dark tunnels of despair, for being there with your smiles and cheerful words. May you have equally wonderful daughters of your own some day.

Gratefully,
Mama

Mumbai
April '99

Dear Bachcha-log,

'Getting involved' with situations that don't directly concern you has often been discussed ad nauseam around the table. Yet, how does one remain 'uninvolved'? Aditya grew up with the gurkha's son. The little boy was around a year old when Aditya was born. They were inseparable through childhood, often eating out of the same plate. I can recall the hours they spent getting together all the paraphernalia for kite-flying during Sankranti, and the fierce competition that would follow on the terrace as they 'cut' kites belonging to enthusiasts on neighbouring terraces. All was well till they grew up into young men and picked their own paths. Moti Singh opted for an early marriage to a lovely young bride while Aditya went overseas to pursue a degree in business and finance.

A year after his marriage, Moti Singh produced a bouncing baby boy. Everybody was delighted. Everybody except the lovely young wife. She looked miserable, her eyes always downcast, mouth twisted. I asked Aditya about it. He shrugged. 'Things aren't working out between them,' he answered shortly. So, I asked Avantika. 'Mother . . . I don't know how that poor girl puts up with his beatings. He is so cruel to her. He didn't spare her even when she was pregnant.' She described a few incidents which terrified me. Not only was Moti Singh abusing his wife physically and in public, but she was being deprived of regular meals. How would she be able to nurse her infant son? Weren't they at least concerned about his health? I was assuming they'd have figured out the fact that a lactating mother required nutrition to breastfeed her baby. Obviously they hadn't. Avantika and I talked about the problem at length and I told her to intervene the next time she saw Moti Singh striking his wife. A week after our conversation, Avantika was woken up by the cries of the young woman. She rushed to the balcony to see Moti Singh kicking her as she bent over a bucketful of soaked clothes—his family's wash—at the common tap in the compound. Avantika rushed downstairs and told Moti Singh to stop at once. Far from feeling ashamed of his actions, he whirled around and told Avantika to stay out of his affairs. She threatened to call the police. He threatened to beat her up for interfering in a 'family matter'. Two weeks after the incident, Moti Singh's tormented wife ran away, leaving her baby behind. I silently applauded her escape. Had she stuck around he might have killed her.

We shall never know what the young girl was being 'punished' for in this sadistic manner. But it was important not to stand around watching mutely while a helpless victim was being brutalized. This is just one isolated incident. There have been several other, equally horrifying ones that have led to discussions at home about 'staying out of it' because it's 'none of our business'. Or taking a stand, getting involved and trying to make a difference, even a small one. It's hard. It's thankless. Often, it's very frustrating. But it's also important not to be a passive bystander. Injustice has got to be addressed, even if—or particularly when—it doesn't affect you directly.

A couple of years ago, I was in the car with Arundhati, Anandita and their friends when we saw the man who goes from house to house in our area, collecting junk and old newspapers. He was beating his wife, in the middle of a busy street near our home. By the time we realized what was happening, our car had passed the traffic signal. I told the driver to turn around and go all the way back to that spot.

One of the other kids piped up, 'But Aunty . . . we'll get late for the movie.' Another said, 'So what? We can't let that poor woman get a beating. Let's go back and stop the fight.' When we got there, the man had shoved the woman into a cab and sped off. I asked the people standing around why they hadn't prevented him from attacking a helpless victim. 'It's between them. A husband-wife maamla.'

All the children were shocked and outraged. 'My mummy always tells people not to behave this way, even when she doesn't know them,' a little girl said innocently. Another added philosophically, 'Chalta hai. People are like that only.' It's true. People are definitely 'like that only'. But is it possible to remain unaffected by brutality? Even if it means putting yourself out for something that could backfire horribly? One must reach out and help the defenceless whenever possible. I don't want to sound preachy. But look at the way we are living our lives today. Shut off from each other, unable and unwilling to extend ourselves even a little, unless there is something in it for us. If we grow so insensitive to our fellow men, we will be the losers. Very often, when something unpleasant happens in school, Arundhati's first instinct is to go to the aid of the underdog—maybe a new girl in their group who's being tormented by the class bullies. She could so easily distance herself from both. But she doesn't. And I'm proud of her. One can't just walk away. One can't leave an accident victim bleeding on the street because of an urgent appointment somewhere. Not everybody is cut out to be a slogan-shouting activist. You don't have to be militant about any of this. Just be human. Help when you can, if you can. And don't expect anything in return. Like that little boy who turned around and snapped after being extricated from a brawl in which he was getting pulped, 'But who asked you to poke your nose in our fight?' See what I mean?

Your slightly bewildered
Mama

....

Mumbai
September '99

Dear Girls,
  This is such a tricky, disturbing subject, I am not sure how I'm going to deal with it. You're aware of the on-line counselling I've started recently. And you've seen some of the e-mail I have been receiving in this context. Well, let me put it this way, you've seen most of it. Some of the messages have been kept from you. Why? Because I didn't know what I'd tell you if you asked me probing questions. The subject is sensitive. But it has to be addressed. So, here it is, without further coyness in the matter. You've heard of incest, of course. At least two of you have. We've been reading reports galore in the media, documenting tragic case studies of victims who have been scarred for life by those they loved and trusted the most—their own flesh and blood. Incest holds such terror for most societies, it is rarely discussed. In fact, it is such a taboo subject, many cultures pretend it doesn't exist. But we know it does. We also know how tragic the outcome is, especially for very young children who are helpless, ignorant and scared. So scared, in fact, that they withdraw into a secret world from which there is no real escape, and they continue to be haunted through life

by the spectre of an abusive family member who exercises a strange power over them.

It is such a very disturbing subject that I, as a mother, don't have the heart to raise it, afraid as I am of ruining the innocence of blissfully unaware young minds. Yet, I am told not to bury my head in the sand and play ostrich. Incest exists. Incest happens. Incest damages. What I want to tell you is that if ever you find yourself in a situation that makes you even remotely uncomfortable, which makes you feel you are compromising with whatever it is you believe in, which is intrusive in any way . . . even if it only a vague feeling of revulsion—say so. Get out of the situation as fast as possible. Report it to someone you trust—an older, responsible person. I am not referring to incest alone here, but any physical contact that is undesirable, unwanted or unpleasant. You must remember at all times that unless you respect your own body you can't get others to respect it. If you are casual, others will be casual too.

Within families (extended ones, in particular) it is not uncommon to find a very high incidence of improper, unwanted and unwarranted sexual conduct—imposed on an unwilling, coerced partner. Most times, these incidents are hushed up for fear of damaging the 'family honour'. What a joke! It is because victims remain silent that the guilty go unpunished. Speak up at all times. Raise your voice—never ever allow someone to take advantage of either your trust or your ignorance. You will know instinctively when something does not seem right. Say so. Do not be afraid of how anybody else might react. It is your body—inviolable and precious. You must protect it at all costs. Very often, a conspiracy of suppression makes family members keep a lid on such a situation. There is the fear of social ostracization. Elders worry that the victim will be faced with rejection at a later date. 'Who will marry my child if the world finds out what happened when he/she was too young to know right from wrong?' Because of such apprehensions, a life is ruined; guilt and self-loathing follow. There is no one to turn to. It should never come to that. All of you should realize that there is always help at hand, no matter what the situation.

A friend of mine told me a pathetic story recently. It involved her own child. For years, the poor kid had lived with her terrible secret, unable to come out with the truth of being sexually abused by a family member, fearing the consequences. Finally, it tumbled out, opening floodgates of hate, resentment and violence within the small, close-knit family. It's going to take years and years of support and love for all of them to come to terms with their unfortunate past. There are thousands of such families in the world. The important thing is to realize that you don't have to endure humiliation; you don't have to keep mum. For if you do, the perpetrator gets away . . . only to torment someone else. Regardless of who it is, you must promise to fight back. That is really the only way. The honourable way. To save yourself, and to save others.

Protectively,
Your mother

Net nannies
and cyber
gypsies

ARUNDHATI

Darling Arundhati,

The first day of your new term as a 'senior' was a big moment for you. I was at the lunch table waiting for you girls expectantly, as I always do. You cut through the kitchen, as you always do, and I thought I heard you say, 'I'm a wreck today.' I was rather startled but tried to cover up by making a joke of it. 'Who wrecked you?' I asked, looking up from my writing pad. You shot me your best wise-teenager look and pointed to a shining chrome badge under your regular school one. 'Not wreck, ma. I said I'm my class rep. Rep. As in representative. What's wrong with you? Aren't you listening?'

Well, this once you were wrong. I was listening. I had merely misheard you. But your remark was a reminder of all the times I may not have been listening. Listening, yes, but not carefully enough. And I felt instantly apologetic about my preoccupation with deadlines, the work pressure which frequently weighs me down, my distracted air, my mental 'absence'. Sorry, Arundhati. After I had admired the badge and congratulated you, we sat down to lunch.

Over lunch, you raised an interesting question. Part of your introductory programme in senior school had included a frank, open discussion in class about 'over-protection'. You had volunteered to speak along with two other girls. You had told your teacher that your parents did not 'allow' you to talk to boys. I didn't know till then that it was an issue. We had never discussed it And you hadn't displayed the slightest interest in the 'building boys'. Then, I remembered something. Only a few days before your school term ended, we had finally got an internet connection—something you had been craving for over the past few months. I had wondered what it was you were so keen on logging into.

The first night after we had made the quantum leap into the Big Void, I had watched you hunched over the computer, your fingers moving furiously over the keyboard. I came and stood behind you quietly—not to spy, but so as not to disturb your concentration. You were far too engrossed to notice my presence. I saw the screen light up. I read the letters 'ICQ'. I noticed your neck muscles straining as you leaned forward to decipher some squiggles. You were muttering under your breath. And then you started tapping the keys with a speed that astonished me. 'Hi. I'm Heat Wave,' you said. 'Hi. Call me Octopus,' someone tapped back. For the next ten minutes, you sent message after message to the Octopus. Innocent words. But what enthusiasm.

'Who are you chatting with?' I asked, trying not to use my mommy-voice. You whirled around, your eyes wide. 'Mom,' you protested, 'you aren't supposed to be here.'

'Why not?'

You looked completely crestfallen. 'Because . . . because . . . I don't want you to read all this stuff,' you said in a small voice.

'Okay,' I answered and moved away.

Sometimes I feel so sorry for you, Arundhati. First, there's me. The hawk-eyed 'mataji' (as all you kids call me). Then there are the four older siblings, who don't quite know where to fit you in—not sure whether they should treat you like a kid sister, or accept you as one of them. And there's Anandita—the absolute bane of your teenage existence. Nothing, but nothing, remains a secret with her around. She makes sure of that. At ten, Anandita can't wait to catch up with you. She refuses to be left out of your life and activities. And it's impossible to shake her off, especially when you most need a little privacy. Sure enough, the night Heat Wave established contact with Octopus, Anandita was there to record the moment, and worse, report everything to 'mataji'.

'Arundhati wants to chat with boys,' she informed me sanctimoniously.

'Before we got our internet connection she used to go to her friends' homes and all of them would chat with boys,' she said, her voice low and conspiratorial.

At that moment, my heart went out to you. I decided to ignore Anandita's attempt at squealing, and talk to you later in an informal way.

'Darling . . . who are these boys you're talking to in chat rooms?' I asked gently.

'They're all from around here, Ma,' you said, a trifle defensively.

'What do you chat about?' I asked.

'School. Music. Movies. Nothing much,' you said, wiggling your eyebrows to indicate your impatience.

I left it there.

And I thought of myself at thirteen. I was also a product of a prissy girls' school. I too had conservative parents breathing down my neck. I was not 'allowed' to talk to boys, just like I was not endorsing your decision to do so. I remember how attractive the prospect of 'talking to boys' was at that time, thanks to parental disapproval. And here I was falling 'plop' into the same trap. Silly. I resolved to ignore your nightly chats. Anandita was clearly disappointed. 'Aren't you going to punish her?' she asked hopefully.

'What for?'

'For talking to boys,' she said with some exasperation.
'Should she be punished for that?' I asked.

Anandita paused. 'I don't know. What age did Avantika
Didi start talking to boys?'

'Why don't you ask her?' I laughed. Anandita shook her
head. 'It's not the same thing. Avantika Didi and Radhika
Didi were in co-ed school. They had to talk to boys.'

And that's where it stayed.

So far, you've shown such a sense of responsibility about
the duration of your 'chats', I haven't had to nag you. I
watch as you stride purposefully towards the computer
after dinner, a clock in one hand to keep track of bedtime.
By 10.30 p.m. you shut down the computer on your own
and pack up. Of course, Anandita is right there, by your
elbow, monitoring each line you key in. She'd love for you
to include her in your chats. But as she herself points out
sagely, 'I'll have to wait for three more years. I'm not a
teenager yet.'

I have nothing against you talking to boys whose families
we know. But I do worry about your talking to anonymous
fellows in a chat room. There is no way of finding out their
identity. No way to control what they say. And that makes
me anxious. These days when you go downstairs to meet
your friends in the garden I hear mixed voices (half-broken
ones of teenage boys, breathless bursts of teenage girls) for
the first time, and feel good about the development. All
these years, you played segregated games, the girls chatting
quietly on the swings or sitting primly, exchanging notes at
the edge of the garden, while the boys indulged in rowdy
games and boisterous fights. These days all of you get
together in some common activity. Scraps of conversation
float up. By now I can recognize individual voices. I've
become familiar with the vocabulary, accustomed to the
peculiarities of different accents; occasional swear words

get picked up by me. But by and large, the exchanges are harmless. Your new-found enthusiasm to take an evening break has not escaped me. I think it's very sweet.

I've also noticed that you pick your clothes with care and take a few extra minutes doing your hair. Anandita (the little spy strikes again) tells me you have a 'crush' on someone. You, of course, deny it vehemently. If true, I'd love to hear it from you, Arundhati. Because, regardless of what you may believe about your mother, I'm not all that rigid or old-fashioned. It's probably very hard for you to accept this but I was thirteen once too, you know. And I did have a crush. Two, in fact. I still savour the sweetness of the memory. So, don't worry. If I'm asking you intrusive questions about 'boys', it is because I belong to the pre-internet generation. I'm suspicious of people I can't see face-to-face and know only through strange-sounding names. I guess I'll get used to this new kind of 'chat', just as my own parents got used to my furtive phone calls and secret notes. Even so, I cannot hold back a word of motherly caution: cybertalk with strangers may seem like great fun to your generation. But fun-without-checks can be tricky too. Which is why the computer is in a public area of the house and not in your room. If you occasionally find me peering over your shoulder as you exchange funny messages with guys named Octopus, just chill (to borrow your favourite phrase). Not only am I overseeing the contents of your exchange, I'm also checking your spellings and grammar. Tell me dear, what exactly is meant by 'Wassup? Nuthin. Kewl? I'm feeling gr8 2day. Luv ya.'

Never mind. I was being nosy. Ignore me.

Yours,
Mama

Mumbai
September '99

Dear All,

You know, children, I have been asking myself a few questions vis-à-vis all of you. Often, while discussing children and how to raise them, with other parents, we've come up against all manner of 'theories'. This is good for children, that is bad for them, you cannot do this any more, you cannot say that. Stuff like that. Frequently, I go through advice columns in various women's magazines and come across what are euphemistically called 'politically correct' guidelines to modern child rearing. I must say they leave me cold. And puzzled.

When I visit the homes of friends with young children, inevitably the topic turns to ground rules. 'Do you allow yours to . . . ?' 'How late can they stay out?' 'Have you ever struck your children in anger?' 'Do you reason with them first—or yell and scream?' I have watched with great interest as young couples battled amongst themselves over the perennial problem all parents face—'how much liberty is too much?' Frankly, there are no clear or easy answers to that one. One has to improvise constantly, practically on a day-to-day basis. The only thing that works in the long run is to go by what your heart tells you. Follow your instincts, be sincere in your approach, and you can't go wrong. All this talk of 'politically correct' conduct towards children has led to a great deal of confusion—for both, the kids and the parents. 'These days one can't say anything too harsh to children,' I've heard my friends say. 'After a certain age, you can't correct them.' Nonsense. So long as kids live in the same house, so long as they are dependents, so long as the house itself runs along ordered lines, I think parents have every right to point it out when children consistently fail to adhere to the house rules—irrespective of how old they are.

In our home, we've been up against this problem often enough. Especially with the older children. I have stuck my neck out, courted disfavour, even got into unnecessary verbal duels over the simple question of 'who's boss'. You might say all this talk of 'boss' is absurd in this day and age. That parents who exercise old-fashioned authority are out of touch with ground realities, that we live in an 'anything goes' era. Sorry, not in this house. To me, a home is not a hostel. Nor is it a five-star hotel with twenty-four-hour room service. Meal times can be stretched somewhat, but not indefinitely. I think it's only fair for working children to inform parents of their plans a little in advance. It is for the sake of convenience—nothing more—that I expect you to call and say you won't be home for dinner. This does not encroach on your rights as an individual. It shows consideration for the person who has planned the meal with not just numbers, but specific preferences in mind. Yes, I know party plans these days are made at the last minute and so on. Fine. A short call cannot possibly intrude into anybody's schedule, no matter how frenetic.

Am I imagining this or do our children sleep far, far longer hours than we ever did, or rather, were allowed to? Regardless of how late we studied, or stayed up chatting, it was understood we'd be up and at the table by 7 a.m, no later. A few concessions were made for me (I am not an early morning person) by my parents, but none for my siblings. Afternoon naps weren't encouraged either ('they make a person slow and lethargic'). As for sleeping at what my parents deemed 'odd hours' (dusk, for example), it was unthinkable for any of us to flop down in bed for a catnap, no matter how exhausted we might be. There was a curfew in place, too, midnight being the cut-off point. After an enormous tussle, we were allowed our own latchkeys. But after the stated hour, an additional safety chain was put in place, making it impossible for us to enter without ringing the doorbell. The Mumbai (Bombay then) of my growing-up years was not your Mumbai. It was far, far safer. Today, if I feel agitated about the late hours you keep it is because I'm concerned about your safety. 'Stop being so paranoid,' you chorus. I'm not paranoid. Merely cautious.

'Discipline' is the dreaded D-word in most families. To me, it isn't the dirty word it once used to be. I see it as a necessary evil, particularly in today's changed times. Sleeping till noon and later on holidays? No way, José. 'Give us a break,' you groan. I do, now that I know your weekends don't start till 1 a.m. on Saturday mornings. 'Nobody gets anywhere before then,' you tell me. And it's true. I find it crazy, completely crazy. But then I suppose my parents must have found it equally crazy that I sometimes went out at 10 p.m. and not 7 p.m., as they'd have preferred it. I've been compelled to 'accept' all these new arrangements—your arrangements—most reluctantly. What choice do I really have?

'Modern' parents find themselves pushed against a wall by children who insist on stretching and redefining the parameters. 'Come on . . . which world are you living in?' I have been frequently taunted, even as you exchange looks and roll your eyes. And yet, when I see some of the walking-talking disasters of your generation all around me, I wonder—is this what you call fun? Do you want to end up this way? When I raise these questions, it's eye-rolling time again. But I think they're pertinent. Fortunately, I haven't had to deal with that other monumental menace—drugs—with any of you. Trust me, I wouldn't have been terribly understanding or accommodating. I would have raised hell and sent you packing to a drying-out clinic. I keep telling you, 'Wait, there is a time for everything. Enjoy yourselves by all means, but don't be in such a frightful hurry. Life will have no surprises for you otherwise.' You find that old-fashioned and amusing. But I have seen the 'seen it all, done it all' types, and felt sorry for them. By the age of twenty-five, it's all over, they're washed up and finished. Twenty-five. Imagine. Life is supposed to take off then, but these people are disillusioned, burnt out wrecks. What will happen to them at thirty? Your generation is a generation in a tearing big hurry. Everybody wants everything at once—instant success, instant riches, instant thrills. If you can achieve it, terrific. But watch out for those skid marks; others have tried and gone off the rails. Don't let that next accident be yours.

Somewhat agitatedly,
Mother

....

Mumbai
September '99

Dear Children,
    Some days ago, I came across a chilling report in the *Times of India*. It was a slap in the face for all the parents who have completely failed to interpret the distress signals sent out by their kids. Interviewed in that feature were several teenagers who spoke with eloquence and pain about

their alienation. Particularly sad was the statement of a young girl who said she preferred to remain outside the house, because she couldn't bear to be in it. The reason? Her parents were constantly rude and abusive towards her. I was surprised by the vehemence of her feelings, and wondered why her father and mother treated her like that. How can any parent use abusive language with a child—any child? Let me qualify that. How can any educated person do that to anybody? And yet here was a twenty-something bemoaning the fact in print.

You know how strongly I feel about bad language in the house. I assume you restrain yourselves in public. At least, I hope you do. We've had arguments over this in the past with you saying, 'But Mother, everybody uses such words these days,' and my retorting, 'I don't care what everybody does. I don't want you to use slang.' Sometimes, I'd overhear the older children on the phone to friends, and ignore the rough conversation. I wasn't about to play headmistress after school hours. But the two little ones had to definitely watch their tongues while speaking to their friends.

It was on a holiday in the summer of '98, that Anandita and Arundhati picked up a few new words from a little boy who was with our group on the trip. When we came back to Mumbai, I heard Arundhati saying 'balls' to something, a trifle tentatively. 'What was that?' I asked, wondering whether I'd heard wrong. 'Nothing, nothing,' she said hastily. It was left to Anandita to roll her eyes and whisper, 'She's been using that bad word ever since we returned from Goa.' I took Arundhati aside and asked her gently, 'Do you even know what that word means?' She nodded her head vigorously and answered brightly, 'Yes. I do know. It means scrotum.' I was floored. Scrotum. Where on earth had she come across that word? She ran to her desk and came back with her biology journal. 'Here,' she said, pointing to the genitals in a diagram. 'It means this.' Okay. I explained to her that it wasn't a very ladylike expression, and little girls had no business using it. 'It's vulgar, darling,' I went on. She started giggling. Anandita joined in. Soon we were all giggling. Till it was time to get serious again. Arundhati said, 'You don't let us use normal words like "shit". That's not fair. It's such a common word.' I provided a few substitutes. Arundhati resorted to the old trick. 'Maybe in your time these words were considered slang. But nowadays we don't find anything wrong with them.'

A few months later, we had to deal with the troublesome 'F' word. I was hearing a bit too much of it around the house from the older kids and I didn't like that at all. Especially since the youngers ones were beginning to think it was a cute idea to repeat it, saying, 'But I'm not saying it. I'm only repeating what Didi said.' That didn't wash either. Soon I was told about all the little girls in the class who had discovered the naughty pleasure of uttering the forbidden word, and were shocking their classmates by throwing it around liberally. It was lecture time once again.

I think the important part of discouraging children to use gutter language is to never use it yourself. Though I used to sprinkle my early books with it liberally, the words were deliberately used in a particular context. There would have been little point in avoiding them, since they represented a certain milieu. But even at that time, my conversation had remained reasonably chaste, except for a very short phase when I cursed away happily much to the disgust of my immediate family. The point is, even as a teenager I didn't use bad language in the presence of my parents or any elders. Slang at school was a different matter. It was freely used by me and my friends, mainly to shock the prudes. We outgrew that once the thrill was behind us. As for Aji and Ajoba, I never once heard them use unparliamentary language, either with each other or towards any of us. Of course they flew into rages, got furious, and yelled. But at all times, they exercised complete control over their vocabulary. We may not have been models of etiquette and good conduct, but nobody could have accused us of being foul-mouthed.

I spoke to a twenty-something working girl who seemed to shun her parents' company. I asked her why this was so, and was saddened by her reply. 'I can't have a decent conversation with them,' she said. 'Frankly, I'm far too embarrassed and so are my friends. Which is why I prefer to stay out. My parents curse each other all day. And if I'm around, I'm cursed too. It's disgusting.' Cursed? By parents? I asked her to elaborate. 'Well . . . even if they want to correct me, they do that so rudely. They call me all sorts of names. Their expressions are so ugly. I'm constantly criticized. And the criticism is very harsh. I can't bear it.'

We've had a few run-ins ourselves. Unexpected outbursts. A show of temper. I've screamed, you've screamed. There have been tears and tantrums. But we always recognized the limits. Never have we flung abuses at one another. There is something known as basic human dignity, regardless of age and gender. It is up to parents to define the outer limits of anger. Sure, people do get out of control when enraged. But there have to be clearly defined lines to the expression of that rage. Hostility between family members is to be expected from time to time (proximity does that to people) but the temptation to say what's uppermost in the mind has to be curbed no matter what the provocation.

I've often regretted my strong words. Or even the manner in which I've reprimanded you. I've never hesitated to say 'sorry'. And our mutual apologies have been transparently sincere. The buck, as in most such situations, stops with parents. Children learn to legitimize abuse if they see their parents doing so. 'If it's okay for them to give gaalis to us, why shouldn't we do the same back to them,' is the attitude. I have a horror of a show of temper in any case. Anger repulses me. It distorts a person's face and transforms the individual so completely, it frightens me. I hate myself whenever I blow my top, and I'm glad there's generally no mirror around. So, the next time you see my face puffing up and my eyes flashing, tap me on the shoulder and say, 'Mother . . . the mercury's rising. Calm down.' I'll consider it a favour.

Coolly yours,
Mama

....

Mumbai
September '99

Dear Children,
   You're going to hate this letter. Do you know why? It concerns your favourite object—the one you cherish above all the others—the telephone—and my feelings about your fixation. Of course, you're aware of exactly how I react each time I hear the instrument ring, but that's not all I want to talk about. I'm a phone-junkie myself, as you well know.

The phone is more than merely a modern convenience for me. I call it my lifeline to the outside world, the one means I have to communicate with goings-on beyond our front door. I use the phone mainly for work-related calls. But I also use it for relaxation. Each time I feel like taking a short break from writing, I reach for the phone and get back to my desk recharged and refreshed after a short chat with Ajoba or your father, or one of you kids, or a friend.

I remember my phone habits used to drive my parents crazy. They could never understand my urgent need to jump on the instrument right after coming back from school/college. There was so-o-o-o much to talk about. Endless conversation, which in retrospect sounds like complete drivel, and a total waste of time. But there was one essential difference. The telephone in my parents' home was fixed in a very public area—in the middle of a long passage that connected all the rooms. The scope for private and extended conversations was strictly limited. The acoustics in our flat being what they were, even whispers carried. This made me very self-conscious and acted as a natural deterrent to long telephone calls. My ten-minute calls could so easily have extended to twenty or thirty otherwise. Besides, we weren't in the call-waiting age back then. Nor did we have cordless phones, extensions in other rooms, or especially dedicated extra lines. My father used to grumble about huge phone bills, just as Daddy does in our home.

I have tried (and failed) to impose 'phone rules'. I don't like the idea of young children lying in bed with cordless instruments and chatting for hours while their parents think they're studying. I'm equally squeamish about the idea of 'privacy' for under-fifteens. While I don't want to be extra-intrusive, nosy or over-curious, I believe I should know what's going on in your lives. Your business at this stage in definitely my business too. No two ways about that. I've often yelled and screamed when you've disappeared into the bathroom with the phone—that's a definite no-no. There's a time and place for each activity. And the loo is definitely out of bounds for phones. You've accused me of being 'weird' for imposing this rule. 'All my friends take the cordless into the bathroom—think of the time it saves,' has been the argument, Sorry. It doesn't wash with me. We've also worked out 'acceptable' timings for receiving phone calls, and 2 a.m. does not figure in that. You say I growl at your friends when they phone any later than ten at night. It's true, I do. I think I'm perfectly justified. Your father and I rarely receive calls at that hour ourselves. I don't think it's either fair or considerate to have your friends disturb the household at any which hour. 'Give us our own extensions in the room in that case,' you've argued. No. That's unacceptable too. For one, you're far too young to be in a position to regulate the hours you spend yakking mindlessly over the phone. A private extension would mean no restrictions on time spent chatting with callers who may not have the same limitation in their homes. I do respect your need for privacy, but only up to a point. I don't want to kick myself later for not having paid attention to say, crank calls, obscene calls, harassment calls, or just unwanted calls. Arundhati, you mentioned how some of your friends were 'allowed' to talk to unknown boys who phone them. You stared at my face to see my reaction. I asked you simply, 'Do you want to speak to strangers—boys or girls?' You shook your head, and it ended there.

Yes, a time will come in the near future when you will receive calls from boys. Fine. You'll be that much older and ready for the conversations that follow. You've seen that happening in the lives of your didis and dadas. It was a perfectly natural progression that went unnoticed. It will happen to you, too, when the moment is right. But even with your older siblings, the rules may be bent only a little; essentially they remain the same. No extensions in the room. No long-distance calls just to say 'hello' and chat. No leaving the phone in the loo. And certainly no calls at unearthly hours, unless it's an emergency. Given the layout of our home, it is the domestics who have to answer. I've explained how unreasonable that is, since they work long hours and need to catch up on their sleep at night. We don't have people working in shifts at home. We can't expect our staff to put in overtime, just to take a few unnecessary calls from boozed up friends calling en route to the next club or party. Come on, that's selfish. Don't you agree?

Meanwhile, I notice some of your pre-teen friends have thoughtfully been given mobile phones by their loving parents. Ten- and twelve-year-olds with their own cell numbers. 'It's convenient,' the parents explain, 'we can keep track of where they are.' Which may also explain why chauffeurs are given identical machines by generous employers. 'The baba log don't have to wait anywhere unnecessarily. All it takes is a ring to summon the car.' Quite. I've loaned you mine on exactly two occasions when you were travelling long distances with your friends and we needed to co-ordinate our movements. You felt very adult, responsible and thrilled. But I also remember how sweetly Anandita sought permission to make 'just one call' to a classmate, only for the kick of dialling the gizmo and getting through from a moving car. It was with a childlike and innocent joy that she made that call—it obviously filled her with awe. I identified with the feeling perfectly and instantly. After all, hadn't I also experienced the same thrill when my family had acquired a much-coveted 'pop-up toaster', and Mother had given us permission to make one toast each? In my time, we asked for new pens and erasers before our exams. Now you demand CD-Roms and internet connections. Fine. But the phone rules stay. Okay?

Your techno-challenged
Mama

....

Mumbai
June '99

Dear Girls,
    We've had this conversation before. It sounds absurdly deja vu. But it came back to me suddenly this morning when I was asked by an eager interviewer, 'When and where did you learn to cook?' I thought back and replied, 'In my mother's kitchen, when I was no more than ten or twelve.'
    The lady raised her eyebrows in surprise. 'Really? You mean your mother gave you cooking lessons that early in life?'
    'No,' I said truthfully. 'They weren't formal cooking lessons at all. It's just that all her three daughters were expected to help out and participate during meal times. I watched my older sisters doing it, and I followed suit. It was a natural part of growing up. These were our "duties", and we couldn't shun them.'
    Don't give me hollow-sounding gender arguments here. Cooking has nothing to do with being a 'typical' housewife. For me, cooking is both a pleasure and a discipline. If you

can feed yourself and others, it's a skill to take pride in, maybe even enjoy. My brother cooks, so does your father. They find it relaxing and challenging. While I don't remember Ashok mama setting foot inside the kitchen in our parental home, today he turns out gourmet meals. I don't understand your resistance to entering the kitchen and learning how to fix yourselves even simple snacks. Do you feel there is shame in that? If you do, it makes me sorry for you. We are increasingly moving towards a time when domestic help will be hard to come by. What then? Who knows, by the time you girls set up your own homes, cooks might be obsolete. You'll say, 'We'll worry about that then; meanwhile, don't nag us to cook.' Fine.

In my case it was not an option, let me tell you. Had the decision been mine alone, I might have resisted getting anywhere close to a stove. The point is, we were expected to assist our mother, even though she did have a maid around. We were assigned other 'duties' as well. Which is why I can iron a shirt perfectly (it's quite an art, I'll have you know). I can scrub the dishes, make beds neatly, wash clothes, sweep and swab, hang clothes up to dry (again, not as simple a task as you imagine), make pickles and papads (an annual ritual), and fry puris and fish as good as any professional, if the need ever arises. You may think I'm boasting. I'm not, I'm merely telling you that there is no shame in any of this. And that children should participate more fully in the running of the home. In this age of computers and modern technology, most urban kids are completely indifferent to domestic discipline. I've met women in their mid-twenties who've boasted foolishly about 'not knowing a thing around the house'. How pathetic. It is their house, their space, yet they're not involved with it. Kids breeze in and breeze out, treating their home like a hostel (but even hostels have some rules).

Anandita is showing signs of being interested in the sort of things that interested me at her age. I encourage her to bake cakes, cookies or even chop up vegetables for salads. I want her to get used to the idea of a kitchen, to feel that it isn't an alien, out-of-bounds area. I'd like all of you to feel the same way, to spend a little time in there, at least finding out where things are stored and how. Two of you like curd—do you know how to set it? If I were to ask you to fetch jeera for me, would you know what to look for, or even where the jar is kept? You watch me in the kitchen, on those occasions when I get into my magic cooking phase. I know you appreciate what I produce, even when it's not up to scratch. All you need to do is hang around. I don't need to sit you down and issue instructions. By merely taking an interest, you will learn. By observing what goes into which dish, you'll understand. By actually picking up a kadhai, or whipping up eggs, you'll get the hang of it gradually. Who knows, you might even surprise me someday by cooking a meal for me. I look forward to that with enormous joy and anticipation. Meanwhile, tell me—what exactly is haldi? Is it a liquid? Is it a nut? A powder? A spice? A lentil? Or a cosmetic? Your favourite dish as reward for whoever comes up with the right answer first. Go for it.

Yours despairingly,
Mama

The heart
goes on

RANADIP

Dear Arundhati and Anandita,

Remember the day our loving, faithful, dependable driver, Vinayak, died? Of course you must. He was such an integral part of our lives. If our home functioned efficiently, if our day-to-day existence ticked along like clockwork, a lot of that domestic efficiency was because of Vinayak. When you, Arundhati, were much younger, you used to bully him mercilessly. As for you, Anandita, he was willing to walk to the end of the earth to please you.

For nearly a year, we watched him die. Initially, we didn't know what was wrong with him and teased him about his weight loss, saying he looked like a 'hero' with his paunch gone. Along with his shrinking belly, his sparse hair began to disappear too. We put it down to a scalp infection and got him a medicated shampoo. We noticed he slept longer and longer hours in the car and we yelled at him for being lazy. Even at his energetic best Vinayak was a slow coach. But now, he dragged his feet. Often his breath would be short after climbing a few steps. It was you kids who realized things were not as they appeared when Vinayak started refusing snacks. He was a great one for sharing your tiffin, buying forbidden colas and gum and telling you not to inform me about his little treats. He was also uncharacteristically generous when it came to spending money on you during festivals. He'd invite you to his home and spoil you silly—cheese dosas, Peppy chips, pastries, chocolates. I'd be touched. We were his family, really. He spent far more time in our home than in his own. He was more involved in our lives than in his own small family's. He was there when the two of you, the youngest, were born.

He was there when I took you for your shots to the pediatrician's. He was there on your first day at play school when you cried. And he was there to plan your birthday parties with as much enthusiasm as I felt. I'd consult him about the decorations, he'd help to blow up the balloons. I'd forget to pick up candles for your cakes, he'd rush to G.D. Somani store to get them. He knew all your friends, their homes, and even their little idiosyncracies. Everybody trusted dear Vinayak, felt safe with him at the wheel. I trusted more than just his cautious driving. He'd be the one I'd send to the jewellers to drop off an old necklace for restringing. And Vinayak it was who'd go to the bank to fetch money. I can't think of a single aspect of our lives in which Vinayak didn't participate in some way. Ferrying Aji to the hospital, taking Ajoba to the dentist, making sure Tuts got to the vet for his periodic check-ups. Vinayak was the one who kept track of whose clothes were stuck at which laundry, whether there were unpaid bills pending, or even whether my column deadline had been missed (he delivered some of the hand-written ones).

When I realized he was dying I wondered how all of us would manage without him. Vinayak and I spoke Marathi to each other—that in itself was a big bond. The idea of a replacement with whom I wouldn't be able to communicate in my own language was unsettling. Vinayak knew that. Yet he hand-picked a non-Marathi-speaking successor. I wonder whether that was done deliberately—Vinayak's little way of keeping our dependence on him alive through unfair comparisons. The last time he came home before his long hospitalization, it was to say goodbye to us all. By then, he'd become gaunt, hollow-eyed and unrecognizable. This wasn't our roly-poly, jolly Vinayak at all. But how could he be? Wracked with pain and fever, he was a

ghost-like figure, grey, drawn and desperate. He showed me
his medical files. Not a word was spoken. We looked at
each other in silence. The verdict was clear. It was only a
matter of time now.

He asked the maid with whom he did the daily round of
shopping, for the usual writing pad—the one in which he
used to painstakingly take down my instructions. 'I want to
write the list today,' he said, his voice low, his writing
feeble. Under his breath he added, 'It will be the last time I
do it.' You were all away from the house. I put my arms
around him as he began to cry . . . like an anguished child.
'I'm dying,' he wept, 'my guarantee period is over.' The
other domestics also began to sniffle. I told him to keep his
spirits up. He mentioned he had one unfulfilled desire. 'I
have never been in an airplane. I want to know what it feels
like.' I promised I'd take him to Ahemedabad where he had
some relatives. I was determined to make it happen, no
matter how frail he was. I thought it through. A
return-flight—why not? It was his dream. Not such an
impossible one either. But after that formal goodbye to the
only real life he had known during his adult years, Vinayak
never made it back.

When we visited him in hospital, weak as he was, his
concern was for you kids. He wanted you to sit down
comfortably on proper chairs, not stand around his steel
bed. He gestured to his sister to fetch a few colas. This,
coming from a man who could barely move his eyes. I could
see death hovering over him. It didn't make me cringe. I
wasn't afraid even for Vinayak, because he wasn't afraid for
himself any longer. I was amazed by his quiet acceptance.
He was waiting to die. There was no hope. But there wasn't
any anger either. I touched his cold forehead: the skin was

grey and scaly. Silent tears formed in his eyes. I couldn't hold back my own. His arms were punctured with needles.

His mouth looked dry, his tongue thick and swollen. His speech was slurred. I remembered the 'other' Vinayak—cheerful, easy-going, helpful. And oh so dumb. I say that fondly. It was something of a joke—Vinayak's dumbness, especially his consistent mispronunciation of certain words and phrases. I nearly chuckled at the memory of Vinayak referring to the Pavement Club (which Radhika used to attend faithfully) as 'Table Cloth'. And his complete inability to recall street names.

The man who lay dying on a sturdy steel bed with an incongruous red blanket covering his skeletal frame, was another person altogether. Only his kindness remained. He gestured to his sister to get fresh coconut water for me, knowing I never drank colas. I stopped him . . . and then changed my mind, realizing how important it was for him that I have the offered drink. A doctor strolled up to check the charts. I was relieved to see he was human and affectionate with Vinayak. I spoke to him privately. 'It's better for him to go home. We cannot do anything more,' he told me bluntly. The doctor was right. It was decided that Vinayak would spend his last days in relative comfort. When the time came to say goodbye, you kids cried along with him. In a way you were glad to get out of that depressing hospital ward (colourful fairy lights and streamers celebrating Diwali, notwithstanding). I had noticed your expression as we walked in, eyes dilated with horror and revulsion, lips twisted, noses turned up. It was your first time in a public hospital, and you were clearly overwhelmed by the sights and sounds around you—patients lying on thin mattresses spread on the floor, some howling in pain, wounds oozing, grimy bandages, relatives with morose expressions getting ready for the long nights of vigil ahead. Definitely depressing—and scary, too.

When we left the hospital, all of us were quiet. Very quiet. Anandita was the first to break the silence. 'Is he going to die?' she asked. I didn't want to lie. I nodded. Arundhati looked out of the window at the paper lanterns swaying from several balconies. Suddenly Anandita giggled, 'Did you notice Vinayak's new hairstyle? He looks ganja.' That was her way of dealing with a grim situation. Arundhati hushed her up disapprovingly. 'How can you talk like that? Poor chap. He's so sick.' I hastily changed the subject. A week later Viniyak was no more. I heaved a sigh of relief. Vinayak had been set free from pain and sorrow. He had died a dignified death in his house in his own bed, with his sister and a friend by his side. My only regret was that I hadn't been able to fulfil his last wish. No flight to Ahmedabad for poor Vinayak. But a longer, a much longer one, to heaven-knows-where. So long, dear, faithful, good soul. May you wander to different worlds, closer to the stars than you'd ever have been in a 737.

Yours in anguish,
Mother

....

Mumbai
March '99

Dear Children,

Religion is awfully hard to discuss. I mean, I can't sit you down one day and announce solemnly, 'Okay family, it's time to discuss God.' But I do know it's important to you, to all of us, to find a few answers to that eternally perplexing question, 'Does God exist?' Frankly, I don't know. Ask that of a believer and you're likely to hear an impassioned endorsement. Since I have never been a believer in the strict sense of the word, I don't want my confusion to become your confusion, my ambiguities to become your ambiguities.

You've often asked me whether I'm 'religious', expecting a straight-forward response—which, I suppose, is a short and simple 'no'. No, I'm not religious, in that I do not adhere to a specific set of beliefs. I do not pray regularly. I have never fasted for religious reasons. Nor have I asked for any special boons against the performance of specific rituals. Like fasting for twenty-one Wednesdays. Or promising a gold crown for my favourite deity at a pilgrimage site. Deep down, I am sceptical and plain ignorant. I know I'd like to believe in a Divine Being. But so far, such a belief has eluded me, and I feel sorry. As a parent, I feel it's important for you to know exactly where I stand in this regard. But as of now, I'd love to find that out for myself.

As I'm growing older, I can sense a change within me. There is a strong need to believe. This didn't exist earlier. Life was happening to me at such a frenzied pace—who needed God? Pujas? Temples? Prayers? Chants? Yet, I had grown up with it all. I can smell the agarbattis, hear the soft tinkle of the little brass bell, taste the slightly acrid tulsi leaves. Our tiny kitchen shrine had a small framed picture of Ganpati, and another carved image in dark sandalwood. There was a beautifully proportioned Bal Krishna cast in five metals (now installed in our own shrine at ·Alibag). Each morning, after his bath, Ajoba, bare-chested, clad in a towel wrapped tightly around his waist, would enter the kitchen, ignore the cooking odours and the constant clatter of pots and pans, remove his slippers, and worship silently, his ritual unchanging. At the end of his short prayer, he'd go back into his room and read aloud from his well-thumbed book of shlokas.

Shoe-flowers. Bright red shoe-flowers—Lord Ganesh's favourite flowers. And a garland of durvas (fresh, green shoots of a particular grass). Our gods were never without these adornments. Even though nobody compelled us to pray, we did so on our own, whenever we felt like it. The kitchen was a dark and strangely comforting part of a home crowded with six individuals of wildly differing temperaments. I used to pray before exams—fervently, desperately, not really expecting God to respond positively to my last-minute appeals. Even so, I didn't want to take any chances.

I notice you, Arundhati, always but always carry a tiny image of Ganpati with you to the exam hall. This is a completely untutored gesture. I remember a time last year when some girls made fun of you, asking mockingly, 'Do you expect God to write your papers! If you've studied, you'll do well. If you've bunked, you'll fail. Then nobody will be able to help you. Not even God.' You had been in tears narrating the incident to me. I had consoled you saying, you should continue to take the image with you, uncaring of silly barbs. But I could see uncertainty in your eyes as you nodded through your tears. Like me, you also drew an 'Om' on your exam sheets, initially without much thought, later, out of superstition. One day you asked me why I always started my new projects with that particular symbol. Was it because I needed luck? Or something else? I replied that it was a combination of several things. Most writers are superstitious. Besides, I remembered how, as children, we were taught to worship Saraswati through a graphic design that represented the Goddess of Learning. Only Kunda knew how to draw it faultlessly in one continuous stroke on a slate. This was something we did on the first day of Diwali. Our father would tell us to bring out our pens, text books and exercise books, after bathing at dawn. Then, with utmost reverence, the symbol would be etched and the invocation to Vidya would begin. At the time I thought this was enough effort to see me through my exams. But somewhere, the memory stayed strongly embedded, and it invariably resurfaces these days at the start of any new writing project. There are other little practices, too. I'm not sure whether or not to dub them 'religious'. But I do adhere to a set pattern, like 'offering' the advance copy of my book to Ganpati, placing it at his feet and seeking blessings. I pray with all my heart before I start something new, my eyes screwed tight, my entire being tense and focused. Of course, it's an act of utter selfishness. It's a need-based prayer.

At other times I do say a casual 'hello' to God. You do that too, Arundhati. Just a cheerful greeting to tell the Divine One he is in your thoughts. I pray before drifting off to sleep (like you again, Arundhati) but sometimes I forget. I've tried repeating short mantras five, ten, twenty times, but found my attention wandering. I want to meditate, but my mind is far too restless. I want to calm down, but there's too much stuff happening inside my head.

Yet, I don't want to influence you by my own lack of belief. As children we were exposed to traditional worship every day. With you, it's a sporadic thing. I drag you to the temple on your birthdays and we attend the annual Durga Puja at a sarvajanik celebration. I look forward to the occasion, knowing how important it is to Daddy. Ashtami is a particularly auspicious day during the 'pujas'. We make it for the pushpanjali and aarti, all of us in new clothes. It's a good feeling. It's also one of the few days of the year on which we become a small part of the large Bengali community in Mumbai—that's important. We greet people we only meet annually, and a special warmth binds us as we participate in the worship of the Devi. The atmosphere is charged. I love the fragrance of dhoop mixed with marigold. I love the chanting of the priests, the sound of the dhol and cymbals. It's the closest I get to what can be described as a 'religious experience'. I'm both attracted to and scared by spiritual mumbo-jumbo. I don't wish to brainwash you into believing. But I do want to expose you to this aspect of our life (Daddy's and mine). It is an integral part of our upbringing and I don't want to deny you that. We also have our annual Satyanarain Puja at home on Arundhati's birthday. All this is vital, for you will recall it some day and then decide for yourselves. Just as I was left to do. Without that early exposure, I might have floundered today and not known where to look for solace. The power of prayer is strong indeed, even if it is mechanically repeated. That's what Ajoba tells me. That's what I feel. Each year Daddy and I visit our family deity at Mangeshi in Goa, and each year the experience means more and more to us. Whether it's only the sense of continuity we cherish, or something deeper, I can't say. I only know it's increasingly important to both of us to make it to the temple and offer prayers.

I watch your father each morning while he prays. I cast my eyes over his arrangement of images; there is democracy in his selection. We have them all—the entire Hindu pantheon along with a beautiful ivory Pieta, a slightly chipped Buddha, a rosary, a crucifix, a conch shell and all the other deities cheek-by-jowl—a perfectly compatible family of 'gods' who receive his prayers impassively and fairly. Daddy also prays faithfully to his late parents every day, twice a day. His beliefs are far more deep-rooted than my own rather shallow and sceptical ones. And yet, I know that I am gravitating to a period in my life when I shall turn increasingly to God, and tap into that side of me that even I don't completely know. Meanwhile, I want you children to follow your own path—question, seek, learn, reject. That is the only way. Then, some day when we talk about this subject again, we might actually have answers that will surprise us both. Won't that be wonderful?

Yours spiritually,
Mama

....

Mumbai
April '99

Dear Kids,

Help me. I have difficulty understanding the contemporary (and very 'in') concept of 'giving space' to you. What I think it means is—mind your own business. Am I wrong in assuming that? Well. How does a parent do that? Your business is my business. Sorry, but that's how I feel. I cannot *not* be involved in your lives. Do you find that unreasonable? I guess I have the answer. The problem is, I'm not comfortable with it. I want to be involved—yes, in everything. And suddenly I feel guilty about my need. How selfish, I say to myself. 'Poor kids. They must find my interest in them so oppressive.' Do you?' Do you feel I don't leave you alone? All of you are pretty outspoken. I comfort myself with the thought that had it been so, you'd have yelled, 'Get off my case, mother.' So far I haven't heard those words.

Yet, from time to time, I feel like an intruder. I think back and try and recall parallels from my own life. The concept of privacy was alien to us when we were growing up—we were a family and families did not need privacy. That's what we were raised to believe. Family meant sharing everything—thoughts, time, emotions. Would you believe that we, the children, were forbidden from locking our room (I used to share it with my sisters). 'Why do you need to lock the door?' Ajoba would ask imperiously. 'What are you hiding?' Once or twice. I had brought up the 'p' word and he had exploded. 'What nonsense,' he had said, 'children don't need privacy. We are your parents. We have the right to know what's going on in your lives.' And that's where the debate had ended. Like all other debates in our home. I'm sure we must have resented this aspect of our existence, but we didn't argue. Not about this. And not about anything else either.

'Space' is a comparatively new word. But I suppose it means the some thing. I hear it all the time. From you. From all the TV kids on music channels. Everybody is looking for space and I find that rather strange. What is this space thing? Has it got to do with secrets? If so, I can understand. I grew up with secrets too. Not many, but a few that I held close to my heart and felt possessive about. My parents didn't feel bad about them, because they never found out. In any case, these 'secrets' were so foolish, so childish, they affected nobody. Today, it's a whole new world out there. In my parents' home, there was just one phone and it was in the living room. The only way we could protect ourselves from being overheard was by speaking in whispers. Which I did. That was the only insulation. Most of your callers are known to me. I consciously avoid listening to your conversations, but I do get the gist of what's going on. Ditto for mail. I would never ever open your letters. But since I'm the one who sees them first, I do know what the postman has been slipping into the mailbox. Fortunately, there is enough openness in our communication for me to not pry (I'd hate to do that). But let me tell you, I do enjoy it when nervous young people call for one of you and start stammering. It reminds me of the effect Ajoba's growled 'hello' used to have on various acne-scarred young men who'd phone for me and hang up at the sound of my father's voice.

I only fear your 'secrets' could harm you. Maybe my fears are exaggerated. But I'm not being nosy when I ask, my voice exaggeratedly casual, 'What's the plan?' or 'Where are you going?' or 'How will you get back?' I lie awake at nights worrying about your safety. You (the older ones) laugh at my anxieties and say, 'Aren't you forgetting something? We are over twenty-one, Mother. How long are you going to take care of us?' Only as long as I'm alive, I half joke. And then I remind myself about your 'space' and back off. For a while.

We talk. We talk a lot. We talk more than most people I know. Sometimes we call one another ten times in a day but there's still so much left unsaid. My sisters find this neurotic. They even said so. 'Isn't it a sign of insecurity?' they ask worriedly. 'No,' I replied, 'it's a sign of good communication.' I thought so. I still think so.

Relationships don't operate on convenient time slots. I cannot possibly tell any of you, 'Look, I've pencilled you in

between 10.15 a.m. and 10.25. If you miss that slot . . .
sorry . . . I won't see you or take your calls till 6.45 p.m.' I
admit I'm not always one hundred per cent receptive to
these interruptions. Sometimes I'm trying to beat a
deadline. Sometimes, I'm more than usually preoccupied.
Sometimes I need to concentrate on the work at hand. But
you aren't supposed to know all that. Or be 'considerate'.
I'm your mother. And there can be no priorities more
important than you.

This afternoon, I received a call from Anandita. She was
in tears. A newly-hired driver had informed her that he
needed to run an errand for me which would require her to
remain unattended in a parked car on a busy street. She
sounded frightened. 'I'm scared, Mama,' she said. I told her
to come right home and forget the errand. Her call was
'inconveniently' timed. In less than twenty minutes, a peon
would arrive to pick up my column. After I put the phone
down, I couldn't get back to my unfinished writing; I was
too concerned about Anandita's agitated state.This was a
panicky ten-year-old girl calling to express her fear. She
needed me. Simple. The column could (and did) wait.

My mother's life was different. Her family was her only
priority. She didn't have deadlines either—well, she did, but
they had more to do with getting the family's meals ready
on time. She was accessible round-the-clock. And in that lay
our security. It was so reassuring to know we could barge
into the kitchen or even my parents' bedroom at any time,
and get a sympathetic hearing. Of course, she'd also get
bugged from time to time. But I don't recall her ever telling
any of us to get lost because she was too busy or had
something more important to attend to. If she could extend
this day-and-night service to us, why shouldn't I? How can I
not offer the same to my children?

And yet, they want 'space'.

Okay, kids. One day, I'll seriously give it to you. All the space you want. All the space you think you need. And then let's see what happens. Is that fair? I think so.

Your 'spaced-out'
Mama

....

Mumbai
September '99

Dear Radhika and Avantika,

A day will soon come (perhaps sooner than I'm mentally prepared to deal with) when you'll come to me and announce your intention of getting married. Of course, I won't be taken entirely by surprise, but I still wonder how I'll handle it. With grace, I hope. We've discussed marriage in abstract terms several times. We haven't always agreed. Radhika has stated her views quite emphatically. So have you, Avantika. Radhika's opinions have reflected her radical stand on most issues. Avantika, yours has been a more conventional approach. But both of you have agreed that more than anything else, marriage is about commitment. You have to believe in marriage in order to make it work. And once you commit, you have to put in a lot of effort to keep it not merely going, but running at an energetic pace.

I've met some of your suitors. I can't really say I've been crazy about any of them. But that's spoken like a protective mother hen—nobody is good enough for my baby-jaans.

It's not that actually. It's never been a question of 'good enough'. I've only asked myself one question: 'Will this man make my daughter happy? Will he look after her, care for her, cherish and respect her?' That has been my simple test. Sorry, the few specimen I have met so far have failed it.

Mothers have a way of sensing these things (on the other hand, mother can also go hopelessly wrong). But I think we know instinctively whether or not someone is 'good' for our children, good as in stable, loyal and honest. I'll add 'hardworking' too—those are the criteria. Everything else is icing on the cake. When you girls seek a life partner it should not be for the wrong reasons ('Oh Mother, he's so cute, so charming, so witty, he makes me laugh'). I remember being alarmed, Avantika, by the over-dramatic courtship rites of an early suitor—flowers at midnight, proposals in the middle of traffic jams, poems at high noon and a steady stream of corny jokes. 'We look so good together,' the vain man once declared as you were leaving to attend a birthday dinner. It was all about 'visuals'—your looks off-setting his own. A rake is a rake. Perhaps you girls have led far too protected a life to recognize one. I tell you to trust my experience if nothing else. You reply that you'd rather rely on your own feelings. Fair enough. I've had such conversations with Aji myself. But at the end of the day all that you really need is a partner you can count on, someone who makes you feel loved, someone who helps you realize your potential.

Today, both of you are bright, young, confident women. Your self-worth is determined by you . . . and not some fellow putting you up on a pedestal or pulling you down. Life is looking good, you're looking good. You've met other young men, liked a few, hated the others. Avantika, you seem to be in a stable loving relationship right now. As you put it, 'I'm happy. He's happy. For now, that's more than enough.' You're right. This isn't the time for decisions—hasty or otherwise. I want you girls to be self-sufficient, to travel, to keep your minds and hearts open, to meet people—all kinds of people—and only then decide on who your husband will be. Marriage involves many responsibilities, and even though I hate the word, 'sacrifices' too. Priorities change, so do fears. And you need to attain a certain level of maturity and calm. We've seen too many 'young' marriages break up. So many of your friends who took the plunge at age twenty or twenty-one are back in their parents' home, often with a kid or two. All this before hitting twenty-five. Most of them say the same thing—they were not emotionally ready for marriage. Well, we don't want to be caught off-guard, do we? Which is why dear girls, think and think again. But when you do meet the right man, and your heart tells you he's the one . . . go for it. Take the plunge with our blessings.

Concernedly yours,
Mama

....

Goa
March '99

Dear Little One,

Yes, you Anandita. You will always be my 'little one' even when you're a young woman yourself. Do you remember asking me one day, your large, expressive eyes wide with curiosity, 'When will you die? In your sleep? Or in hospital?' I was slightly taken aback at the intensity with which you asked me these morbid questions. But I also knew what had brought them on. We had just lost our first dog, Marciano. We had watched him fall sick and die. It had been difficult and painful for all of us to come to terms with the loss. For you and Arundhati, this was your first exposure to death. The finality of it had puzzled you. I remember your asking over and over again, 'I know he's dead. But when will he come back?' 'Never' is a tough concept for a child to comprehend. How does one explain 'never'? Impossible. At least it was for me. 'We won't be seeing him again,' I said. 'That is because he was sick and then he died. But what about after he gets better and comes back?' So, I tried again. 'He won't be coming back.' 'Why not?' 'Because he is dead.' 'I know that. So what? Why can't he come back?' 'Because he has gone to God.' 'I know that too. He can always meet God and then come home.' 'No. That's impossible.' 'Why?' 'Because he has gone forever. Once someone goes forever, they do not come back.' That's when you paused, withdrew and asked me when I would die. 'I don't know,' I said, my voice calm, my gaze steady. 'Why don't you know?' 'Because nobody knows.' 'Why doesn't anybody know?' 'Because God decides.' 'But then God knows, doesn't He?' 'Yes. He does.' 'So, why can't we just ask Him?' 'Well, He doesn't reveal it to anyone. That's His special secret.' 'Why does God need secrets?' 'That's a good question. But I don't have an answer.' 'If I ask God to tell me His secret about you, I'm sure He will. I'll ask Him tonight, when will my mama die.' 'Okay. And if He does tell you, don't forget to tell me.' 'I won't tell you. It will then be my secret.'

I laughed and changed the subject. But it didn't end there. You raised it again, a few weeks later. It was Marciano's birthday. He would have been two. 'Why did he die so early? I asked God and he didn't tell me,' you said. I explained that the poor dog was born with an ailment and it was better that he died without suffering further pain. You turned your face away and said, 'I hope you die without pain. Not now. But later, when you're older and I'm older.' I patted your hand and told you not to worry. Surprisingly, I didn't feel all that disturbed by your preoccupation with my death. I didn't find it ominous. I didn't get nightmares worrying over your probing questions. Instead, I wanted to reassure you about your anxieties, help you come to terms with what is, after all, inevitable. I will die someday, and life will still go on for you. We still miss Marciano, even after the arrival of King Tuts in our lives. We aren't being 'disloyal' to Marciano's memory by transferring our love to King Tuts. We love them both—but differently. Fortunately, your interests changed rapidly and so did your questions. You haven't asked me, 'When will you die?' for quite a while now. Perhaps because you are far more concerned by another death—Leonardo Di Caprio's in *Titanic.*

Alive and kickingly yours,
Mama

....

Mumbai
July '99

Dear Radhika and Avantika,
    This year both of you took independent trips of your own. Radhika, you went to Bhutan which, for long, was

your dream destination. And Avantika, you went off to London. To me, these trips were more than mere holidays. They signified a major shift. Suddenly, I realized, you girls were all grown up. You didn't need us to organize vacations for you any longer. In fact, you probably didn't want to tag along on family holidays henceforth. On one level, I understand perfectly; on another, I feel a bit sad. It would have happened soon enough. Both of you are in your twenties, with good friends of your own. Your time is no longer my responsibility. I don't have to tear my hair out wondering how to entertain you. You have things figured out pretty well—including what you want to do with your leisure hours. Gone are the days when you'd moan and groan about how 'bo-r-r-r-ing' things were during summer and I'd wrack my brains wondering how to stop you from going mad—and driving me mad with you.

With Bhutan and London behind you, you proved two things—that you were going to be making your own travel plans in future and that you'd be happy doing so unaided. Frankly, I was quite impressed by the manner in which you went about the whole thing. You fixed your itineraries on your own, you contacted the travel agent, you shopped around for cheap tickets, you organized your accommodation, and you merely informed us of your plans.

Initially, I was a little taken aback, even hurt. Why was I not 'consulted'? I felt obliged to make a few noises expressing my disapproval. I talked about risks and safety factors and how dangerous it was for young girls to take off on their own. Both of you handled my concerns cheerfully . . . and carried on with your plans. My 'sanction' had ceased to be anything more than a formality—if that.

We spoke to each other after you left. I could tell from these calls that you were flying free and loving every moment of your independence. Though you did say you were missing home, I knew those words were meant to comfort me. And it was very sweet of you to bother to do that.

Radhika, you came back a week or so before Avantika. Bhutan had turned out to be all that you had visualized, perhaps more. With a borrowed handycam, you had video-taped the trip lovingly, captured the sights and sounds forever, and then edited it down to a neat film. Avantika, you came back not just with hundreds of pictures, but also a scrapbook detailing the places you'd gone to and your impressions of them. But what touched me the most about both you girls was the time and thought you had invested in bringing back gifts for the family. Knowing my weakness for pottery and ceramics, Radhika, you picked some lovely things—a miniature tea-set, an ash tray, a plant holder, a cute set of bathroom accessories. And you, Avantika, zeroed in on my passion for sunglasses by buying me an extravagant pair that you said was 'worn almost exclusively by movie stars'. You also brought me some wonderful coffee, another weakness. Through these gifts both of you demonstrated not just your generosity but also your involvement.

Gift-buying is an indicator of how well you know a person. Also how much you care to invest in terms of time while buying a present. Anybody can give a gift, provided the person has money to spare. You girls weren't exactly loaded with extra cash. You could so easily have spent all of it on yourselves. After all, there really is no ceiling as far as shopping is concerned in a young girl's life. Instead, you thought of each and every member of the family. For all of us you brought back well chosen, appropriate gifts. I really appreciated the effort and sacrifice. I know you'll laugh and say, 'What sacrifice?' But youth is about selfishness. At your age it's hard to think beyond yourselves and your own needs. With the same money you could have bought lots of personal goodies, or maybe spent it on eating out and excursions. That you chose to make others happy was a wonderful gesture. I haven't worn the 'movie star' sunglasses yet. But I'm touched that you thought me worthy and glamorous enough for them, Avantika. As for Radhika's presents, I've divided them up between our two homes, where they will be constant reminders of your sentiments.

Thank you girls, and it's good to have you back.

Your overwhelmed
Mama

....

Mumbai
July '99

To Rana and Aditya,

I don't know why, but I find it a little hard to talk to you in this way. Unlike your older sisters, whom I feel I have the absolute right to address in as forthright a manner as I choose to. With you guys, I feel awkward. I fear you'll laugh at me, exchange looks and say, 'Is she ill or something?' At twenty-six and twenty-three respectively, you are working men with a life of your own. A life I catch an occasional glimpse of, but don't quite know as thoroughly as I think I know say, Avantika's (maybe it'll be her turn to laugh at this). Or Radhika's (go ahead and laugh, dear).

Sometimes when I think about your lives, and how privileged they are, I feel concerned about your future. While penning this letter, I'm acutely aware of the lives of thousands of young men—men exactly your age—who are on our borders fighting a fierce battle at Kargil. Each day on television, I see the horrific images of death and destruction and wonder whether they affect you the way they affect me. In my mind, I constantly superimpose your faces over those of our brave soldiers and wonder what must be happening to the mothers and other family members of these men while the tension on the border continues.

When I first heard the news about Flt. Lt. Nachiketa's capture, my heart went out to his mother. What must she have endured for those few days when she knew her son was being held in captivity in Pakistan? The lady's words were brave indeed and India felt justly proud of her, when with supreme dignity she said she was unafraid and proud of her son. I tried to visualize her in her own home, lying awake at night while the rest of the country slept peacefully. I put myself in her place, and wept silent tears. I couldn't get rid of that image for months. The young pilot's smiling face after his release kept haunting me. What if it had been either of you in that aircraft?

It made me think, forced me to think—about your lives. I recalled some of the conversations we've shared over the past few years. Of course, comparisons are awful and I have always felt you boys are blessed in every way—good looks, good health, good grades, good jobs, even good girls—you've got it all. Sometimes I worry that it may have happened a bit too easily and a bit too soon. When I voice my fears, you dismiss them by saying, 'Stop being paranoid.' You think I'm over-reacting. And you point out that you've worked hard to get to your present positions. There's no denying that. I watch you keeping long hours at the office and on many levels, I admire the independent decisions you've taken. Rana, you knew very early in life that it would be a career in advertising for you. And you, Aditya, have a pucca businessman's blood coursing through your veins.

Both of you decided at a frightfully young age to strike out on your own. Whatever you've achieved so far has been on your own steam without any help from the parents. In Aditya's case, he was determined to study in America, and managed to convince everybody that the experience would be worth every cent spent. Rana decided to scout around for a job right after graduation and found one almost immediately. We were sceptical (as parents of highly individualistic children tend to be), and wondered whether it was the right move. Today, some four years later, we believe it was. In your terminology you guys are 'all set'. True. But what next?

There have been girls—serious involvements and casual relationships. We have differed on your dealings with them. Perhaps I don't understand the new equation, but I believe there has to be some sort of a commitment in such situations. You tell me 'things have changed'. I'm sure they have. But that much? I watch a succession of your women file in and out of your lives and I wonder what it's all leading up to. 'We're friends. Good friends,' you insist. I immediately think of all those clichés associated with movie-star quotes. Yet, I have seen how smoothly old girlfriends become 'buddies' in your case and how comfortable all of you are in the fresh alignment. It doesn't make sense to me. I worry about the girls; you advise me to save that for someone or something else. I lecture you not to be so light-hearted about romance, and you insist that's how the girls want it too. I'm not so sure.

A few years from now, you'll be looking for life partners. You seem to be very clear in your heads about the sort of person you're seeking. There will be responsibilities and pressures that will affect the easy pace of your present existence. How will you cope then? Your generation is still searching for an identity. At least, that's how I feel. Behind that 'cool' facade there is much insecurity. How on earth will you create bonds that endure? So far the girls I have met have seemed unlikely candidates. I guess you've felt likewise, since none of the link-ups have endured beyond a few months. Better that than an early divorce, I say.

Perhaps I should teach myself to relax. The problem is, I get overwrought. It's so much easier to have a heart-to-heart with your sisters than with you. I hold back. I try and make intelligent guesses. I play fill-in-the-blanks. Is it like that with most mothers of my generation, I wonder. People assure me that both you guys are okay. 'Thank the Lord. They don't do drugs,' they say half in wonder. 'Look at all the other kids these days.' I think to myself, 'Good heavens. Is that what I'm supposed to thank God for, that my children aren't drug addicts?' What a sad comment on your generation. Virtue by default. Well, that isn't the yardstick I've employed for you and I'm not about to change that. Yes, I've nagged. Yes, I've been overbearing. And yes, often I haven't 'connected'. But through it all, there has been just one consistent wish for both of you—that you live your life with integrity and pride. I don't care about your 'achievements'. I don't care whether you win laurels, medals or awards. Like any mother, I want you to do your best and be happy, without compromising on the values we've tried hard to imbibe in you. Treat women with respect and be kind to the less fortunate. As long as you do that, I will be able to enjoy my sleep.

You see, the problem is really quite simple—I haven't understood what it is that your generation cares about (besides material success). Maybe you yourselves don't know. Once you can define that for me, I really will relax and get off your case. Promise. But tell me it isn't just money that matters. All else is forgiven.

In grave doubt,
Mother

....

Pune
September '99

Dear Little Girls,

I don't understand the fuss over kids not being 'allowed' to watch *Baywatch* and similar 'wicked' serials from the West. I've talked to semi-hysterical mommies who've reacted in horror when I said, 'Yes, my kids watch it sometimes. But not with any degree of sustained interest. They prefer *Small Wonder*.' 'You mean they watch that dirty serial in front of you? My God. Don't you switch off the TV immediately? All those "nanga" people kissing-wissing. It's disgusting.' I shook my head and smiled. They shook theirs and grimaced. I guess that was one more confirmation of my depraved mind. I was weird, and irresponsible. I 'allowed' young children to watch dirty-dirty programmes on television. What's more, they heard me say that I often watched the same along with the kids.

Frankly, you and I found *Baywatch* boring. That settled matters. We stopped watching it. If only parents would 'allow' their children to make up their own minds about irrelevant issues like this. They don't because they have no faith in their offspring's judgement. But more, much more than that, they are control freaks who want to monitor each and every action, word and thought of their children. Upto a point, this is a good policy. There is such a thing as responsible parenting. But when it becomes extreme (as in exercising an autocratic control over the remote panel) resentment is bound to develop. I find it easier to defuse tricky situations by discussing them openly with the two of you. At ten and fourteen you have minds of your own and specific points of views. It's my job to listen. Preferably with interest.

Concerning *Baywatch*, we began to see the odd episode while idly channel surfing. Arundhati commented on the skimpy swimsuits worn by the women in the serial. She thought the actresses were 'shameless'. Anandita giggled at that comment and added her own—'I think the men are shameless too.' I stayed out of it. I noticed with some amusement that both of you covered your faces at any display of physicality. Anandita did so more to copy you, Arundhati. I asked why. 'We feel shy,' you choroused. And I understood that perfectly. In our culture, it's rare to see even husbands and wives being overtly demonstrative in front of the children. I never saw my parents embracing or kissing. There is a sense of privacy about such displays—and we accept that without questioning. Little girls either genuinely feel coy when they see adults in such situations or they feel they ought to. I'm not sure which it is. And it doesn't matter. By the time you are fifteen or sixteen, you'll take that and more in your stride. There's time enough for it.

But as of now, I hardly consider watching or not watching *Baywatch* a big issue in our house. After a few episodes, we switched off completely. But I am certain that had I made a big number out of your not watching it, you'd have gone to a neighbour's to do so. Just to find out what was so very objectionable. Or just for the thrill of being naughty. I know the feeling. I've done similar things in the past myself. So don't look at me like that and say, 'But Ma . . . how could you think we'd . . . ?' Of course there are parents who worry legitimately about the long-term effects of such TV shows on their children. For us in India, the cable revolution is not even a generation old. We really and truly do not know the long-term consequences of having these sort of shows beamed into our homes. It will be your generation they'll use as guinea pigs. The effects will be evident ten, perhaps twenty years, from now. Meanwhile we will have to deal with the changed situation, as generations of equally bewildered parents have, adopting a healthy dose of humour as we go along. I have noticed that if parents can only find it within themselves to laugh at a few tricky developments, the nasty edges get blunted. I've often chuckled over Pamela Anderson's silicon experiments with you girls, and reduced the actress's mammary obsession to a joke. Not everything, alas, can be converted into a giggle. I do feel responsible, even concerned, about what we see on the small screen. Yours is a highly receptive, impressionable age—you absorb everything quickly, like sponges in a hurry to bloat. The good thing that I've noticed is how soon you tire of some of the shows most parents consider 'objectionable'. They don't seem to engage your imagination sufficiently and you move on swiftly to something else.

There is no one single way of dealing with this problem. I know parents who restrict and control TV viewing very strictly. What happens is that their kids sneak off to the neighbour's to watch forbidden shows or they wait for the parents to leave home before pouncing on the television. I've also heard of domestics forcing children to hire pornographic video-cassettes from a library while 'saab-memsaab' are partying somewhere. Here, an additional problem enters the picture—guilt. The kids often suffer long bouts of it, knowing they're disobeying instructions. I'd rather you ask me about a show—not seek my permission, but talk to me about what it is that draws you to it. It is only through discussion that we can arrive at a consensus. Maybe we can watch the show together and exchange opinions on it. What do you think?

It has rarely happened that we've disagreed on content—be it *Baywatch* or any other programme. I've checked them out, raised points, clarified, argued, criticized, but never banned. Downloading porno sites from the net is another contemporary concern confronting parents. Since the computer sits in a doorless study next to our bedroom, chances of you kids surfing indiscriminately are pretty remote. I think you've been pretty responsible yourselves and have prescribed your own limits. Which is the way it should be. I'd hate to play ogress in your young lives, or even chief censor. I'd rather you knew for yourselves what's right under the circumstances. Happily, I know that you do.

Confidently,
Mama

Mumbai
February '99

Dear Vanti,

There was a period—mercifully a really, really short one—when you toyed with the idea of modelling. I suppose it was inevitable. You were seventeen and pretty. There were tempting offers. Plus you held the trump card in your hand—'But you modelled when you were my age, Mother. So why can't I?' I have to confess I went through some tense months while we argued away. Fortunately for me, your resolve began to disappear gradually. Not because I wore you down (I consciously avoided playing 'overbearing mom'), but because your interests shifted. You no longer considered modelling a 'cool' option. You were pretty sure you didn't want to join the rag-tag band of giddy veejays (yes, those offers came as well). But I can tell you I was worried, given the perspective. Here I was lecturing to you about the pitfalls of the career while you stared at me disbelievingly. 'How come you survived in that world?' you asked. 'How come you enjoyed yourself? Why do you think I won't be able to cope?' I tried to explain that today's was a different world from the one I had set foot into. This was nearly thirty years later. A lot had changed. Back then, we were clumsy amateurs passing free hours before the camera, not hard-nosed professionals negotiating tough deals. There was less of a dog-eat-dog spirit, less competition and consequently less stress. Look around you, I had urged. Check out the scene. Do you really think you'd be able to fit in? Do you want to deal with the pressures of permanent diets, permanent make-up, unearthly wake-up anxieties, and permanent tension over contracts and lousy working conditions? At seventeen, for God's sake?

We were on our annual holiday in Goa. There was a hot-shot campaign being shot in the same hotel. The photographer was a friend of mine. He asked permission to shoot a few casual frames of you. The look in your eyes said it all. I would have felt like a mean, petty mother to deny you the opportunity. I said yes. I also assured you I wouldn't hang around or breathe down your neck during the shoot. You went off excitedly to our family friend, Prasad Bidappa, India's most accomplished style-guru, who was also holidaying with his family, and asked him to hold your hand and be with you through the session. He was only too delighted, more because he shared my views about your modelling fancy. 'Don't worry,' he assured me privately, 'let her see the nitty-gritty for herself. I guarantee she'll get disillusioned, without our having to influence her. You know how our Vanti is—this is clearly not for her.' He was right. Once the excitement of being shot by a top-notch photographer wore off, you confessed you hadn't really enjoyed the experience. 'Why didn't you tell me it would be so boring?' you asked. I smiled a secret smile. Good. I wouldn't have to do anything more. My work was being undertaken by professionals.

We came back to Mumbai. You saw the pictures. You didn't like them. 'I look awful, Mother,' you cried. 'It doesn't even look like me.' Yup. I agreed. But that's exactly what make-up does. It transforms a person completely, makes one unrecognizable. The disillusionment was not complete, however. 'Maybe the lighting was harsh and . . . we were shooting informally without all the equipment,' you reasoned. 'Maybe,' I said laconically. 'Perhaps I didn't strike a rapport with the photographer.' 'Perhaps,' I echoed. 'I should take another crack at it. Please, please, please. Speak to Gautam mama. I'll do anything to be

photographed by him,' you said. I nodded. Little did you
know Gautam (Rajadhyaksha) and I had already discussed
the subject. He had prepared me for the prospect of your
getting modelling offers when you were fourteen years old.
'Watch out,' he had said. 'Avantika will be spotted. And
people are bound to ask her to model. What do you feel
about it? What does she herself want?' I had expressed my
views frankly and he had supported them whole-heartedly.
'You're right,' he had told me, 'it's not for our girl. But let
her try it, if only to get it out of her system.'

I phoned him to convey your request. He readily agreed.
Once again, you didn't want me around. He thought that
was a good idea. 'Leave her to me,' he said, 'I'll take great
pictures. The best. But I'll also keep talking to her casually
about my own experiences in the field.' Which he did. You
narrated them to me later. The photographs were fabulous.
I must say even I was surprised. My little girl was a big girl.
How lovely you looked. Once again the disappointment
was yours. 'I hate myself in photographs,' you declared, 'I
don't look like me.' Gautam and I rejoiced. Clearly you
weren't cut out for this particular career option. Or else you
would have fallen in love with your own images and dreamt
about seeing your name under the lights.

It was at age twenty that you made your appearance on
the cover of *Femina*. With that done, your enthusiasm
vanished almost as suddenly as it had appeared. You
thought you looked pretty 'weird' on the magazine, but its
appearance alone meant something—everything—in your
circle. I guess that was reward enough. You danced with
glee when the compliments started rolling in—but the thrill
didn't last for too long. Modelling offers that followed were
treated with indifference. And since that cover the whole
modelling thing seems to have been taken out of your

system. I haven't heard you mention it even once over the past year. In fact, when a top Hindi film director offered you a role in his new film, it didn't take you even a minute to turn him down. All of us heaved a huge sigh of relief. It was over. The modelling bug had crawled down the tube forever. Now if only my parents had dealt with it with equal indifference. Who knows, maybe I too would have stopped in my tracks after my first *Femina* cover. That's life, I guess, darling. An endless series of 'who knows' and 'why nots'. Right?

Your relieved
Mama

....

Mumbai
June '99

Dear Children,
    I know this hasn't really been an issue in our family, but I've heard you mention it as being one in your school/college/workplace. Often, I've walked in on conversations about so-and-so being 'so fair' or 'so dark' and wondered why precious time was being wasted on such an inconsequential subject. I've picked up stray remarks. 'Poor thing, she's so dark that nothing suits her.' And I've been aghast. Since the dark-fair debate has not really been an issue at home, we haven't had the chance to discuss it. Yet, I know you cannot be entirely unaffected by its implications, considering it is a national obsession. None of

you girls has ever come to me with a request to buy you a cream that promises instant fairness. You boys haven't ever discussed a potential girlfriend in terms of the colour of her skin.

As far as complexion care is concerned, I've said exactly the same things to all of you, which is to look after your skin by keeping it scrupulously clean. Fortunately, all six of you are blessed with healthy skin. The occasional spots and pimples have been dealt with, adopting grandma's tips. Other than that, we haven't really invested much thought in the issue. Sometimes, I've chanced upon a comment here or there about an actress's appearance ('Aishwarya is so beautiful . . . and so fair'). But I know that these 'colour' discussions have taken place in your classrooms. 'So-and-so is so dark, yaar. You can't see her on a moonless night.' Once or twice I've heard your friends chatting: 'No chance for that chick, yaar. She's blacker than a tavaa.' I was told of the insensitivity of a maid who had asked a four-year-old girl whether she was adopted. All because the child happened to be ten shades darker-skinned than either of her parents. We've heard kids describing a classmate as 'kallu' or 'kaliya', and been shocked by it. Quite often, it's adults who are responsible for creating this colour prejudice. Foreigners coming to India frequently comment on the apartheid practised by us. It has been going on for centuries. But how does one root it out?

I remember how you children had reacted on our trip to the United States. It was the first time you had seen black people in such numbers and at such close quarters. Little Anandita had displayed fear—no, terror, when a black had occupied the seat next to her on the subway. I had seen her shrinking, her eyes dilated with fear. She had asked me in Hindi whether he was likely to attack or kidnap her. I had been momentarily stumped by her reaction. After all, it wasn't a subject that had come up for discussion in our home. How come she had responded in this manner? On probing she said it was a maid who had told her that all 'negroes' were bad people.

Around that time, a black family had moved into one of the apartments in our complex. Anandita would frequently ride in the same elevator and stare at the newcomers in fascination. Their presence in the building had generated a lot of curiosity among the staff. Lift attendants claimed the family was aggressive and rude. The other maids physically restrained their wards from entering the same elevator. Soon the rumour spread that they consumed human flesh. Nobody, but nobody, was willing to greet them. 'They are wild people from the jungles of Africa,' I overheard Anandita's maid announcing. I promptly corrected her. She told me I didn't know the truth. 'These people are dangerous. They think like animals, behave like animals. One has to be very careful. They could do anything at any time.' She went on to narrate some cock-and-bull story about how innocent children had been attacked in the elevator. I later discovered what had actually happened. A bunch of bratty kids had made some deeply offensive remarks about the lady's hair and skin, which she had understood. She'd shouted at the children and threatened to report them. I asked Anandita's maid if she knew the facts. 'What facts? These people look like bhoots. They are bhoots,' she insisted.

She was an illiterate woman who didn't know better. But you do. Whenever I hear nasty remarks about a person's appearance, I check you immediately. We Indians come in all colours. Isn't that lovely? I think so. In our own family, we can find such a range of shades. From biscuit to toast.

The important thing is to make sure you look after yourself. A healthy skin is a beautiful skin. Who cares about a few shades this way or that on the colour spectrum?

The best policy of all is not to indulge in comments that are personal. If you cannot find nice things to say to someone, don't say anything at all. And never ever draw attention to whatever it is the person is sensitive about—weight, height, colour, hair, nose, breasts, legs. These attributes are in God's hands. It doesn't require any skill to be born with beautiful eyes or glossy hair. Appreciate beauty by all means, but don't condemn anybody for not possessing it. Ask yourself how it would feel if someone were to point a finger at you, or laugh at your physical attributes (or lack thereof). Recently, you told me about a little boy in the building (the one you play football with) who was being teased mercilessly in the garden downstairs for bleaching his face in an attempt to look fairer. It wasn't his fault. His mother had forced the poor fellow to undertake the treatment. You said he had started crying, unable to handle the taunts. I'm not surprised. How foolish of the mother to attempt to lighten her son's skin. Just as we were discussing this, a neighbour's maid walked in. She had caked her face with talcum powder. You girls began to giggle. I confess I was tempted to do the same, till I realized how hard it must have been on the woman, being rejected by one and all only on account of colour. Seeing our amused expressions, she actually explained why she had plastered so much powder on her face. 'When I go for job interviews, employers reject me for being so dark. I stand a better chance with powder. That way, they can't make out how dark I really am.'

In a country obsessed with light skin, is it any wonder there are so many 'get-fair-quick' products available in the market today? Successive maids would often advise me, 'Why not add some haldi powder to the atta?' I used to scrub you clean with chick-pea flour when you were infants. Turmeric powder added to the flour was supposed to make you fair. I know mothers who want dark-skinned daughters to go in for all sorts of ridiculous beauty treatments. The girls lose their confidence and withdraw into a shell, often never to emerge again. Isn't that tragic? I was saddened when you told me about a little girl from your class, Anandita, who'd been kicked out of a group because the other girls found her 'too dark'. She was also made fun of for using far too much oil in her hair. The little girl was so traumitized by the incident that she stopped attending school for a week. It took a great deal of gentle handling from your teacher to get her back into class.

Isn't it ironical then, that some of your friends spend thousands of rupees on expensive tanning lotions from abroad? For what? For getting their skins to look noticeably darker. 'A tan is fashionable, Mother,' you tell me like I don't know. Fashionable it may be. But it does make fair, pale skin look darker by several shades. The very same pale, fair skin that our culture so values. So many crazy contradictions. You know what? You shouldn't really bother with any of them. Every tone, every shade, every tint has its own beauty. You only have to teach yourself to look for it. Right?

Sagely,
Mama

....

Mumbai
11 August '99

Dear Arundhati and Anandita,

One shared experience I shall cherish forever was the incomparable thrill of watching this millenium's last solar eclipse with you. For days before the celestial event, we had been discussing the pros and cons of observing the eclipse. There was such utterly confusing information appearing in the newspapers, we couldn't make up our minds—how dangerous would it be? Were our filters good enough? Would we risk damaging our eyes if we peered at the phenomenon through multi-layered, fully exposed negatives?

The previous night had been a late one for Daddy and me. I was bleary-eyed and exhausted. At four o'clock in the afternoon you girls burst in after a long day at school. Arundhati stomped her feet and promptly burst into tears wailing, 'But where are the special solar goggles? You had promised me . . . now we won't be able to see a thing.' I answered rather gravely that in any case it would be near impossible to spot the sun, given the ink-black monsoon clouds hovering over the horizon. 'They'll go away, Mama. They know we want to watch the eclipse,' Anandita muttered absently, more to cheer you up. Her comment enraged you further. 'Stop talking rubbish.' I rubbed my sleepy eyes and told you girls to calm down while I fished out strips of old negatives and cut enough pieces to go around. By now, Deepa and Rohini were completely involved, which surprised me. I thought the maids would be huddling in their room, curtains drawn. Obviously your enthusiasm broke through their superstitions, for they were peeping out of the balcony along with you and urging the clouds to part.

It was five minutes to five o'clock. Nothing, but nothing, was visible behind the thick cloud cover. I was feeling let down, and recalled my last experience of watching the solar eclipse from a deserted maidan in South Mumbai. It had been a feeling like no other and I had hoped for a repeat. I started describing that incident to you, as all of us hung out over the rails of the balcony and gazed skywards. There were ten minutes left. I narrated an amusing story I had heard from a neighbour upstairs. She had been at her in-laws' home in Jaipur, expecting her second child, during the previous eclipse. Her grandmother-in-law bundled her up in an attempt to 'save' her from the sun after sealing every possible orifice in her body with well-kneaded dough. 'My belly-button was also closed up,' the neighbour laughed. 'She applied mehendi on my palms, nails and the soles of my feet, so as to cool me down and protect me from the strong rays of the eclipsed sun.' You girls were too glum to listen. Arundhati was sitting on the floor cutting up pictures for a history project, refusing to look at the sky, when suddenly Anandita screamed.

'It's happening. Look, look.' All of us grabbed our tiny pieces of negatives and gazed up to see that the clouds had indeed lifted to reveal a bitten-off orb. From then on, it was peek-a-boo time. Arundhati, a worried frown on her serious little face, searched for 'holes' in the dark cloud blanket, predicting fairly accurately the time it would take for the sun to show through. I didn't want to leave it to nature alone. We decided to do our cosmic bit. 'Come on, girls,' I said, 'let's all recite the Gayatri mantra,' and for good measure, I asked Anandita to slip in the cassette so that we could chant it along with the professional singers. I'm convinced our efforts paid dividends because the clouds moved off dramatically, giving us a clear and glorious view of the eclipse.

We yelled, screamed and cheered lustily, much to the astonishment of indifferent passersby, who either did not know what they were missing or didn't care. Life went on as usual on the busy street below. The parking bay was crammed with cars, chauffeurs idling against the bonnets. Office-goers entered and exited the commercial complex next door without glancing at the sky. Hundreds of people went about their lives completely unaffected by the spectacle. I found that surprising, and a little depressing. Is this how focused our city has become on the business of making money, that nobody has the time or interest to stop even briefly, to look up and to marvel at nature's glory? Really, it came as something of a shock that this wondrous, magical sight had left our city-slickers so totally unmoved and untouched. Time is money in Mumbai. This was proved once again on the eleventh of August when nobody stopped to stare. After all, the minutes were ticking away, each micro-second adding up to bigger and bigger bucks.

Meanwhile, you remember Deepa blowing the conch and startling people five floors below our home? At some point during the progression of the eclipse, I had thought of the beautiful conch shell (a present on my fiftieth birthday from Sudip, our dear friend in Delhi) sitting silently on the altar. Why not blow it lustily on this auspicious occasion? The more we chanted our mantra and the more Deepa puffed out her cheeks and blew on the conch, the bigger grew the clear space around the sun. We had done it, we gloated. We had chased away those nasty clouds.

At its peak, the sight was incredibly beautiful. Arundhati, you were gripping my arm so tightly, I could feel your nails digging into the flesh. Anandita rushed from the balcony to the bedroom window. By now, Daddy had joined us too. In any case, it was a special day for him and me. The solar eclipse coincided with our anniversary—a double treat. By the time it reached near totality, the light had altered. It was a pale silvery-gold, like no light I've ever seen. And it was being reflected off the surface of the incoming tide outside our home. The tiny waves glittered in an unnatural, unreal way, like a scene from a sci-fi flick. I pointed the effect out to you girls as we grabbed phones to share the sight with Avantika and whoever else was interested in listening to our high-pitched, stream-of-consciousness babble. I couldn't take my eyes off the water. It wasn't moonlight. It wasn't sunlight. It was its own light. Eclipse light. At once silver and gold, shimmering with a strange power. I was mesmerized.

The moon was racing ahead. The sun took on a crescent shape. I thought to myself—now there's a neat role reversal. The thin sliver gleamed evilly, as if taunting us earthlings with its awesome force. We switched filters. The sliver went from midnight blue to tangerine gold. We gasped at its beauty and wondered why all those busy people rushing in and out of the adjacent building were so unmoved by a once-in-a-lifetime event. Your father, finally irritated by my frequent comments about their lack of interest, snapped at me to shut up and concentrate on the dramatic spectacle outside our balcony, which was changing by the second.

Since it wasn't a total eclipse in Mumbai, I rushed to watch its progress on television. I found the coverage abysmal. Who wanted to see an overpainted anchor gushing away foolishly, her vocabulary of ten adjectives getting rapidly exhausted, till she was reduced to using 'spectacular' every two seconds? I took a quick peek at our altar. I had been told to protect the gods from the shadow of the moon. They were out of its range. I checked the puja flowers I had ordered for a post-eclipse thanksgiving prayer. They were waiting patiently in a banana-leaf packet. Daddy and I had planned to visit our favourite Shiva temple at Colaba later.

The sun was lower on the horizon now. It was close to 7 p.m. The sky had changed its garb and was clad in pale orange streaked with gold. I watched the dying moments of the eclipse with mounting sadness. Arundhati was busy calculating how old she'd be when the next one came around. 'Eighty-eight,' she announced happily. Anandita, as usual, got her sums all wrong. 'And I? I'll be about fifty,' she announced uncertainly. Arundhati heaped scorn on her counting skills, which promptly led to a flood of tears. Through her sobs, Anandita enquired, 'And how old will Mama be?' Before Arundhati could say anything, I smiled and kissed her forehead. I didn't have the heart to tell Anandita, my youngest child, 'Your mother will be long dead by then, darling.' But her innocent question once again brought home the fragility of the moment, with mortality raising its head. How could a ten-year-old possibly connect the two? What does an eclipse have to do with death?

As Daddy and I drove to the temple, after I had adorned the gods at home with flowers, we were both a little thoughtful, a little silent. This wasn't just the last eclipse of the millenium for both of us. It was also the last eclipse of our lives. The thought that our children would be there to witness it without us, was a sobering one. Of course, we all have to go. But we don't have to think about our going. Yet, on 11 August, my mind was full of that certainty. Of how delicate existence itself is. I was here, Daddy was here, along with two vibrantly alive children, sharing one of the most memorable natural occurrences together. This moment would never return. Never. Soon it would join the bank of shared memories. Ten years from now, we would recall what the eclipse had meant in all our lives. Maybe nothing, maybe something. For me it would be a frozen recollection worth preserving, worth cherishing. A stillness I could touch, always precious. Very special. Very sacred. Very pure.

God bless you, my dear, dear little ones.

Yours cosmically,
Mama

....

Mumbai
August '99

Dear bachcha log,

I use the address (bachcha log) with a tinge of irony. It was during Rajiv Gandhi's short burst at the top (our desi version of Camelot) that the words 'baba log' and 'bachcha log' gained popular currency. They were flung around in a sneering, derogatory way. The terms referred to spoilt city brats who lived in cocoons with no notion of life outside their penthouses. If they got into politics, it was to try out a new fad and see how it worked for them. I don't remember which journalist had dubbed Rajiv Gandhi and his cronies 'baba log', but whoever it was, the description was apt. It is with the same emotion (but with more affection) that I'm calling you 'bachcha log'. Another election is upon us.

Today's papers are full of Sonia Gandhi filing her
nomination papers from Bellary—last night Daddy and I
watched the unfolding of the drama on television. Two of
you were in the room then, but seemed totally disinterested.
You were busy discussing the latest Hindi film in town
(*Taal*) and wondering what to do with your free day.

The next morning, Arundhati came to me to say she was
working on a project on politics. That interested me.
'Where do I begin?' she asked. 'How about the
newspapers?' I replied. She scanned the headlines briefly
and put the papers away. 'I only need twelve lines,' she
informed me. Wow, I said to myself. A twelve-line project
on politics. That's impressive. But was it possible? Then I
thought, 'How come these children—older ones
included—are so totally cut off from what's going on in the
country? How come they remain unaffected and ignorant?
Don't all these changes make any sort of impression on
them? It wasn't as if the home environment was a sterile
one, free of political opinions. Anything but. Daddy and I
discuss current topics, the latest developments, relevant
issues constantly. Aren't you guys listening? Even if politics
bores you, something must filter down surely.

I, for one, had waited eagerly till I was old enough to
vote. The year in which I turned eighteen was an election
year. I was thrilled to line up at my polling station, wait in a
long queue, only to get that all-important black dot on the
index finger of my left hand. Before leaving to cast my vote,
I had discussed the candidates with my father, sought his
opinion, disagreed, and voted for a communist (it was in the
'60s, remember?). I had come away feeling proud, adult,
responsible and involved. I had followed the counting of the
votes closely. Felt sorry that my candidate had been
thrashed, and generally gone around airing my half-baked

views with complete authority. By the time the next elections came around, I was more blasé, better prepared, but still enthused.

So many years and elections later, I can honestly say that I haven't missed even a single one. Of course, my enthusiasm levels have been steadily waning, but not my sense of duty. It is a duty, you know. By not voting, you are abdicating an important responsibility. You are declaring your apathy, even contempt for the country's future. And that isn't fair. You live here, you enjoy a great many privileges, you are who you are because of where you were born (for better or worse). How then can you not connect with what's happening around you? Perhaps it's the schools and colleges that have failed to inculcate these values in you. I know ours did. Perhaps we as parents have been a bit self-conscious about voicing our feelings in this matter. But Daddy and I both feel very strongly nationalistic, you know that. We argue a lot, and disagree on several political points. So what? You've sat in on many a debate and heard our views. Daddy is far more politically passionate than I am (that's the Bengali in him). I see things more dispassionately. Our viewpoints rarely overlap, but the important thing is that they exist. And that you are frequently in the audience while we thrash out our differences, rarely conceding even a single point. Yes, we are vociferous. Sometimes—especially when Ajoba is at our home for a meal—the voices are so raised, so animated, it's possible for an outsider to believe we are waging our own war. But those are the sort of emotions politics raises. You cannot remain cold or detached.

Four of you are old enough to cast your votes in this most crucial of elections. I would want us to go together to the polling booth to do so. But I'm preparing myself to deal with turned up noses and bored expressions. You might say, 'But who gives a damn?' or 'What does it matter whom we vote for . . . it's the same bunch of crooks anyway.' That's not just cynical, that's awful. It's also taking the easy way out. I don't see you reading the newspapers thoroughly. You go straight to the sports pages after taking a quick look at the entertainment section. Aditya is pretty well up on the financial news these days. Radhika reads the front page. But the rest of you just about know what's going on, and that's thanks to television. You cannot insulate yourselves to such an extent. There are times when I'm tempted to quiz you, ask simple elementary questions about the state of the nation. Ask you who the finance minister is, for example, or who is contesting opposite Sonia at Bellary. But I keep quiet. Perhaps I don't want to embarrass you—or myself—by asking. This makes me feel sad. It is for your generation to push for change. It is your future we are talking about. You are the ones who will shape India's destiny. To do that you must feel a sense of belonging. You must feel involved. You must feel you can contribute something—even if it's nothing more than a little time—to the country. Without that investment, you have no right to expect any returns.

So kids, keep the flag flying.

Yours,
Mama

. . . .

Mumbai
August '99

Dear Kids,

Nobody likes a war except the arms lobby. We never had to deal with the subject of war or peace, till Kargil happened. It was then that the worst three-letter word in the English language became a reality for all of us, even though we were thousands of miles away from the action. This was India's first televised war. It crept into our homes and hearts before we knew it. Twenty-four hour live coverage kept us posted about each and every development on our borders. For me, personally, it brought back terrifying memories of the two previous wars with Pakistan, especially the one fought in 1967.

Bombay was shrouded in darkness night after night as air- raid sirens wailed and anti-aircraft guns boomed over the harbour. I was in college at the time and trying to appear brave and grown-up, but with very little success. Come nightfall, and I'd coil up with fear, my ears waiting for the spine-chilling sound of the sirens, my body tense, my heart pounding. I seriously considered running away from home, since Aji and Ajoba weren't paying heed to my requests to flee Bombay and go as far away as possible. I had suggested Kolhapur, for some reason. But everybody had laughed and gone about their work as if nothing had changed. For me it was the end of the world. I was mortally afraid. I spent every tense second anticipating the worst. I invested hours in thinking up reasons why the Pakistanis would target our specific residential area (we were close to the naval installations, the atomic energy plant, the main railway station and the port).

I tried on several occasions to involve Ajoba in an academic discussion. I'd even charted out the flying course of fighter jets taking off from a base near Karachi. 'They'll be able to get here in under an hour. If they fly low, they'll escape radar detection. Maybe they'll be flown by Kamikaze-style pilots. Even if they drop just one bomb, we'll be dead. But they'll probably go in for cluster bombing.' Ajoba decided I had been watching far too many films. I felt belittled and slighted. Even the 'mavshis' didn't take my theories or anxieties seriously. They'd pat me sweetly at night and say, 'Okay, okay, go to sleep.' I'd lie awake for hours waiting for the whistle of all those undetected bombs. When the late evening sky was lit up with naval flares fired from warships encircling the harbour, I thought I was dead. I remember crawling under the bed and staying put. These were my last moments on earth, I told myself, my fingers pushing the cotton wool I used to stuff into my ears, still further. Of course, nothing happened. But the trauma remains vividly etched in my memory. Soon, it was all over. We took down the black sheets we had covered our doors, windows and ventilators with. We relaxed and discussed how inconvenient black-outs and curfews were. We wondered about people who had lived though years and years of violence and conflict. I agreed it was a triumph of the human spirit. Unfortunately, mine was found wanting.

This was strange, even peculiar, considering my lack of fear in circumstances most people would find scary. I was not a ninny. Anything but. Given a confrontational situation, I was the last one to run away. Why then did those sirens make my blood run cold? I asked a lot of people that question, since I couldn't explain my abject terror even to myself. What sort of fear psychosis was this? 'Something to do with your past life. Maybe you died in the last war.

Maybe you were a soldier in World War II.' Maybe. Who knows?

I believe in full stops. When one dies, it's final. It's only our vanity that leads us to believe there is another life in the hereafter. We don't wish to let go, that's all. So we fantasize about all our births—past, present and future. We want to believe we are eternal . . . that our souls live on. Nonsense. When it's over, it's over—finito. Anyway, the '67 experience may sound paranoid today, but I can tell you it paralysed me. That's when I decided I would never ever support a war. Any war. War has an ugly face. War kills, maims, destroys, annihilates. Yet, here we were, a little over thirty years later, dealing with just such a possibility. Kargil stopped at our borders. But who knows what might have happened had the hostilities carried on?

Even though Kargil was a distant war (in Mumbai, anything beyond Juhu beach is considered 'distant'), all of you felt strongly about it. And it wasn't only because of television. I could see your involvement. But more than that I could sense your revulsion—we'd watch that coverage and your faces would change. Anandita, in particular, seemed very angry about India being at war. 'Why can't the two countries just talk about their problems? Why must they fight?' Arundhati was very moved by the sight of body bags—regardless of which country they came from. 'Pakistani soldiers have families who love them too,' she cried, after seeing a particularly sad clip showing unclaimed bodies lying on the mountainside waiting for identification. For your generation, war is something that takes place in a Steven Spielberg film. Even for mine, it was a remote nightmare. We were lucky we grew up in times of peace (if not harmony). I have experienced riots first-hand, but you haven't. I have seen hatred in the eyes of crazed mobs out to lynch the first victim. You haven't. I have seen looting and assault, arson and carnage. How fortunate you are to have been spared such traumatic sights.

Our faujis and jawans touched your hearts. How long will that memory last? How strongly will you feel about it a few years from now? Strongly enough to protest the next time a war looms on our borders? Strongly enough to mobilize public opinion against it? To speak out, to say it is wrong and sad and serves no purpose? I'm confident you will. But if, for any reason, your direct involvement in helping our soldiers is sought, I'm equally sure you'll be ready to provide it.

Your generation is far more practical than mine; you realize the futility of war. You know our planet's survival depends on preventing armed conflicts. You know how fragile the world really is. You value life more because you understand the threats to it, far better than we ever did. Your aims and ideals are different, too. You want to live and let live, more than anything else. You cherish the moment, celebrate the present and anticipate the future with hope and the sort of optimism that youth brings. To live fearlessly is to live fully. It's a shame we needed Kargil to remind us of that.

Sadly,
Mama

....

Mumbai
August '99

Dear All,

Two days from now, we'll be celebrating raksha-bandhan. In our home it isn't the biggest festival. But even so, we do mark it with an exchange of simple rakhis, sweets and small presents. In my parents' home it was one Hindu festival that went unnoticed. Maharashtrians from my background do not participate in this very sentimental ceremony between brothers and sisters. Ajoba would remind us that we did not belong to the warrior caste and therefore we didn't have to seek our brother's 'protection'. However, if we so desired, he and Aji had no specific objection to our tying a rakhi on Ashok mama's wrist. But we never did. Our family celebrated 'bhau-bij' during Diwali—a tradition that we continue to follow. It is a tradition I personally find very evocative and emotional.

But we've introduced rakhis too, and I think all of you enjoy the day and its significance without making too much of it. Rana and Aditya love displaying their crammed-with-rakhis wrists. And you girls like anticipating their gifts and reactions. Of course, before the boys started to earn for themselves, I'd go and pick up a few small gifts on their behalf. Now you bully them into giving you presents, specifying exactly what it is you want.

I love the idea of continuity, and festivals provide it. I'm certain that if we don't break what we've set in motion, all of you will try and maintain that vital link in your future lives too. There is no religious significance in any of this and that's the real beauty. We follow it as a beautiful ritual invested with a lot of sentiment. There have been times when one or the other of you has been fighting or not on talking terms, and all wounds have healed with this small gesture of tying a coloured thread on the wrist of a brother. Nothing more was needed.

Today, my brother is close to sixty. And yet, when we meet for the annual aarti during bhau-bij, we forget our respective ages, even our married selves. We become just brother and sister, as we once were, part of the same small unit, tied together by the oldest bond in the world—blood. As I prepare the thali for the aarti, my own mood changes. A certain solemnity gets into me. I light the diyas, place a whole supari on a fresh betel leaf, make sure there is kumkum powder and a few grains of rice in a tiny silver container, keep some mithai handy, and approach Ashok mama. He always looks embarrassed. He did so when he was an awkward adolescent who found this moment very 'silly', and he does so today, when maybe he doesn't find it as silly. He sits dutifully enough, and even agrees to wear a topi during the aarti, since we don't perform it with our heads bare. He stares into the flames while I revolve the thali five times around his face in a clockwise direction. Nobody speaks. It's a still and sombre few minutes we share, watched by all of you. Then he places a decorative envelope in the puja thali. Written across it in his neat script (not running hand) is an annual message, properly dated (I have most of these envelopes saved over the years), with a generous amount inside. The notes are always crackling new. He makes sure of that. There's nothing careless about any of this. Once his turn is over, it's yours. While Moyna mami sorts out all the well-picked, thoughtful gifts she has brought for each one of you, we get busy with the aarti—Rana first and then Aditya. It's all a matter of seniority. Radhika first and then Avantika, followed by Arundhati and Anandita.

I wonder if you girls will keep up the practice once you're married and in your own homes. With each passing year, I can see small changes. A little impatience, a little detachment, almost as if it's a mere ritual performed to please the elders. Even so, I don't lose hope. I know how it's all coming back to me now, even though when I was eighteen, it seemed a bit of a bore. Yet, I did want it on one level and would have missed it had my mother announced she was discontinuing the practice. I would have been resentful, too.

Maybe festivals and rituals don't matter to you at this stage. But someday they will, regardless of where you live, which distant city life takes you to. Your mavshis have been overseas for twenty years and more. The Marathi almanac that hangs in their modern, gleaming kitchens reminds them of all the auspicious dates in the Hindu calendar, especially no moon and full moon nights (amavasyas and poornimas). They make sure they carry forward the tradition established by our parents. They fast, they observe centuries-old practices, they rejoice, they celebrate, they pray, as generations before them have done. Imbibe, darlings, imbibe. I implore you.

Beseechingly yours,
Mama

....

Mumbai
August '99

Dear Rana,

A few days ago (27 August) your biological mother Rita would have turned fifty, had she been alive. I thought of her that morning, and said a short prayer. I'm sure you must have thought of her, too. Perhaps you wondered how the day would have been celebrated if she had been alive. All we have now is a beautiful portrait and a few photographs. Poignant reminders of a young vibrant life cut tragically short. I've been thinking of her a lot lately. I don't really know why. That morning, I said to myself, 'Wherever you are, I hope you can see your children, and know that they are fine. You would have been proud of them. Proud of their appearance, their conduct, and what they've made of their lives.'

You turned twenty-six exactly a month before your mother's birthday. We had a small dinner party at home for your close friends. On that night too, as we cut the cake, I sensed her presence. How differently you might have celebrated the evening. Or maybe not. Who is to tell? Still . . . no matter how many years go by, and how rapidly the world around us changes, it is one loss that remains a constant in our lives. I keep asking myself more than a decade later, 'Am I doing the right thing by her? Would she approve? Are her children growing up the way she might have raised them?' I know the answers, of course. Even though I did not know your mother I know that she would have done things in her own manner but not that differently, either. From the little I have pieced together, I sense a certain 'sameness' between us on a few levels. Her childlike enthusiasm, for one. I have it, too. I see it in both you and Radhika. Yet the aching thought continues to nag—you might have been another sort of person with her in your life. Of that there can be no doubt.

Today, you are the eldest of the six children that make up our family. It is a special responsibility. When the time comes for you to discharge it, I'm confident you will do so with honour. I cannot possibly anticipate all the events that lie ahead, but a few are a certainty. Your four sisters will get married someday, and you will have to assume the mantle of Big Brother to them. The age difference between you and Radhika is just fourteen months. It's two years between Aditya and you, five between Avantika and you, nine between Arundhati and you, and sixteen between Anandita and you. Growing up surrounded by so many girls, you have taught yourself to deal with their moods and demands. Mainly, you've learnt to hang on to your sanity and sense of humour, even under annoying circumstances, like coming home and finding your room overrun by ribbons, bows, odd pieces of girls' clothing, scrap books, socks, abandoned shoes, geometry boxes, Enid Blytons, crayons and paints. You've lost your shirt a few times and hollered, but at most times, you've chided them gently and thrown their belongings out of the room—with a smile. Despite the age difference between you and the two youngest, you've indulged their kiddish prattle and put up with their pranks. In return, they have reciprocated your affection through naked hero worship. I recall Arundhati's comment as a five-year-old when she came up from the garden one evening and announced, 'I have seen God.' 'What does he look like?' I had asked curiously. 'He looks just like Rana dada—big and strong.' Now that's an image worth living up to, wouldn't you say?

In a year or two, you'll find the right woman and move into a home of your own. The girls tease you about it and demand, 'When are you getting married? Make it soon, so that we can grab your room.' Daddy teases you about it, too. But I rarely do. To me, you're still the mischievous kid I met sixteen years ago, aged ten then. The awkward little boy with funnily shaped ears and a shy smile, who has since grown into what the girls describe as a 'cool dude', lean and fit and tall, thanks to a carefully monitored regimen. You work hard and play hard. We don't see you around the house all that much any more. Your schedules are packed with so much activity, home is a place to shower, change, relax, make calls and eat the occasional meal.

Ten . . . fifteen years down the line, you will be assuming a different role—that of a parent yourself. I'll be watching that development with enormous interest—if I'm still alive. I've seen you with your sisters when they were little. I've seen an affectionate, protective streak in you, the one you so successfully hide from the world. Beneath that nonchalant facade I've glimpsed the 'other' Rana—sentimental, emotional, and, if I may say so, a trifle unsure. I've watched you in your various relationships, negotiating your way carefully around landmines. The diffident little boy I first encountered hasn't entirely disappeared—he's just cleverly disguised, that's all. So far, you have not had to shoulder any real responsibility; you are still the young son of the house. The eldest child, but still a child. Our child. At work, you may be an entirely different person—a man. Your colleagues may know aspects of your life we never will. That's okay. This letter is being written to remind you of the role you will assume when we are no more. It is you who will represent us. It is you who will bear the family name and carry on the Dé tradition. You will head the clan—small as it is. It is you your sisters will turn to for whatever it is they might need—advice, moral support or just familiar bantering. Hopefully, all of you will continue to be as close and loving towards one another as you are at present. But these things cannot be predicted. Who can tell what lies ahead? To you, we entrust the well-being of the girls in future. I am sure you will do what needs to be done by them when the occasion arises.

It isn't such a large family, when you look at it. To the outside world, our set-up seems unwieldy and huge. But none of us has ever felt that way, or experienced panic over an unmanageable situation. On the contrary, we have not only derived strength from one another, but we've also had a great deal of fun. We have taught ourselves the art of peaceful co-existence. To date, I can't remember a single ugly encounter that has threatened the bonds of the family. Arguments galore, yes. Differences of opinion . . . temper tantrums . . . spontaneous outbursts . . . sure, sure, sure. The normal drama of any family. We've survived pre- and post-adolescent blues, young adult angst and job anxieties. Today all of us are veterans in the field of living together without committing either harakiri or murder. Perforce we have mastered tolerance and patience while dealing with so many different temperaments and preferences.

You will remember all those times when the little ones drove you mad . . . badgering you for small change, pestering you to drop them at their friends' home for Hindi tuitions, forgetting to give you telephone messages from your girlfriends-of-the-moment, and embarrassing you in front of these very girls by dropping the names of ex-s—yes, they shamelessly eavesdropped on your calls, spied on your goings-on, reported on your activities and even ate up your carefully hoarded Pringles. It can't have been easy, especially when you needed privacy, space, peace, to sort yourself out. Yet, you rarely lost your cool.

I was looking at old albums just the other day. I smiled at some of the candid camera moments captured during our holidays. The expressions on the faces of all you kids are interesting and telling. As a fourteen-year-old, you, Rana, can barely disguise your disgust at the conduct of the others in public places . . . restaurants or airports. Later, you look like you'd prefer to be anywhere else on earth but with all of us. At around seventeen, you have clearly disowned us all. You appear aloof and detached in the pictures—like you're saying to the world, 'Hey, I don't really know or care who these people are.' By twenty you seem a little more relaxed, but still distant. The message? 'Sorry—can't help the family I was born into . . . don't look at me like that though . . . I'm different.' On our last big holiday together, over two years ago, you finally did what any sensible man would. You took off on your own whenever you could. We didn't see too much of you on that trip to America. It was a definite turning point in your life and ours. You didn't come back with us, either, preferring to stay back in New York to pursue courses in copywriting. When you did return after a couple of months, you were different, in that you seemed far more self-sufficient; your food habits had changed and so had your outlook. For the better, I might add. The kids saw less of you. You switched jobs. Your hours were extended. You stayed out much more, got home later and later.

The girls, meanwhile, were similarly steering their own course. Arundhati was a teenager by now. Radhika was enjoying her job. Anandita, still very much the baby of the family, was the only one who parked herself in your room regardless. Avantika, of course, had moved on—a new set of friends, new diversions, new passions, new distractions. That left Aditya, also in the process of finding his niche in the overcrowded job market, equally preoccupied and self-engrossed. Family get-togethers continued to be warm, noisy and full of good-natured banter. But now, there were three men and three women present in the room—plus two children. I observed the dynamics shifting, with curiosity and a little apprehension. How was it all going to work out finally? How will it? Frankly, I don't know. But I no longer fret over it. Somehow, I feel optimistic and upbeat about the future and your capacity to handle whatever it brings. You will always be the leader of the pack. It will be your initiatives that hold the family together. There will be change and challenges ahead. It will be up to you to handle those. How you deal with the crises to come will define your responsibilities. For there will be crises—there inevitably are.

For all the roles you will be called upon to play in future, my prayers and blessings are with you. I may not have given birth to you, but fate has cast me in a small role while raising you. I have watched with pride as you came into your own as an individual. There is still one responsibility left for me to discharge—that of a grandmother. I look forward to that . . . and sincerely hope I shall be worthy of it when the time comes. Till then . . . till such time as you have a 'baba' or 'baby' of your own, you're still the 'bachcha' of this home. The big bachcha maybe, but a bachcha nevertheless. Many a time, I look at Rita's portrait watching over me as I sit writing at the dining table. It is such a startlingly lifelike likeness, I feel as if she might talk to me . . . ask me a few woman-to-woman questions . . . discuss you . . . Radhika . . . the other kids . . . discuss me . . . my life . . . my work . . . and in some way assure me that she believes I have done the right and fair thing by all of you. That would be my greatest reward.

God bless,
Mummy

....

Mumbai
September '99

My Beloved Children,

The monsoons are ending. Ganpati utsav is round the corner. Avantika will be choosing her 'murti' soon. For ten days there will be aartis and flowers and naivedya. Her altar will be decorated with colourful buntings and garlands. The house will be filled with the fragrance of incense, and the tinkling sounds of tiny cymbals and brass bells. Twice a day, Lord Ganesh will be honoured with special prayers and devotional songs. On the last day, his journey to the sea shall begin. Avantika will walk the entire route, her eyes moist, her voice tear-choked as she says her goodbyes—'Ganpati bapa, morya, pudhchya varshi lavkar ya.' Again, I wonder how it will be when she marries. It was Avantika who started the tradition of installing Ganesh at home during the festival. She was a mere child then. Her fervour and faith remain unshaken. Will they be strong enough to ensure the tradition remains unbroken in her marital home? After all, inviting Ganesh to be a member of the family once a year is not a casual passing fancy. Once established the practice has to be carried forward . . . unbroken . . . by the family of the person who has started it. So far, Avantika has discharged her duties admirably, and with the same level of enthusiasm and belief. But what of tomorrow?

The festival season is about to begin, Navratri followed by Diwali. And then the biggest moment of this century—the countdown to the millenium. So far our plans remain somewhat vague and uncertain. We are hoping all of us can be together . . . will be together, as the clock begins to strike the midnight hour. I had imagined the occasion would leave me cold. But as the moment approaches, I find my pulse quickening. I suspect, our elaborate travel schemes will fall through after all, and we will in all probability be in our garden at Alibag, under all those magnificent trees we've personally planted. The night air will be cool and fragrant. We will hear the neighbour's dog barking. There will be champagne, cake and cigars. The family of biscuit-coloured owls which resides in the hollow of the jamun tree will fly low silent sorties over our heads. There will be music playing and much laughter. Someone will be cold, someone sleepy. But everyone will be happy. Happy to be together.

We will link arms as we always do on New Year's Eve. We will find our magical spot on the dew-laden lawn and sing 'Auld Lang Syne', our voices in different but not discordant keys. We will experience love, great love. We will think of those absent and miss them. We will remember those no more, and mourn them. We will look at one another and smile, perhaps through tears. Happy tears. I shall hug you close and kiss your eyes. Seal them with a quick prayer. For you. For me. For the whole world. Yes, it will be such a moment. We will be one . . . as the ships' sirens herald an age and the night sky explodes with a million fireworks . . . as our voices trail off . . . 'let's drink a cup of kindness yet . . . for Auld Lang Syne' . . . My heart will thud against my chest painfully . . . audibly . . . I'll seek your eyes . . . and close mine. That moment . . . too special . . . too precious . . . too sacred . . . for anything but the silence of deep and abiding gratitude.

With all my heart, here's to you. To us.

To Love.

Your mother

....